The Politics of Reality Television

Reality television is global. Transnational television companies and international distribution networks facilitate the worldwide circulation of popular shows; the 1990s in particular saw the growth of media companies that specialize in the development of reality television formats that are easily adaptable to local variations. While the industrial history of the global migrations of reality television is well established, there has been less consideration of the theoretical and methodological implications of this expansion.

The Politics of Reality Television encompasses an international selection of expert contributions which consider the specific ways these migrations test our understanding of, and means of investigating, reality television across the globe. The book addresses a wide range of topics, including:

- the global circulation and local adaptation of reality television formats and franchises
- the production of fame and celebrity around hitherto "ordinary" people
- the transformation of self under the public eye
- the tensions between fierce loyalties to local representatives and imagined communities bonding across regional and ethnic divides
- the struggle over the meanings and values of reality television across a range of national, regional, gender, class and religious contexts.

The Politics of Reality Television proposes ways in which we can think through the international dimensions of reality television in the context of highly mobile media, politics, and publics. It offers a global, comparative examination of reality television alongside empirical research about the genre, its producers and consumers.

This book will be of interest to undergraduate and postgraduate students on a range of Media and Television Studies courses, particularly those on the globalization of television and media, and reality television.

Marwan M. Kraidy is Associate Professor of Global Communication at the Annenberg School for Communication at the University of Pennsylvania. His books include *Reality Television and Arab Politics: Contention in Public Life* (2009) and *Hybridity, or, The Cultural Logic of Globalization* (2005).

Katherine Sender is Associate Professor of Communication at the Annenberg School for Communication at the University of Pennsylvania. Her books include *Business not Politics: The Making of the Gay Market* (2004) and *Makeover Television and its Audiences* (forthcoming).

Shaping Inquiry in Culture, Communication and Media Studies

Series Editor:
Barbie Zelizer (University of Pennsylvania)

Dedicated to bringing to the foreground the central impulses by which we engage in inquiry, the *Shaping Inquiry in Culture, Communication and Media Studies* series attempts to make explicit the ways in which we craft our intellectual grasp of the world.

Explorations in Communication and History
Edited by Barbie Zelizer

The Changing Faces of Journalism
Edited by Barbie Zelizer

The Politics of Reality Television: Global Perspectives
Edited by Marwan M. Kraidy and Katherine Sender

The Politics of Reality Television

Global Perspectives

Edited by
Marwan M. Kraidy and
Katherine Sender

Routledge
Taylor & Francis Group

LONDON AND NEW YORK

First published 2011
by Routledge
2 Park Square, Milton Park, Abingdon, Oxon OX14 4RN

Simultaneously published in the USA and Canada
by Routledge
270 Madison Avenue, New York, NY 10016

Routledge is an imprint of the Taylor & Francis Group, an informa business

Editorial selection and material © 2011, Marwan M. Kraidy and Katherine
Sender; individual chapters © 2011, the contributors

Typeset in Baskerville by Taylor & Francis Books Ltd
Printed and bound in Great Britain by
TJ International Ltd, Padstow, Cornwall

British Library Cataloguing in Publication Data
A catalogue record for this book is available from the British Library

Library of Congress Cataloging in Publication Data
The politics of reality television : global perspectives / edited by Marwan M.
Kraidy and Katherine Sender.
p. cm. – (Shaping inquiry in culture, communication and media studies)
Includes bibliographical references and index.
1. Reality television programs–Political aspects. I. Kraidy, Marwan, 1972–
II. Sender, Katherine.
PN1992.8.R43P65 2010
791.45'72–dc22
2010010089

ISBN 13: 978-0-415-58824-9 (hbk)
ISBN 13: 978-0-415-58825-6 (pbk)
ISBN 13: 978-0-203-84356-7 (ebk)

Contents

List of figures and tables

Figures

Tables

Notes on contributors

Mark Andrejevic is an Associate Professor at the University of Iowa's Department of Communication Studies. He is also a postdoctoral research fellow at the University of Queensland's Centre for Critical and Cultural Studies. He is the author of *iSpy: Surveillance and Power in the Digital Era* (2007) and *Reality TV: The Work of Being Watched* (2004). He has published numerous articles and book chapters on surveillance and digital media, including "Faking Democracy: Reality TV Politics on American Candidate" in K. Riegert (ed.), *Politicotainment: Television's Take on the Real*, Oxford: Peter Lang, pp. 83–108 (2007) and "The Discipline of Watching: Detection, Risk, and Lateral Surveillance," *Critical Studies in Media Communication* 23(5), pp. 392–407 (2006).

Nick Couldry is Professor of Media and Communications at Goldsmiths, University of London where he is Director of the Centre for the Study of Global Media and Democracy. His interests include media power, ritual dimensions of media, audience research, media ethics and the methodology of cultural studies. He is the author or editor of seven books, including *The Place of Media Power: Pilgrims and Witnesses of the Media Age* (Routledge, 2000), *Media Rituals: A Critical Approach* (Routledge, 2003), *Listening Beyond the Echoes: Media, Ethics and Agency in an Uncertain World* (Paradigm Books, USA, 2006) and (with Sonia Livingstone and Tim Markham) *Media Consumption and Public Engagement: Beyond the Presumption of Attention* (Palgrave Macmillan, 2007). He is currently working on books on mediation and society, and voice.

Fabienne Darling-Wolf is Assistant Professor of Journalism in the School of Journalism and Theater at Temple University in Philadelphia. She also teaches and supervises graduate students in the school's Mass Media and Communication Doctoral Program. Dr. Darling-Wolf's research focuses on processes of mediated cultural influence and negotiation in a global context, paying particular attention to how such processes intersect with gendered, racial and ethnic identity formation. Because of Japan's longstanding engagement with cultural hybridity, much of her previous work has focused on the Japanese media environment. Originally from France, her research is also influenced, however, by the works of francophone scholars and aims at destabilizing essentializing dichotomies between various parts of the world, including those between "East" and "West." Her current research reflects this emphasis.

Laura Grindstaff is an Associate Professor of Sociology and a member of the Graduate Group in Cultural Studies at the University of California, Davis. Her teaching and research focuses on American popular culture as it relates to issues of social inequality. Her first book, *The Money Shot: Trash, Class, and the Making of TV Talk Shows*, won the Distinguished Scholarship Award from the Pacific Sociological Association and the Culture Section Book Prize from the American Sociological Association. She has published numerous articles and book chapters on matters of popular culture, and is currently finishing a second book, with co-author Emily West, about gender, sport, and cheerleading.

Sean Jacobs is an Assistant Professor of African Studies and Communication Studies at the University of Michigan in Ann Arbor. He is a former political researcher for the Institute for Democracy (Idasa) in Cape Town, South Africa and co-edited a book on South Africa's former leader, *Thabo Mbeki's World: The Ideology and Politics of the South African President* (Zed Books, 2002). He has published articles in the journals *Media, Culture and Society* and *Politique Africaine*. He is writing a book on the relation between liberal democracy, globalization and mass mediation in postapartheid South Africa. His journalism and opinion has appeared in *The Nation* and the UK *Guardian*. He blogs at http://theleoafricanus.com/.

François Jost is Professor at the Sorbonne Nouvelle-Paris III University, where he is Director of the Centre d'Études sur l'image et le Son Médiatiques (CEISME), and teaches television analysis, narratology and semiology. He is invited in numerous universities all around the world. He has authored numerous books and articles on cinema and television, including *L'Œil-caméra* (1987), *Le récit cinématographique* (with A. Gaudreault, 1990), *Un monde à notre image* (1993), *Introduction à l'analyse de la télévision* (1999), *La télévision du quotidien* (2001), *L'Empire du loft* (2002), *Realta/Finzione* (2003), *Comprendre la télévision* (2005), *Le Culte du banal* (2008), *Le Téléprésident* (2008). He has directed several films, written some screenplays for TV and published a novel (*Les Thermes de Stabies*, 1990).

Yngvar Kjus (Ph.D. 2009 University of Oslo) wrote his doctoral thesis about event programming (part I available at www.duo.uio.no/publ/mediekomm/2009/93490/kjus_utenArt.pdf) and has published articles about the co-production of television and new media in *European Journal of Communication, International Journal of Communication* and *Journal of Media Practice*. He has previously worked as Media Analyst in the Norwegian Broadcasting Corporation (NRK), and is currently Advisor in the Norwegian Media Authority.

Marwan M. Kraidy writes about global communication and the media-politics-culture nexus in the Middle East. He is Associate Professor of Global Communication at the Annenberg School for Communication at the University of Pennsylvania. Kraidy has published *Global Media Studies: Ethnographic Perspectives* (Routledge, 2003) and *Hybridity, or, The Cultural Logic of Globalization* (Temple University Press, 2005), and more recently *Reality Television and Arab Politics: Contention in Public Life* (Cambridge University Press, 2009) and *Arab Television Industries* (British Film Institute, 2009). He has published articles on reality television in *First Monday* (2006), *Transnational Broadcasting Studies* (2006), *International Journal of Communication* (2007), *International Journal of Middle East Studies* (2008), *Middle East Journal of Culture and Communication* (2008), *Journal of Communication* (2009), and *Television and New Media* (2009).

Tania Lewis is a Senior Research Fellow in Sociology at La Trobe University, Australia. She has a strongly interdisciplinary background, having trained in cultural studies, American studies and medicine. Her research interests include the green "turn" in popular culture, ethical consumption and lifestyle media and culture. She is currently conducting a comparative study of lifestyle television in Asia with Fran Martin. Tania is the author of *Smart Living: Lifestyle Media and Popular Expertise* (Peter Lang, New York: 2008) and editor of *TV Transformations: Revealing the Makeover Show* (Routledge, London: 2009). Her personal website can be found at http://www.tanialewis.net/.

Gareth Palmer teaches Television at the University of Salford. He has published extensively on television and governance. In 2003 he published *Discipline and Liberty* with Manchester University Press. In 2007 he organized the First International Conference on Lifestyle Television which brought together a range of scholars from three continents to debate the rise and effects of this powerful new genre. He has edited a collection for Ashgate: *Exposing Lifestyle Television: The Big Reveal* (2008). Palmer is also active in Media Production. Over the past 18 months he has been involved in producing and writing a series of interactive DVDs concerning health and the community. His next book will focus on Television and the Body.

Aswin Punathambekar is Assistant Professor in the Department of Communication at the University of Michigan. His research and teaching revolve around globalization, cultural industries, and new media. His current book project provides a historical account of changes in the Bombay media sector and examines the operations of film, television, and dot-com companies as they grapple with the challenges of imagining "Bollywood" as a global cultural industry. He has published articles on these topics in *Biblio*, *International Journal of Cultural Studies*, and *Gazette: International Journal for Communication Studies*, and has also co-edited an anthology of essays (*Global Bollywood*, NYU Press, 2008). He blogs about these and other topics at BollySpace 2.0 (http://bollyspace.wordpress.com).

Katherine Sender is Associate Professor at the Annenberg School for Communication, University of Pennsylvania. She is the author of the book *Business, not Politics: The Making of the Gay Market* (2004) and a new article, "Queens for a Day: *Queer Eye for the Straight Guy* and the Neoliberal Project," in *Critical Studies in Media Communication* (2006), as well as many other articles on GLBT media and marketing. She is currently working on a new book on audience engagements with makeover reality shows, *Makeover Television and its Audiences*. She is also the producer, director, and editor of a number of documentaries, including "Off the Straight and Narrow: Lesbians, Gays, Bisexuals, and Television" (1998), and "Further Off the Straight and Narrow: New Gay Visibility on Television" (2006).

Beverley Skeggs is Professor of Sociology at Goldsmiths, University of London. She has published *The Media: Issues in Sociology* (1992); *Feminist Cultural Theory* (1995); *Formations of Class and Gender* (1997); *Class, Self, Culture* (2004); *Sexuality and the Politics of Violence and Safety* (2004, with Les Moran) and *Feminism after Bourdieu* (2005, with Lisa Adkins).

Zala Volčič is a Postdoctoral Fellow at the Centre for Critical and Cultural Studies, University of Queensland, Australia. She is interested in the cultural consequences of nationalism, capitalism, and globalization. Her major area of research interest is in the relationship between collective identities and mass communication in the Balkan region. Recently, she has published different articles, including "The notion of 'The West' in the Serbian National Imaginary" in *European Journal of Cultural Studies* (2005); "Blaming the Media: Serbian Narratives of National(ist) Identity" in *Continuum: Journal of Media & Cultural Studies* (2006), and "Yugo-nostalgia: Cultural Memory and Media in the Former Yugoslavia" in *Critical Studies of Mass Communication* (2007).

Helen Wood is Principal Lecturer in Media Studies at De Montfort University in Leicester, UK. She is author of *Talking With Television: Women, Talk Shows and Modern Self-reflexivity* (2008), University of Illinois Press, and has recently co-edited the working papers of the Birmingham Centre for Contemporary Cultural Studies for Routledge (2007). She has published a number of articles on television and reception in journals including *Media, Culture and Society*, *European Journal of Cultural Studies*, *The Communication Review* and *Continuum*. She is co-grant holder with Professor Beverley Skeggs for the ESRC project on reality television, "Making Class and the Self through Televised Ethical Scenarios."

Acknowledgements

We would like to thank the people who helped in the formulation of this book. In addition to the authors, we appreciate the support and labors of the colleagues and students involved in the project: Valentina Cardo, from the University of Leeds, who was involved in conceptualizing the project; Tara Liss-Mariño, Oren Livio, Adrienne Shaw, Briar Smith, and Keren Tenenboim-Weinblatt, the Annenberg School for Communication graduate students who helped devise the program for the symposium from which these chapters come, and some of whom introduce the sections below; Barbie Zelizer, director of the Annenberg Scholars Program in Culture and Communication and Routledge series editor, whose advice about and support for both the symposium and the book has been invaluable; and Michael Delli Carpini, the Annenberg School's Dean, whose enthusiasm for and contributions to the project were fundamental to seeing it to fruition.

Marwan Kraidy and Katherine Sender
March 2010

Permissions

Chapter 1

Real worlds

Migrating genres, travelling participants, shifting theories

Katherine Sender

In March 2009 two reality television stories hit the British press: one described the successes and conflicts surrounding *Afghan Star*, a regional version of the UK's *Pop Idol*;[1] the other the death of Jade Goody. Goody was a young British woman who achieved fame (or notoriety) on the British *Big Brother* series and went on to convert her designated fifteen minutes into a sustained celebrity only enhanced by her death from cervical cancer.[2] Together, these items exemplify many of the themes collected in this book: the global circulation and local adaptation of reality TV formats and franchises; the production of fame and celebrity around hitherto "ordinary" people; the fierce loyalties to local representatives; the imagined communities bonding across regional and ethnic divides; and the struggle over the meanings and values of reality TV across a range of national, regional, gendered, classed, and religious contexts. Both examples demand, if in different ways, that we think through the global migrations of reality TV from a variety of perspectives and in the context of highly mobile media, politics, and publics. *The Politics of Reality Television: Global Perspectives* presents new research that comes to grips with this protean genre.

The case of *Afghan Star*, a local adaptation – or rip-off – of the singing competition formula, highlights the increasing ease with which formats and participants travel across national boundaries. While sharing the Western focus on pop music of its precursors, *Afghan Star* competitors nonetheless inflect their performances with Afghan musical motifs and styles, dress more modestly than *Pop Idol* viewers are used to seeing, and decline to dance. For all its local adaptations, *Afghan Star* exemplifies the migration of a genre from its European beginnings, as well as the movement of personnel across borders: the show's star presenter, Daoud Sidiqi, refused to return to Afghanistan after travelling to the US to promote a documentary about the show,[3] and has been replaced as host by a part-time Afghan flight attendant.

Coverage of *Afghan Star* and Sidiqi's defection says as much about Western perspectives on the meeting of globalized media and Muslim cultures as it does about the details of the show itself – perspectives on reality television that *The Politics of Reality Television* is intended to complicate. Journalist Simon Broughton described Afghans as a music-loving people in recovery from the years of

Taliban prohibitions on listening to music. *Afghan Star*, hugely popular among Afghan viewers (the final was watched by an estimated third of the population), carries the hope that it will "unite Afghanistan's diverse ethnic groups and help bring an end to conflict."[4] Sidiqi is quoted as saying that the show's aim was "to take people's hands from weapons to music."[5] Even members of the Taliban apparently supported the female contestant from Pashtun in a show of regional pride. As in other countries, Afghans voted for the winner by mobile phone. The journalist described this as the "first taste of democracy"[6] for many Afghans. A television show can heal where civic processes have failed: as one fan argues, "*Afghan Star* is better than politics ... Politics bring misery."[7]

Before we too quickly celebrate the mass mediated move from the silent days of the Taliban to cultural unity and democracy on a commercial music stage, Broughton's article reminds us of the risks of participating in a show like *Afghan Star*, particularly for women: "Many Islamists disapprove of music and dance as incitements to licentious behavior."[8] When a female contestant, Setara Hussainzada, moved to the music onstage, "it cause[d] a storm of protest, even among her fellow contestants. 'Dancing may be liked overseas, but Afghans don't approve,'" says one. Someone from her hometown rails, "She brought shame to the Herati people ... She deserves to be killed."[9] The article celebrates Western reality television formats that can be imported into and adapted by a non-Western country with a notoriously oppressed history. The shows not only reconnect Afghans to their musical traditions and passions but also heal ethnic rifts and induct fans into the processes of technologized democracy. The article reminds British readers how essentially repressive and sexually reactionary a society Afghanistan is, confirming a dominant Western view of Islam as inherently authoritarian and oppressive.

The second media story in March 2009 also exemplifies the transnational flow of formats and cast members, here in a volatile moment of post-colonial conflict. Jade Goody – young, working class, and poorly educated – joined the cast of the British *Big Brother* show in 2002, and skillfully maintained a media profile in the tabloid press and on shows such as *The Weakest Link*, taking her from a life of privation to that of a highly visible millionaire by 2004. She reentered the *Big Brother* house in 2007, in *Celebrity Big Brother* (ironic because she was a celebrity largely because of being on *Big Brother* in the first place), where she was held responsible for a racial bullying scandal during which the Indian Bollywood star Shilpa Shetty was called a "bloody Paki bitch."[10] Tremors of this scandal were felt as far as the British House of Commons, where a Member of Parliament tabled a motion to reprimand the *Big Brother* housemates for their behavior and Channel 4 for its failure to prevent racism in the house.[11] After a very public apology, met with due grace by Shetty, Goody then participated in the Indian version of *Big Brother*, *Bigg Boss* (2008). While on this show she was told she had cancer and withdrew for treatment. After she learnt that her illness was terminal in early 2009, Goody married her boyfriend, baptized her children, and died, all in the glare of media publicity: *OK!* magazine reportedly paid £750,000 for the photo rights to her wedding.[12]

Goody's celebrity depended in part on how she was seen as representative of far more of the British population than is usually visible on national television; according to *Guardian* journalist Aida Edemariam, "Many of the things for which Goody had been scorned – being out of her depth, overweight, lower-class, inarticulate – were things with which millions identified."[13] Or, more positively, after her funeral came this headline from the British tabloid newspaper, the *Sun*: Goody was a "star [who was] one of ours just like Princess [Diana]."[14] But her celebrity had been enhanced – and not necessarily in a good way – by her participation in *Celebrity Big Brother* and, with other housemates, her racially-inflected bullying of Shetty. Implicit in both the *Sun*'s and the *Guardian*'s acknowledgment of Goody's representativeness was that the Shetty contretemps revealed as much about the discrepancies between Goody's working-class upbringing and Shetty's privileged one as it did about their respective racial entitlements. In the process of Goody being summarily evicted from the house and the ensuing debate about racism in post-colonial Britain, her reputation as a lower-class, ignorant bully was consolidated, even if it was somewhat redeemed by her immediate contrition and later work towards cervical cancer awareness and screening. Jade Goody's celebrity trajectory demonstrates how a reality TV show can become a touchstone to consider not only class and gender representation in the UK, but also how the movements of reality show genres and participants across borders raise questions of multiculturalism and national identity in a British post-colonial context.

Each of these news stories demands investigation into an increasingly complex interplay among the meanings of nation, gender, class, celebrity, politics, and globalism on the terrain marked out by reality television. This anthology gathers contributions to the burgeoning field of reality television studies from a number of perspectives. A central theme concerns how we must think differently about reality television when we move beyond narrowly text-based studies carried out on shows from the US, the UK, and Australia. Much of this defamiliarization means looking at shows and their reception outside the Anglo context, but it also includes looking at Anglo shows from new perspectives: within their institutional frame, in the context of labor studies, in the cultures of their production, and through alternative frames for audience engagement with the texts. "Global" here is not meant to inclusively represent work that focuses on each part of the world, as if that were possible, but offers a way of thinking more expansively about places and approaches that complicate narrowly text-focused studies.

The chapters gathered here engage with a number of recent routes of enquiry. One is a productive field of research that looks at the policy and political economic conditions of the global production and distribution of reality shows.[15] As Madger points out, challenges to state sovereignty by broadcast media are far from new, and "state control over media systems or cultural expression is rarely absolute."[16] The pace and scale of international distribution of reality formats has accelerated, however, since the 1990s, boosted by the expansion of distribution networks and the consolidation of global media corporations.[17] Most significantly for reality TV, the 1990s saw the growth of media companies that specialize in the development of large numbers of reality TV formats that are easily adaptable to local variations. "These companies generate program ideas, sell concept rights, provide detailed production manuals, offer consultancy services, supply computer software, and create graphics and set designs to aid licensors in localizing formats," McMurria explains.[18] Reality TV companies are highly concentrated in Western Europe, and are epitomized by Endemol (originally based in the Netherlands), a network that produces formats for *Big Brother, Deal or No Deal, Extreme Makeover: Home Edition, Fear Factor, Star Academy,* and thousands of other non-scripted programs, and by FremantleMedia, which began as the UK's Pearson Television and owns the *Pop Idol* formula that has spawned at least 35 local variations (not to mention proliferating derivations such as *Star Academy* and *Afghan Star*). Reality television shows have proven to be highly profitable in many countries, drawing large audiences to cheap-to-produce shows with proven formulae that are flexible enough for local modification.[19]

Rather than positioning the global spread of reality television formats as another example of US or even Anglo cultural imperialism, however, new work suggests that the relationships among global formats and their local implementations are specific, contingent, and unpredictable. Each nation that develops and adapts reality formats does so in a particular policy environment that navigates between (at least) commercial demands, expectations about public interest programming, and local tastes. Transnational television companies looking to enter new markets must often meet quotas for local programming designed to protect national television industries; by using local talent and crews, these adaptations often take on a strongly local flavor.[20] The direction of flow of formats, as well as their adaptability, challenges the assumption of US cultural imperialism in reality TV, contradicted by the success not only of European producers and exporters, but also by formats coming from Asia. Japan's competitive cooking show *Iron Chef*, for example, has a US and an Israeli version in addition to its inevitable field of impersonators. Institutional analyses investigate the development of increasingly adaptable reality formats that migrate easily among markets. They also address the unevenness of formats' success in local contexts depending upon taste circumstances, lived environments, expectations of social mobility, policy constraints, and so on.

A second theme in the book considers from both global and methodological perspectives the Foucault-inspired critique of reality television that dominates much text-based analysis of shows in the US, the UK, and Australia. This perspective takes as its starting point neoliberalism, which purports to minimize government interventions in the market and in social life, to govern "at a distance"[21] (although where neoliberalism might be in the aftermath of the economic crisis of 2008 is anybody's guess). Neoliberalism demands flexibility and responsibility from citizens, emphasizes rationality and consumer choice as an ideal mode of social planning and decision making, and prioritizes privatized responses to social issues. A top-down model of power is incompatible with neoliberalism; Foucault argued that the preferred mode of citizenship in contemporary Western societies was governmentality, a productive orientation that promotes self-consciousness, self-monitoring, and adjustment – all under the rubric of choice and freedom.[22] Scholars working in the US and the UK, especially, have argued that reality television shows are uniquely well placed to model this new kind of citizenship. Reality programs emphasize professional expertise and wise consumption to solve what might otherwise be imagined as social, not personal, problems, and promote the judicious application of techniques of the self (by attending to appearance and self-esteem, for example) to engineer one's own happiness.[23]

Central to governmentality is the use of surveillance in the cultivation of good neoliberal citizens. Drawing from Foucault's earlier work on the Panopticon,[24] which extends the condition of constant surveillance from the prison to society, scholars have argued that reality television production and its attendant new technologies model conditions for perfect monitoring as a form of soft discipline.[25] Made possible by discreet and highly mobile recording technologies, shows such as *Big Brother* and its online counterpart are based on the premise of constant surveillance. Critics of governmentality argue that external surveillance cultivates self-monitoring both in reality show participants and in the audiences who watch them.[26]

As persuasive as these arguments might be, neoliberalism is not an undifferentiated global phenomenon but is articulated differently in regional and national contexts.[27] Likewise, the local articulations of reality television formats may be so distinct as to make its governmental imperatives unrecognizable. In what ways must we reconsider governmentality and surveillance in reality television shows, without privileging rationalism and responsibility, and while acknowledging specific taboos on representing, for example, individualism, competitiveness, exposure, and shame? Must we think differently about self-monitoring as a mode of government in political systems where state surveillance is the norm?

A third theme of this anthology augments narrowly text-based analyses of shows with field research that explores the production and reception of the shows. Despite the solid foundation of ethnographically-oriented studies of media production,[28] research investigating the production of reality shows is relatively underdeveloped (notable exceptions to this include work by Mark Andrejevic, Laura Grindstaff, and Vicki Mayer).[29] As with earlier cultural production research, ethnographic studies of reality TV production encourage us to rethink the presumption of a single unified "message" that reality texts promulgate, and to look at them instead as products of necessary compromises among professional, economic, and generic constraints. Further, production studies of reality television recognize the particular professional and labor circumstances of the reality television industry that employs cheap, highly mobile, non-unionized labor working under temporary contracts. These workers experience, if at a different moment in the production process, the same conditions of flexible capitalism that audiences are presumed to accept through the texts. Focusing on the production of a US reality show, Grindstaff's chapter in this anthology contributes a framework to this new area of research that might be fruitfully adapted to other locales.

Related to production studies is more ethnographically-focused attention on people who watch reality television and participate in reality-related media communities online. As with cultural production studies, attention to reality television audiences is relatively new; examples include Nabi et al. who focus on a uses and gratifications approach in a US context, and Hill, who looks at audiences of reality TV within the specifics of British public interest programming.[30] Concurrent with the growth of reality television has come the interrogation of the very idea of "the audience," a concept which has been problematized as an artifact of both market research and scholarly audience research. We want to bring together questions about the very meaning of "the audience" with shifts in the global distribution and reception of reality television, where audiences are no longer (if they ever were) organized along national boundaries but become reconfigured mediated communities both sub- and transnationally.[31] How might the global migrations and local variations of shows and formats draw attention to the shifting place of the nation within new mediated communities? In what ways might reality television be particularly well placed to mediate, imagine, and rework ideas of national identity and belonging? How might new technologies that accompany reality television – the internet in particular – intersect with these tensions between national imagined communities and niche programming?

A fourth theme of this collection, and one that is close to my heart, is how reality television has opened up space for more complex representations of gender and sexuality. Although there has been much work in this area in relation to Anglo reality television shows, especially those in the lifestyle format, Kraidy is among the very few authors who address gender and sexuality as it plays out in non-Western reality shows.[32] My earlier work on *Queer Eye for the Straight Guy* in the US attempted to account for the show's success with both gay and women audiences.[33] Although the US version of the program debuted with promising ratings in both Australia and the UK, these were short lived, and the local adaptations of the format in both these countries were complete flops. Shows succeed and fail for many reasons, but it is striking to me how unexportable *Queer Eye* seemed to be: are there such different histories of gay politics and representations in both Britain and Australia that the show makes less sense there? Conversely, why was the US version's spin-off, *Queer Eye for the Straight Girl*, also an immediate flop? Duggan has argued that neoliberalism's proponents have successfully persuaded citizens, in the US at least, that both global and domestic affairs are a cool matter of economic policy and technical expertise.[34]

She argues instead that policies and expertise play out in our most intimate lives, through the family, sexuality, and health and, I would add, through media representations of gender and sexuality. Although underrepresented here, I hope to see comparative studies of how reality programs must contend with themes of gender and sexuality as they play out through struggles over nationalism and modernity.

The Politics of Reality Television collects together twelve original articles that take different routes to understanding reality television in a rapidly changing media landscape. They assess how migrations of technologies, labor, audiences, and formats test our understandings of reality television across the globe, as well as the means of investigating these migrations. How does the global expansion of the reality genre broaden thinking about "identity" as a performance of national, gendered, racial, sexual, and ethnic belonging, to see it as a kind of labor – including emotional labor? What can production studies tell us about negotiations between participants and producers, not least about the belief that participants are merely dupes or celebrity-seekers? How can reception studies challenge the assumption of governmentality – viewers' willing submission to surveillance and models of good citizenship – by investigating how audiences assess reality shows' moral judgments and displays of feeling? Finally, how can we think about mediated politics beyond the familiar frame of journalism and current affairs to look at the ways that nationalism, regionalism, gender, sexuality, and other workings of power play out in the representations of intimate and mundane life offered by reality television?

More than half of the essays collected here address reality television outside of the Anglo context. The remaining chapters encourage alternative approaches to reality television that might be productively deployed in light of the changing economies of media distribution. We have collected the chapters in four sections. The first section, *Producing Identity*, looks beyond familiar critiques of identity representation in reality shows to ask how identities are produced by participants within quite narrowly constraining contexts. Each chapter investigates how producing identity for reality television constitutes a kind of labor, from Andrejevic's analysis of the unpaid labor of the child participants on the US show *Kid Nation*; to Jost's assessment of the claims to labor rights and overtime pay by contestants in the French show *L'Ile de la Tentation* (*Temptation Island*); to Grindstaff's ethnographic study of the negotiation of sorority identity in *Sorority Life* – including through cast members' and producers' emotional labor. In different ways, each chapter considers the institutional, economic, and legal frameworks in which identity is not simply depicted, but actively co-produced by participants and production personnel.

The second section, *Laboring the Self*, investigates how a particular subgenre of reality television works through contemporary ideas about "the self" in a mediated and commercial context. Lifestyle shows address the personal and domestic habitus of everyday people with the aim of self-improvement: cooking and gardening shows, home improvement programs, makeover shows, wayward children and pet shows, and so on. These programs have garnered much scholarly critique for their emphatic class and gender norms, and for the uses of surveillance and models of good behavior designed to reform participants – and, presumably, the audience – in ways compatible with the demands of neoliberalism. Palmer begins the section, outlining neoliberal critiques of lifestyle television. Lewis takes up this theme, questioning the extent to which neoliberal approaches to the self must be rethought in non-Anglo lifestyle shows. Wood and Skeggs's novel approach to audience research considers how gender and class norms are mediated by audiences' identification with lifestyle shows' participants. Collectively, these chapters demonstrate that we must move beyond thinking about reality TV as a single genre that reproduces discourses of good citizenship in a consistent fashion, and suggest that reality subgenres – from makeover shows to docusoaps – rework ideas of citizenship in sometimes quite unexpected ways.

The third section, *Performing the Nation*, addresses how the global spread of media technologies and reality television formats encourages national and ethnic allegiances, reframes a nation's imagined past and present, and forces us to rethink the idea of a national and regional public through a mediated lens. Volčič and Andrejevic question how producers of *That's Me*, a Balkan *Big Brother*-style show, hoped to promote Balkan reconciliation through market-driven programming, an effort that in fact enabled a resurfacing of national and ethnic hostility. Darling-Wolf demonstrates how *Star Academy*, a *Pop Idol–Big Brother* hybrid, presents an "imagined reality" of France and Frenchness, where national identity is insistently (and hiply) multicultural even while it effaces its colonial past. Punathambekar's study of *Indian Idol* suggests that reality shows can assemble "mobile publics" from previously hostile local groups (in this case in Northeast India), in order to support regional competitors on a national stage. Each chapter demands that we consider the role of reality television in relation to shifting ideas of nation and identity in the context of highly mobile technologies, media, and genres.

The fourth section, *Migrating Economies*, addresses the political economies of reality television production and distribution. The section begins with Kjus's careful analysis of the adaptation of the *Idols* format to the Norwegian broadcast context, weighing the increasingly interdependent nodes of activity within a complex network of international players. Jacobs's chapter looks at the political economies of *Big Brother Africa*, which was produced in South Africa and distributed by satellite across the continent. He argues that the show not only attempted to cultivate a market for South African goods, but also circulated discourses about race, nationhood, and political engagement beyond that country's borders. Couldry's final chapter investigates the special place reality television formats occupy in reproducing "the myth of the mediated center." If reality programs present rituals that shore up media systems' central place as a privileged source of authority, how differently might this play out in different locations according to local demands for public interest programming, more or less authoritarian political conditions, varying expectations of profitability, and so on? If we are to understand power, authority, government and governmentality not as monolithic forces, but as operating in contingent and particular ways, how can comparative research – across genres, nations, and methods – aid us in this aim?

Each section comes with its own introduction, so I will desist from describing these sections further here. As with all creative and exciting projects, things don't necessarily stay in place, so readers will notice conversations between chapters and sections which, for us, is testimony to the fluid nature of reality TV genres and their migrations across national and cultural borders. The book concludes with a chapter from my co-editor, Marwan Kraidy, who draws upon his research on reality television in Arab countries to signal some fruitful paths for future research.

Notes

1 Jon Boone, "Afghan *Pop Idol* Presenter Takes Off for New Life in West – Opening Door for Flight Attendant Stand-In," *Guardian*, 18 March 2009, 17; Simon Broughton, "Fame, £5,000 – and Death Threats," *Guardian*, 18 March 2009, 21–23.
2 Aida Edemariam, "A Reflection of our Times: Jade Goody Lived and Died in the Public Eye," *Guardian*, 24 March 2009, 12–15.
3 *Afghan Star*, director: Havana Marking, 2008, 87 mins.
4 Broughton, "Fame, £5,000 – and Death Threats," 22.
5 Ibid., 22.
6 Ibid., 22.
7 Ibid., 23.
8 Ibid., 23.
9 Ibid., 23.
10 "Paki," short for Pakistani, is a racial slur used in the UK to describe people assumed to come from South Asia.
11 Owen Gibson, "*Big Brother* 'Racism' is Raised in Commons: MP Calls on Programme to Defend Bollywood Star: Ofcom Receives 7,600 Complaints From Viewers," *Guardian*, 17 January 2007, 7.
12 Edemariam, "A Reflection of our Times: Jade Goody Lived and Died in the Public Eye," 15.
13 Ibid., 13.
14 The *Sun* headline: http://www.thesun.co.uk/sol/homepage/news/article2362089.ece published and received April 6, 2009.
15 See, for example: Michael Keane and Albert Moran, "Television's New Engines," *Television & New Media* 9, no. 2 (2008): 155–69; Ted Madger, "Transnational Media, International Trade and the Idea of Cultural Diversity," *Continuum* 18, no. 3 (2004): 380–97; John McMurria, "Global TV Realities: International Markets, Geopolitics, and the Transcultural Contexts of Reality TV," in *Reality TV: Remaking Television Culture*, ed. Susan Murray and Laurie Ouellette (New York: New York University Press, 2009), 179–202; and Joseph Straubhaar, *World Television: From Global to Local* (Los Angeles, CA: Sage, 2007), 179–202.
16 Madger, "Transnational Media, International Trade and the Idea of Cultural Diversity," 382.
17 McMurria, "Global TV Realities: International Markets, Geopolitics, and the Transcultural Contexts of Reality TV."

18 Ibid., 184.
19 Chad Raphael, "The Political Economic Origins of Reali-TV," in *Reality TV: Remaking Television Culture*, ed. Susan Murray and Laurie Ouellette (New York: New York University Press, 2009).
20 McMurria, op. cit.
21 Andrew Barry, Thomas Osborne, and Nikolas Rose, eds, *Foucault and Political Reason: Liberalism, Neo-Liberalism and Rationalities of Government* (Chicago: University of Chicago Press, 1996), 8.
22 See, for example: Michel Foucault, "Governmentality" in *The Foucault Effect: Studies in Governmentality*, ed. Graham Burchell, Colin Gordon, and Peter Miller (Chicago: University of Chicago Press, 1991); Nikolas Rose, "Governing 'Advanced' Liberal Democracies," in *Foucault and Political Reason: Liberalism, Neo-Liberalism, and Rationalities of Government*, ed. Andrew Barry, Thomas Osborne, and Nikolas Rose (Chicago: University of Chicago Press, 1996), 37–64; and Richard Sennett, *The Culture of New Capitalism* (New Haven, CT: Yale University Press, 2006).
23 Toby Miller, *The Well-Tempered Self: Citizenship, Culture, and the Postmodern Subject* (Baltimore: Johns Hopkins University Press, 1993); Laurie Ouellette and James Hay, *Better Living through Reality TV: Television and Post-Welfare Citizenship* (Malden, MA: Blackwell, 2008); Nikolas Rose, *Governing the Soul: The Shaping of the Private Self*, 2nd edn (New York: Routledge, 1999); Katherine Sender, "Queens for a Day: *Queer Eye for the Straight Guy* and the Neoliberal Project," *Critical Studies in Media Communication* 23, no. 2 (2006): 131–51.
24 Michel Foucault, *Discipline and Punish: The Birth of the Prison*, trans. Alan Sheridan (New York: Vintage Books, 1995 [1977]).
25 Mark Andrejevic, *Reality TV: The Work of Being Watched* (New York: Rowman & Littlefield, 2004); Ouellette and Hay, *Better Living through Reality TV: Television and Post-Welfare Citizenship*.
26 Gareth Palmer, "'The New You': Class and Transformation in Lifestyle Television" in *Understanding Reality Television*, ed. Su Holmes and Deborah Jermyn (New York: Routledge, 2004), 173–90.
27 See, for example, Lisa Rofel, *Desiring China: Experiments in Neoliberalism, Sexuality, and Public Culture*, Perverse Modernities (Durham, NC: Duke University Press, 2007).
28 See, for example: Barry Dornfeld, *Producing Public Television, Producing Public Culture* (Princeton, N.J.: Princeton University Press, 1998); Laura Grindstaff, "Producing Trash, Class, and the Money Shot: A Behind-the-Scenes Account of Daytime TV Talk Shows," in *Media Scandals: Morality and Desire in the Popular Culture Marketplace*, ed. James Lull and Stephen Hinerman (New York: Columbia University Press, 1997), 164–202; and Sean Nixon, *Advertising Cultures: Gender, Commerce, Creativity* (Thousand Oaks, CA: Sage, 2003).
29 Andrejevic, *Reality TV: The Work of Being Watched*; Laura Grindsaff, "Self-Serve Celebrity: The Production of Ordinariness and the Ordinariness of Production in Reality Television," in *Production Studies: Cultural Studies of Media Industries*, ed. Vicki Mayer, M.J. Banks and J.T. Caldwell (New York: Routledge, 2009); Vicki Mayer, "Guys Gone Wild? Soft-Core Video Professionalism and New Realities in Television Production," *Cinema Journal* 47, no. 2 (2008): 97–116.
30 Annette Hill, *Reality TV: Audiences and Popular Factual Television* (New York: Routledge, 2005); Annette Hill, *Restyling Factual TV: Audiences and News, Documentary and Reality Genres* (London: Routledge, 2007); Robin Nabi, Erica Biely, Sara Morgan and Carment Stitt, "Reality-Based Television Programming and the Psychology of Its Appeal," *Media Psychology* 5 (2003): 303–30.
31 Straubhaar, *World Television: From Global to Local*.

32 Marwan Kraidy, *Reality Television and Arab Politics: Contention in Public Life* (New York: Cambridge University Press, 2009).
33 Katherine Sender, "Dualcasting: Bravo's Gay Programming and the Quest for Women Audiences" in *Cable Visions: Television Beyond Broadcasting*, ed. Sarah Banet-Weiser, C. Chris and Anthony Freitas (New York: New York University Press, 2007).
34 Lisa Duggan, *The Twilight of Equality? Neoliberalism, Cultural Politics, and the Attack on Democracy* (Boston: Beacon Press, 2003).

Part I

Producing identity

Introduction

Keren Tenenboim-Weinblatt

Questions of identity have come to occupy a prominent place in the literature on reality television, both reflecting and stimulating the growing interest in identity construction within popular culture studies. However, the focus has tended to be on questions of textual representation – and in some cases viewer reception – while concentrating on identity categories such as race, class, gender, or sexuality[1] and largely ignoring aspects of production. The three essays in this section seek to extend our conception of identity beyond the existing parameters of identity-based critiques of reality television and shift the focus of attention from representation to production processes.

Central to this endeavor is incorporating ideas about labor into explorations of identity-related issues in the production of reality television. At one level, issues of labor can be linked to "traditional" identity categories in cultural analyses of reality television. Here, the questions to be addressed are, on the one hand, what are the types and forms of labor involved in the production of different categories of identity, such as race, gender, ethnicity, or sexuality; and, on the other hand, how are the labor practices of reality television gendered, sexualized, or racialized? At another level, the labor involved in the production of reality television becomes, in itself, a component of the participants' identity and a site of struggle and negotiation between producers and participants. At issue here are questions of whether participants in reality television should be defined as workers and of the kind of labor involved in making the participants "be themselves."

Each author in this section addresses one or more of these questions, and together they offer a provocative and multifaceted analysis of the relationship between labor and identity production in reality television; of the complex interactions between producers and participants in the (co)production of identity; and of the legal, institutional, and economic contexts which shape these intricate relationships.

Mark Andrejevic uses reality television to explore the question of exploitation in the new digital economy, while foregrounding the gendered aspects of modes of exploitation that characterize reality television productions. Using a wide range of examples – from the debate over the working status of children participating in CBS's *Kid Nation*, to a lawsuit against the owners of the voyeur-istic website *Voyeur Dorm* for overtime pay to the monitored women – Andrejevic demonstrates how being watched becomes a form of unpaid labor, and how unwaged labor in reality television is related to the exploitation of women's domestic labor in industrial society. However, what is dismissed as the non-labor of leisure and domestic activities in the case of unknown women and children cast members becomes a valorized and well-paid activity in the case of celebrities participating in reality shows, thereby revealing the power structures underlying the distinctions between categories such as leisure, play, and work – distinctions which become increasingly contested and untenable in the new digital economy.

The contestation over the definition of participants' status in relation to the spheres of work and play is at the center of François Jost's essay, which moves the discussion of labor and identity to the French context, while focusing on the show *L'Ile de la Tentation* (*Temptation Island*) and a lawsuit filed by contestants on the show against the producers. In this lawsuit, the plaintiffs claimed that their activities on the show should be recognized as work under the French labor laws rather than being defined as play or as an enriching adventure. Jost examines the complex ways in which the intrinsic malleability of the reality television genre – that is, its flexible anchorage within the worlds of the real, the ludic, and the fictitious – in interaction with the inherent tension between being oneself and playing a typecast role on reality shows, are used by producers and participants to negotiate the contestants' status and identity.

Laura Grindstaff shifts our attention to another type of labor involved in reality television productions – emotional labor – and to the ways in which it is used by both production staff and participants to coproduce the participants' identity and their status as "ordinary celebrities." Drawing on an ethnographic study of MTV's *Sorority Life*, Grindstaff explores the construction of performative contexts in which the participants' "ordinary" identity is produced, as well as the gendered and ethnicized dimensions of these constructions. Similarly to Jost, Grindstaff examines the implications of the increasingly blurred distinction between acting and playing oneself on reality shows, but also emphasizes that the performance of everyday life within a celebrity framework does not eliminate but rather protects and reproduces the hierarchy between "ordinary" and "real" celebrities.

The innovative comparative perspectives offered by the essays in this section – individually and collectively – shed new light on both the uniqueness of reality television as a cultural phenomenon and the ways in which we can use it to understand broader trends in the new media environment. Thus, Mark Andrejevic compares the labor practices in reality television to those of internet websites as wide-ranging as *Voyeur Dorm* and *Facebook*, while using reality television to con-ceptualize modes of labor and exploitation in the broader digital economy; François Jost's essay allows us to compare the legal and discursive contexts sur-rounding reality television in France to the US contexts analyzed by the other contributors; and Laura Grindstaff shows the similarities and differences between daytime talk shows and reality television in the production of identity and the expenditure of emotional labor. Each of the three essays opens new avenues for thinking about the interactions and negotiations between producers and participants in the production of participants' identities. As such, they go beyond traditional approaches to media research, which locate and investigate identity construction in either the shaping of the text by the producers or the negotiations between the audience and the text. Investigating identity negotiations between producers and the characters that inhabit the texts is an area of research to which reality television may more readily lend itself, but it can also be applied to other media settings, from the relationship between journalists and news sources to that between photographers and their subjects. The three essays in this section show us that reality television can be the place from which we can start moving in this direction.

Note

1 See, for example, Gray Cavender, Lisa Bond-Maupin, and Nancy C. Jurik, "The construction of gender in reality crime TV," *Gender & Society* 13, no. 5 (1999): 643–63; Susan J. Douglas, "Young women learn harmful gender stereotypes from reality TV," in *Reality TV*, ed. Karen F. Balkin (New York: Greenhaven Press, 2004), 61–63; David S. Escoffery, ed., *How Real Is Reality TV? Essays on Representation and Truth* (Jefferson, N.C.: McFarland & Co., 2006); Kathleen LeBesco, "Got to be real: mediating gayness on *Survivor*," in *Reality TV: Remaking Television Culture*, eds Susan Murray and Laurie Ouellette (New York: New York University Press, 2004), 271–87; Ji Hoon Park, "The uncomfortable encounter between an urban black and a rural white: the ideological implications of racial conflict on MTV's *The Real World*," *Journal of Communication* 59, no. 1 (2009): 152–71; Christopher Pullen, "The household, the basement, and *The Real World*: gay identity in the constructed reality environment," in *Understanding Reality Television*, eds Su Holmes and Deborah Jermyn (London: Routledge, 2004), 211–32; Rebecca L. Stephens, "Socially soothing stories? Gender, race and class in TLC's *A Wedding Story* and *A Baby Story*," in *Understanding Reality Television*, eds Su Holmes and Deborah Jermyn (London: Routledge, 2004), 191–210; or a special issue of *Critical Studies in Media Communication* on "Race & Reality TV" (vol. 25, no. 4, 2008).

Chapter 2

Real-izing exploitation

Mark Andrejevic

Watch out for the people who insist, with the fervor of original insight, that reality TV is not *really* real. While attempting to take the promise of the genre all too literally, they nevertheless have not been quite literal enough: it is, after all, called reality *TV* – and those two letters mark an important qualification. They invoke not just the forms of editing and re-presentation that we associate with television programming as a cultural artifact but also, and of primary concern to this chapter, the redoubling of reality whereby daily life, once captured by the camera, is transformed into a commodity. It is the alchemy that this chapter seeks to explore, not so much for what it might tell us about television aesthetics, programming, or production processes, but rather for its relation to recent transformations in realities external to and broader than the televisual realm. The goal of this chapter, then, is to take reality TV as an object to think with – to explore the ways in which the monitoring process becomes productive and comes to serve as a form of exploitation of the work of being watched. At issue in such a formulation is the notion of exploitation, which this chapter will attempt to clarify by arguing that, at least in certain respects, the valorization of the work of being watched generalizes forms of exploitation stereotypically associated with aspects of women's labor in industrial society. In this regard, reality TV and its aesthetics of voyeurism and spectacle provide a model for thinking about the generalization of exploitation in the "social factory" – a realm in which the production of surplus value isn't restricted to the workplace proper, but extends into the realms of leisure, domesticity, and consumption.[1] To put it in terms outlined by Corsani, we might describe the alchemy wrought by the redoubling of reality – its capture and repurposing in a monitoring-based economy – as contributing to the "becoming woman" of exploitation in the digital era: "The becoming-woman of labor would concern the very nature of labor, its being as an activity that produces economic value, goods and services on the basis of extra-economic human qualities such as language, relational ability, and affectivity."[2] The result, she argues, is what might be described as the generalization of forms of exploitation hitherto associated with (although clearly not limited to) the realm of women's unwaged labor in industrial society: "precariousness, instability and atypical contractual forms will no longer be exclusively the feminine condition, but will encompass all of human activity. By entering the labor market, women will have exported what had been their condition to the rest of the world."[3] This chapter explores the way in which the model of reality TV might be used to interpret shifts in the mode of labor and exploitation associated with the "putting to work" of spheres beyond the realm of wage labor proper in the interactive era.

Malleability

In his contribution to this volume, François Jost usefully highlights an important aspect of reality TV by describing the "malleability of the genre." Associated with this malleability are recurring forms of indeterminacy: between fact and fiction, labor and leisure, reality and artifice. Jost incisively focuses on the labor angle: much is at stake for producers in determining whether reality TV cast members on shows like *Big Brother* – or its French cousin, *Loft Story* – are to be defined and treated as skilled or unskilled laborers, or merely participants in what amounts to an extended game show. If they are laborers, then they may well have the right to demand to be paid as such – threatening the economic model that has made reality TV a global programming staple. It is one thing to be able to assemble an entire cast of characters for a cash prize far less than the combined salaries of actors and writers for a fictional format, and quite another to have to pay untrained performers professional-level wages for their unscripted contributions. Would that mean having to pay cast members on other types of game shows?

And yet, the contributions of reality TV cast members are undeniably valuable, in the sense that they generate profit for reality TV producers. As Jost neatly demonstrates, the malleability of the reality format allows it to deflect criticism of reality formats – whether for being potentially psychologically damaging or exploitative of cast members – by dismissing the reality of the shows, and portraying them in terms of what he calls the "ludic world" invoked by the remarks of the president of the channel that broadcast *Loft Story*: "It is a game; It is not reality."[4]

In this regard the malleability of reality TV resonates with the malleability of reality itself associated with developments facilitated by digital media technologies. Just as we might locate and relocate instances of reality TV in relation to the three realms invoked by Jost – play, reality, and fiction – we could engage in similar attempts at remapping other contemporary practices that take place in a monitored context. When we are engaged in social networking on a commercial Web site such as *Facebook*, are we entertaining ourselves, socializing, or working (generating value for a third party)? The same question might be asked about reality TV cast members: are they playing, working, or socializing? If they might be considered, in some contexts, to be doing all three, how do we sort out these various functions when it comes to providing a critique of the kind of work that is increasingly coming to characterize not just some corners of reality, but also the online economy?

One of the issues facing any such critique is to sort out the question of what might count as exploitation in a context in which pleasurable activities engaged in by people as they build social relationships, entertain one another, and share information about themselves are transformed into a commodity-generating activity – whether in the form of participation in a commercial television show or of generating marketing data for a new generation of targeted advertising. In her discussion of the "free labor" provided by participants in the online economy who willingly moderate chat rooms in exchange only for access to online services, Tiziana Terranova suggests that such productive activities can, in some contexts, be described as both voluntary and subject to exploitation: "Free labor is the moment where this knowledgeable consumption of culture is translated into productive activities that are pleasurably embraced and at the same time often shamelessly exploited."[5]

The challenge put forth by such accounts – and they multiply across the terrain of scholarship devoted to the exploitation of consumer labor – is two-fold: to determine the difference between exploited free labor and "free" free labor and to explain how non-coerced activity might be construed as being somehow subject to exploitation. This chapter uses the example of reality TV to offer some preliminary attempts to answer such questions – it does so not in order to offer a critique of the forms of exploitation associated with the genre, but to think through the broader question of exploitation in sectors of the economy where value-generating labor comes to spread throughout the realms of leisure, recreation, and sociability – an economy associated with what Terranova, invoking the Italian Autonomists, describes as the "social factory."[6] As a prelude to this discussion, the chapter considers how what Jost describes as the "malleability" of the realms of leisure, recreation, sociability and labor associated with reality TV models what Corsani describes as "the confusion between production and reproduction that is scrambling the categories of political economy, and making the borders between the time and space of life and those of so-called 'productive' labor seem to disappear, in order to account for the phenomenon of 'setting affect to work' or 'setting life to work.'"[7] Such an analysis, it is worth pointing out, is confined to those sectors of the economy in which value is generated via the capture and use of activity that takes place beyond the space and scope of the workplace and the waged labor that takes place within it. Given the ways in which digital media technologies have been put to work to generate value in a variety of ways, this chapter focuses on the way in which reality TV illuminates the logic of only one subset of the digital economy: that in which unwaged activity is put to work.

Laboring in the reality TV camp ... or dorm

The conveniently indeterminate character of labor in reality TV has been an ongoing issue in the economics of the genre. In the United States, both the Screen Actors' Guild and the Writers' Guild have been concerned by the way in which reality TV productions have claimed exemption from union pay scale for cast members and story editors.[8] By contrast, in France, a court ruling has established that participants in at least some forms of reality TV are subject to the protection of existing labor law, and in the United Kingdom, the government is considering the protection afforded to children on shows like *Britain's Got Talent*, after one 10-year-old contestant broke down and cried during the show's semifinal episode.[9] Nevertheless, in the United States, the threat of expanding network reliance on reality TV has been used to discipline labor in the face of impending contract negotiations and threatened walkouts. The contested status of reality TV cast members received a brief burst of publicity recently in the media debate over the status of 40 children, aged 8–15, who were recruited by the producers of a show called *Kid Nation* to take over an ersatz "ghost town" in New Mexico. This was part of a staged experiment to answer the question, "Can these incredible kids build a better society, can they succeed where adults have failed?"[10]

The very fact that there was a public debate over the question of whether children who had been taken out of school and away from their parents to participate in a commercial TV show in exchange for $5,000 and cash prizes were actually *working* is testimony to how far reality TV producers have been able to push the envelope. The children were subject to contracts, signed by their parents, that stipulated they do "whatever they were told by the show's producers, 24 hours a day, 7 days a week" and that even though they could be paid for their participation, "those payments or the agreement to be fully under the producers' direction did not constitute employment under the producer's interpretation and therefore was not subject to any state or federal labor laws."[11] The media reported that a state labor inspector was turned away from the set during production, and that the New Mexico attorney general was investigating whether the production had violated state labor laws.[12] Invoking the "ludic" realm described by Jost, the show's creator, Tom Forman, defended the use of children to make money by claiming that they "were not working; they were participating" and compared being on the show to "going to summer camp."[13]

The media discussion focused on whether or not the children were enjoying and benefiting from the show, and if so, whether that exempted the producers from the charge of exploitation. Supporters of the show and parents defending themselves for signing over control of their children, many of them aspiring actors, emphasized the benefits of the children's "experience" on the show. The mother of one 10-year-old participant praised the show publicly, saying her child "came home a stronger, more confident and more self-reliant child."[14]

The show's creator and executive producer, Tom Forman, similarly described it as a social experiment, suggesting, somewhat disingenuously, that it was like a documentary: "They [the children] took part in an experience. We followed them some of the time with cameras."[15] Another parent echoed the producers by describing her child's experience on the show as comparable to summer camp: "I don't think that she or I feel that she worked any of the time she was there ... She feels like it was summer camp. And I guess that would be a summer camp with cameras. This was a fun adventure for her."[16] Given that parents were prevented from speaking publicly about the show without CBS approval under threat of a $5 million fine, it is perhaps not surprising that their public comments tended to echo the network's public relations strategy.

However, the very fact that both children and parents were bound by contract indicates the type of control they had "freely" relinquished to producers. The children's contract, obtained by the *New York Times*, stipulated that producers would be able to portray the children any way they liked for as long as they liked: "CBS and the production companies, Good TV Inc. and Magic Molehill Productions, retained the rights to the children's life stories 'in perpetuity and throughout the universe.' And that right includes the right to portray the children either accurately or with fictionalization 'to achieve a humorous or satirical effect.'"[17] The ability to extract this type of concession without salary, limitations on working hours, or the provision of a tutor to make up for lost school time is testimony to the power differential between producers and individual parents, who were unprotected by collective bargaining provisions because the children were not professional actors.

The claim of freedom from control as a defense against criticism of the treatment of cast members gets to the heart of an implied definition of exploitation: if control of one's creative activity is surrendered under conditions structured by power relations, then exploitation is at least a possibility. If, however, control is retained, and its byproduct is captured by others, then exploitation is – or so the argument seems to run – not an issue. The implicit assertion is that even if surveillance can transform everyday activities into value it nevertheless cannot transform allegedly spontaneous activity (free of the observer's control) into exploitation.

A similar question was posed in a very different context by the case of *Voyeur Dorm*, a soft-core adult entertainment Web site. This paid young women a salary and provided them with free room and board to live in a house filled with cameras that relayed images of their daily lives to online subscribers. As part of their agreement with producers, *Voyeur Dorm* residents were required to participate in scheduled activities, such as sunbathing semi-nude and chatting with subscribers online. The women were paid a weekly salary for the required activities, but sued the Web site's owners for overtime pay, claiming they were working the entire time they were in the house – including when they were sleeping, which, according to their lawsuit, they had to do in accordance with policies set by their employers.[18]

I first learned of this lawsuit when I was contacted by lawyers who said they were working for *Voyeur Dorm* looking for reality TV scholars to discuss the case. I declined to work for them, but was intrigued by the point they made: that this seemingly marginal case was one that could have important ramifications for the reality TV industry. If it were determined, for example, that being watched while sleeping counted as a form of labor, the ability to get cast members to work for free or far below minimum wage on reality shows would be called into question. When I told the attorneys that I believed appearing on reality TV was indeed a form of labor, they tried an alternative argument: that portraying oneself on camera might be described as a form of creative labor which could therefore be exempted from overtime rules under US labor law.[19]

The implications for reality TV turned out to be overblown, as the case was apparently settled – there is no judgment in the court records. Of central interest to this chapter, however, is what to make of the claim that being watched in the *Voyeur Dorm* house constituted a form of labor. The employers apparently agreed that the activities they required (scheduled chats with subscribers, for example) could be understood as work and compensated as such, but the further question remains: whether generating value by being recorded while going about the activities of one's daily life might be understood as work – and, if unpaid, as a form of exploitation. Unsurprisingly, the media coverage tended to take a somewhat mocking tone toward the notion that being paid to live in a large house with a pool could count as work. The *Miami Herald*'s account led off with a description of women spending their days "playing topless Twister and strip pool," and quoted the dismissive observation of a *Voyeur Dorm* attorney that "It's not taxing work."[20] Perhaps not, but it was labor that reportedly generated multi-million-dollar revenues for *Voyeur Dorm*'s owners, presumably based not just on the scheduled "shows" staged for subscribers, but also on the ability to log in at any time of day or night to observe the house's residents.[21]

Exploiting non-labor

It should perhaps not come as a surprise that much of the activity that gets dismissed as the non-labor of everyday life on both *Voyeur Dorm* and *Kid Nation* is that of daily household life: typically unremunerated work associated with the domestic sphere. Those who dismissed the notion that the women or children were working implied that even the alchemy of the camera cannot turn what people might be doing anyway into productive labor (even though, clearly, both *Voyeur Dorm* and *Kid Nation* were highly contrived environments). By contrast, when celebrities let the cameras into their homes, these same elements of domestic life are legitimized as value-generating activities – if only by virtue of the revenues they attract. The family of heavy metal rock star Ozzy Osbourne, for example, reportedly earned some $85 million over three years for exposing the details of their daily lives to MTV viewers.[22]

When it comes to promoting celebrity reality shows, it is the very domesticity of the activities being shown that constitutes their promotional appeal. Thus, for example, an online promotion for the rapper Snoop Dogg's show *Father Hood* includes the voiceover, "He's a rapper he's an actor, he's a *baby sitter*? ... Shante's away and Snoop's in charge."[23] Taking care of the kids becomes, thanks to the introduction of a camera, not unpaid domestic labor, but a directly productive economic activity and, consequently, a valorized activity for a star who has, in some respects, built his career on a hyper-masculinized image. What was dismissed as productive labor when it came to (non-celebrity) women and children becomes the latest way for even (or perhaps especially) male stars to profit directly from the activity of their domestic lives.

What the comparison between celebrity and "amateur" reality TV highlights is how the balance of power determines who benefits from the value-generating activity of being watched. In both cases the activity of cast members, captured by the camera, generates a product that can be sold. However, those who have already accumulated celebrity drawing power and capital are clearly in a position to capture a larger portion of the revenues that flow from their contributions.

Taken as a model for transformations in the broader interactive economy, the case of reality TV can be used to think in more general terms about the ways in which monitoring transforms forms of leisure and domesticity into directly profitable activity. Users who sign on to a site like *Facebook*, for example, "freely" enter into a transaction that provides them with something they desire in exchange for agreeing to have their personal information collected, aggregated, sorted, and, in many cases, sold. As in the case of reality TV shows like *Kid Nation* or *Big Brother*, the activities *Facebook* users engage in are not traditionally understood as wage-earning labor per se, and yet they generate value in the form of information commodities that can be bought and sold. At the same time, they create the content that makes the sites popular and hence desirable to advertisers.

We might talk about the demographic data they generate as another form of "user-generated content" – not the intentional result of the creative, participatory activity of users, but a by-product of this activity captured by virtue of the interactive capacity of networked digital technology owned and operated by commercial entities. That such activity is productive in the narrow sense of generating value seems clear; whether or not it is subject to the form of exploitation that is the target of a critique of capitalist political economy requires further clarification.

We might also think of the interactive generation of data about user behavior as a form of what recent critical literature on the interactive economy calls immaterial labor, albeit with a twist. Maurizio Lazzarato describes immaterial labor as comprised (in part) of the "activity that produces the 'cultural content' of the commodity."[24] In this account, such labor "involves a series of activities that are not normally recognized as 'work' – in other words, the kinds of activities involved in defining and fixing cultural and artistic standards, fashions, tastes, consumer norms, and, more strategically, public opinion."[25] In this regard, the work corresponds to what Hardt, also following Lazzarato, describes as the "affective" form of immaterial labor which "involves the production and manipulation of affects and requires (virtual or actual) human contact and proximity."[26]

The logic described by such critiques is one in which the free and spontaneous production of community, sociality, as well as shared contexts and understandings, remains both in principle autonomous from capital and captured by it. Thus, the form of labor in question tends to be "free" in the sense described by Terranova: both unpaid (outside of established labor markets) and freely given, endowed with a sense of autonomy. As Hardt puts it, "In the production and reproduction of affects, in those networks of culture and communication, collective subjectivities are produced and sociality is produced – even if those subjectivities and that sociality are directly exploitable by capital."[27]

Such a formulation allows us to describe reality TV shows as thematizing the direct capture of affective labor by serving as "factories" for valorizing the work of building social relations, manipulating affect, fixing cultural standards and norms (think *Queer Eye for the Straight Guy*), and so on. By creating scenarios in which this activity can be captured on camera and sold as an entertainment commodity, reality TV renders it *directly* economically productive.

The interactive economy facilitates a similar transformation whereby, for example, social networking sites capture and repurpose the forms of immaterial or affective labor associated with building, maintaining, and extending social relationships online. This labor both provides the content of the Web sites and a wealth of information economies for those who own the site and monitor the activity of its members. The capture of personal information is becoming the economic machine driving the customized, targeted, and "accountable" model of interactive online advertising. Not only do users provide the content for popular Web sites, but they also provide a reflexive form of user-generated content: the data about their online activities.

Critical accounts of affective or immaterial labor in the online economy tend to give less attention to this second, less obvious form of user-generated content, echoing the commercial sector's emphasis on intentional forms of self-promotion, self-expression, socialization, and creativity. It seems fair to describe these intentional forms of activity as freely given. It is less clear that monitoring-based forms of reflexive user-generated content – data about users' online activity – is similarly freely given, at least to the extent that informed consent and intentionality might be construed as necessary conditions of free production. Whether or not either form might be construed as a form of exploitation, other than in the sense that they are used to create value for a third party, is a very different question.

The notion of exploitation is both a problematic and, as this chapter suggests, a crucial one for the development of a critical approach to the productivity of the interactive economy. As outlined in the work of critical scholars, the term "immaterial labor" denotes both autonomy from capital and an exploitable surplus. Raising the specter of exploitation suggests that the production of community, sociality, and subjectivity is, at least in one important way, analogous to that of the more "material" forms of labor associated with industrial production: it can generate surplus value that is captured by the mechanism of capitalist exchange. The notion of exploitation is frequently invoked but less often defined in the post-Marxist critical literature. In his critical analysis of postmodern branding, Adam Arvidsson, for example, observes that the "context of consumption" (the shared meanings associated with particular brands) created by consumers is subject to a process of "exploitation."[28] He seems to mean by this simply that consumers generate the raw (and "immaterial") material that is used by capital as a means of enhancing brand value and profits: capital appropriates forms of productive free creative activity that nevertheless remain external to it. The apparent assumption is that if one entity profits from the activity of another, exploitation by definition obtains. It is a critique that conserves a Marxist conception of exploitation while rejecting the Marxist formulation of the power relations internal to capital that structure wage-labor relations. What distinguishes free labor from wage labor is that the former is not subject to the same relations of coercion – this is what makes it autonomous from capital. A notion of exploitation without coercion runs the danger of reducing exploitation to a matter of choice – as evidenced, for example, by the familiar rejoinder that those who don't want to be exploited need only withdraw: they will not go hungry if they do not go on *Facebook*, shop online (or go on reality TV, for that matter). Despite the repeated invocation of the concept, the question remains as to whether a critical notion of exploitation can be applied to free labor. If, as Terranova observes, "free labor is not necessarily exploited labor," how are we to tell the difference?[29]

In the most general terms, a critical, Marxist conception of exploitation implies, as Nancy Holmstrom argues, "forced, surplus and unpaid labor, the product of which is not under the producers' control."[30] In capitalism, Marx argues, exploitation takes place in the wage relation whereby the surplus value generated by labor (not captured by its exchange value) is appropriated by capital.[31] The Marxist account discerns the coercion built into the "free" exchange whereby labor is commodified and sold as reliant upon the compulsion to earn a living under conditions in which workers are left with nothing to exchange for the means of survival but their labor power (thanks to the forcible privatization of the means of production). This form of compulsion should not be ruled out in the case of reality TV – consider the statement of one prospective cast member for the second season of *Kid Nation* that she wants to be on the show in part because "we're kind of in a situation of us needing money."[32] However, many of the shows (including *Kid Nation*) offer financial rewards so much lower than the minimum wage that their wage-earning potential is largely speculative. In the case of the online economy, it would be even harder to make the case that participation takes place under the threat of compulsion, despite the fact that some online services are becoming increasingly important to certain sectors of the labor market.

"Feminizing" labor

How then might one relate the notions of compulsion and exploitation to the capture of value generated in non-waged forms of value-generating activity – the type of exploitation invoked by Corsani in her account of the "feminization of labor"?[33] Holmstrom makes a crucial link between exploitation and alienation to suggest one way in which the capture of the fruits of free labor might be construed to partake of the logic of exploitation (which is not to trivialize other forms of exploitation, but rather to note a shared logic of underlying coercion).[34] For Marx, Holmstrom argues, the appropriation of control over workers' labor represents more than a means for capturing surplus value: it simultaneously reproduces the alienation of workers from the product of their labor: "Being congealed labor, the product is in some sense part of the producers. When it is taken away from them, they are thereby diminished, impoverished, denuded."[35] It is a formulation that draws from the description of exploitation in the *1844 Manuscripts*, where Marx forcefully elaborates the wages of estranged labor: "The worker places his life in the object; but now it no longer belongs to him, but to the object ... What the product of his labor is, he is not. Therefore, the greater this product, the less is he himself."[36] It is worth recalling this overtly humanist formulation if only to note how neatly and systematically it anticipates the explicit marketing appeal of the interactive economy: to return control to producers of their creative activity (to overcome the estrangement of the product), to build community (to overcome the estrangement of others), and to facilitate our own self-understanding via self-expression (to overcome self-estrangement). If anyone is directly invoking the language of Marx in the current conjuncture, it is not the critical theorists, but the commercial promoters of the interactive "revolution."

The promise of interactive participation, in other words, takes shape against the background of the forcible appropriation of control over labor power. The ostensible "democratization" of access to the means of media production represented by both reality TV and the internet "revolution" offers to make available to all what was formerly the province of only a privileged few. The offer might be understood as a panacea for the ills of exploitation associated with the lack of control and the forms of estrangement and abstraction invoked by the promoters of new forms of interactivity. The form of exchange that characterizes both formations – that of reality TV and of Web 2.0 – might thus be understood as a *second-order* result of the forcible appropriation of labor power which enhances the appeal of the offer of a modicum of participation or control over the product of their creative activity in exchange for willing submission to productive forms of monitoring.

However, the fact that, for example, our activities on *Facebook* generate value for the site's owners does not mean that they can be compared to factory or office work (waged labor). In this regard, this chapter focuses only on one sector of the economy: the attempt to extract value from unwaged forms of voluntary activity. It thus targets those forms of productivity that are associated with the productivity of unwaged activities specific to digital forms of leisure, consumption, communication, and socialization. It is not meant to provide a general theory of exploitation, but rather to update such a theory – invoked, but often unexplained in Marxist-inflected accounts of the exploitation of immaterial labor – in ways that might facilitate its application to emerging models of advertising-supported and monitoring-based e-commerce. A similar process is at work in the forms of voluntary participation modeled by a show like *Kid Nation*, which, after all, may well have had some of the elements of summer camp described by its producers (without these absolving them of the charge of exploitation). The connection between critiques of free labor and accounts of the exploitation of women's productive domestic activity in the industrial age emerges: they share a common mode of exploitation that differs from the traditional wage-labor model. Women's domestic labor in the context of capitalist industrial production is also unwaged, and yet provided under conditions structured by the forcible separation of the means of production from workers. Hardt invokes "feminist analyses" to describe the ways in which, in the information economy, the forms of affective labor formerly associated with the realms of reproduction and consumption become directly exploitable: "What are new … are the extent to which the affective immaterial labor is now directly productive of capital and the extent to which it has become generalized through wide sectors of the economy."[37] As Corsani puts it, "This is the sense in which one could agree to analyze the feminization of labor as a situation that extends 'the mechanisms of subjection applied above all and historically to women.'"[38] The associated form of exploitation cannot be broken down neatly according to the Marxian formula into "necessary" (to cover the wages, hence costs, of the laborer) and surplus labor time. As in the case of the form of exploitation associated in this chapter with the interactive economy, affective labor is redoubled: time and effort spent building social relations are simultaneously captured by capital.

As an indication of this type of exploitation, we might, following Holmstrom, think not just in terms of profits or surplus value, but also in terms of alienation or estrangement. Such an account depends not just on recognizing the background forms of coercion against which the promise of participation gains its appeal, but also on exploring the ways in which participation, though "freely" given, might be construed as involving "surplus and unpaid labor, the product of which is not under the producer's control."[39] The question to be asked might thus be, in what ways do the promises of participation, shared control and self-expression become self-defeating or self-thwarting? One answer might be illustrated by what this chapter has described as the user-generated data captured by networked, interactive commercial applications. The explicit goal of the capture of this information is to enlist it as a means of influencing consumer behavior and channeling desire. The practitioners of data-driven algorithmic target marketing envision a world in which our own, largely unintentional, revelations about patterns of online socialization, our hopes and fears, our predispositions and preferences, can create marketing appeals tailored to time, space, personality, and context that move us without our knowing why or recognizing the results of our own actions turned back upon us to serve ends that are not our own. Such an outcome marks the return of the very forms of estrangement it promised to overcome.

Notes

1 On the social factory, see Tiziana Terranova, "Free Labor: Producing Culture for the Digital Economy," *Social Text* 18, no. 2 (2000): 33–58, 34.

2 Antonella Corsani, "Beyond the Myth of Woman: The Becoming-Transfeminist of (Post-)Marxism," *SubStance* #112, 36, no. 1 (2007): 107–38, 127.

3 Corsani, "Beyond the Myth of Woman," 124.

4 François Jost, "When Reality TV is a Job", this volume, p. 31.

5 Tiziana Terranova, "Free Labor: Producing Culture for the Digital Economy," *Social Text* 18, no. 2 (2000): 33–58, 37.

6 Terranova, "Free Labor," 33.

7 Corsani, "Beyond the Myth of Woman," 124.

8 Maria Elena Fernandez, "*Kid Nation* Parents Speak," *Pittsburgh Post-Gazette*, 3 September (2007): C6.

9 Eric Pfanner, "The Reality of Reality TV: It's Acting, Court Rules," *New York Times*, 7 June (2009): B1.

10 Collin Levy, "Taste – De Gustibus: Child Labor," *Wall Street Journal*, 7 September (2007): W11.

11 Edward Wyatt, "'Kid Nation' Parents Gave Show Free Rein," *New York Times*, 23 August (2007): E1.

12 Edward Wyatt, "CBS Was Warned on 'Kid Nation', Documents Show," *New York Times*, 22 August (2007): A13.

13 Maria Elena Fernandez, "The New Reality of 'Kid Nation'; Critics Say the Children Were Exploited; Or Was Roughing it More Like Summer Camp," *Montreal Gazette*, 19 August (2007): A18.

14 Fernandez, "The New Reality of 'Kid Nation,'" A18.

15 Broadcasting & Cable Staff, "Former Child Actor Slams CBS' Kid Nation," *Broadcasting & Cable*, 30 July (2007): 10.

16 Fernandez, "The New Reality of 'Kid Nation,'" A18.

17 Edward Wyatt, "'Kid Nation' Parents Gave Show Free Rein," *New York Times*, 23 August (2007): E1.

18 Daniel De Vise, "Being Watched a Full-Time Job, and Then Some, Web Women Say," *Miami Herald*, 22 January (2004): 1A.

19 The Federal Fair Labor Standards Act exempts certain categories of labor including professionals and creative artists from being paid a premium for overtime hours. Put simply it divides forms of labor into those who punch the clock (factory workers, retail workers, etc.) and those who don't (executives, academics, etc.). Lawsuits in which employees have sued for overtime have turned on the question of whether or not the activity in question (newspaper reporting, for example) falls into the creative category.

20 De Vise, "Being Watched a Full-Time Job, and Then Some, Web Women Say," 1A.

21 *MSNBC Reports*, "Look at Me! The Webcam Explosion," MSNBC, 29 August (2000).

22 Jenifer Braun, "Jenny's Dish," *Star-Ledger*, 24 November (2004): 33.

23 Snoop Dogg's *Father Hood* (2008) E! Online, 2008, http://au.eonline.com/on/shows/snoopdogg/index.jsp

24 Maurizio Lazzarato, "Immaterial Labor." In *Radical Thought in Italy: A Potential Politics*, eds Paulo Virno and Michael Hardt (Minneapolis, MN: University of Minnesota Press, 1996): 133–46, 139.

25 Lazzarato, "Immaterial Labor," 139.

26 Michael Hardt, "Affective Labor," *Boundary 2*, 26, no. 2 (1999): 89–100, 97.

27 96–97.
28 Adam Arvidsson, "Brands: A Critical Perspective," *Journal of Consumer Culture*, 5 (2005): 235–58, 251.
29 Terranova, "Free Labor," 48.
30 Nancy Holmstrom, "Exploitation" in *Exploitation: Key Concepts in Critical Theory*, eds Kai Nielsen and Robert Ware (New York, NY: Humanities Press International, 1997): 84–103, 87.
31 Karl Marx, *The Economic & Philosophic Manuscripts of 1844* (New York, NY: International Publishers, 1986).
32 Meghan Daum, "'Kid Nation' Raises Cultural Questions," *Deseret News*, 23 September (2007): p. G06.
33 Corsani, "Beyond the Myth of Woman," 124.
34 Holmstrom, "Exploitation."
35 Ibid., 85.
36 Marx, *The Economic & Philosophic Manuscripts of 1844*, p. 77.
37 Hardt, "Affective Labor," 97.
38 Corsani, "Beyond the Myth of Woman," 126.
39 Holmstrom, "Exploitation," 85.

Chapter 3

When reality TV is a job

François Jost

This text is based on the argument that the success of reality TV arises from the considerable malleability of the genre.[1] Of course, the success of reality TV has multiple causes which are to be found in the intense distrust of citizens at the beginning of the 2000s towards media and politicians. Both the one and the other are blamed, not only in France I believe, but all over the world, for their lack of transparency and, above all, for their incapacity to represent the citizens' daily preoccupations. This atmosphere is a sort of compost on which some programs take root, claiming to remedy the defects imputed to politics and to media. And they succeed particularly well, since it led to this paradoxical situation in May, 2002: 37 percent of ages 18–24 abstained in the first round of votes for the French presidential elections, convinced that it would change nothing in their lives, but they voted massively to decide on the fate of contestants of a constructed reality, *Loft Story*, the French version of *Big Brother*. The result was that the French extreme right leader took part in the second tour.

But, if the revolt of Little People against Big People, and its particular shape that is TV populism, is the context in which so-called "téléréalité" was born, my paper aims to show that it has grown thanks to the perfectly protean character of its genre and of its formats. To understand this fluctuating nature, I shall start with the clarification of the concept of identity by Paul Ricœur. The philosopher shows that this term refers to two very different things: the first is the *sameness*. It designates a numerical identity, a permanence through the passing time of a system's organization, what Ricœur summarizes with the notion of "character," understood "as the ensemble of distinctive features which allow to re-identify an individual human as being the same."[2] In this occurrence, identity is seen from the outside and represents the not-voluntary and not-necessarily aware part of personal identity. "The character encloses at the same time the numerical identity, the qualitative identity, the uninterrupted continuity in change and finally the permanence of passing time."[3] The second sense of identity is *selfhood*, summarized by the question "who am I?" Beyond the changes which we undergo, it translates, from a subjective point of view, the feeling of one's personal authenticity, one's unity and one's continuity, of which Ricœur sees the illustration in two models: the kept word, the promise, which supposes a "preservation of oneself," and a "challenge to time," "a denial of the change";[4] and the ability to self-build one's narrative identity, that is to make of one's life a coherent narrative.

This text aims to show how reality television producers take advantage of this ambiguous duality of identity: first, by giving the appearance of being trust-worthy people through the promise they made of allowing the candidates to be themselves and therefore of expressing their *selfhood*, then by reducing this to the *sameness* of a character prebuilt by the format, up to the point where the candidates came to question the role that the producers made them play. So, reality TV shows us two forces face to face: the producer, the storytelling master, who forges narratives adapted to the target he's aiming at, and the candidate, who tries to win over the spectator, often successfully. To what extent is this televised fight the symptom of a political fight on the scale of society? This is what I shall eventually attempt to answer through the case of *Temptation Island* (*L'Ile de la Tentation*).

The malleability of the TV genre

Usually, the topic of genre is considered from a very descriptive point of view: the analysts enumerate the genres without trying to understand how they are con-nected to one another: for instance, docu-drama, detective series, variety shows and so on. In my opinion, genres are labels first of all that make sense thanks to three "worlds" which are the interpretants of images, that is to say, according to Peirce, a sign by which we interpret another sign:

- Our first "interpretant" of images is, of course, the real world. I do not take the stand that each image needs to be compared with the real world in order to be interpreted, nor that the real world is an absolutely identifying entity which would be the same to all of us. I only mean that our first reflex, when we chance upon an image on television, is to determine if this image refers to our world, says something *about* our world, or not, whatever the idea we have about what this world might be.
- Fiction is second interpretant. To the extent that we think a narrative is fic-titious, we accept events that we would not believe if they were said to be real. So, if I do not believe in witches, it makes no sense for me to anchor *Blair Witch* in reality, but, as far as I consider it to be a fiction, I can enjoy it.
- There is another category, which, in any case, presupposes the respect of rules and which, nevertheless, refers to reality: game shows. This is very obvious for the quiz shows, which obey certain rules (for instance, the period allowed for answering) and in which truth requires a reference to reality. As for the game of role playing, it is close to fiction, but with the difference that it is based on the fact that the player knows full well that it is a conventional role she/he is playing.

Game shows include some genres or some types of discourse that are not ficti-tious: lotteries, answering riddles or jumping with elastic. Besides, fiction is first defined by the creation of a coherent world, whereas the main feature of a game is that it is "gratuitous."

To summarize, the three worlds I have been speaking about may be represented in the following way:

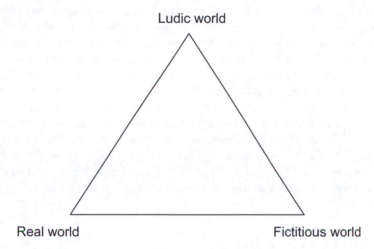

Figure 3.1 The three "worlds" (a)

Instead of being fixed once and for all, the anchorage of a genre within a world is very variable, and depends on the way it's used by the various actors of communication: the producers, the channels, the mediators, the archives, the institutions measuring the ratings, the institutions of regulation and, naturally, the televiewers. If certain genres are more naturally anchored within such or such a world (news within the real world, series within the world of fiction), the skill of these new genres launched by contemporary television is to be positioned at equal distance between the real world, the world of fiction and the ludic world. Therefore, these genres may be endowed with different meanings according to the arguments that seem best adapted to the conquest of the public. From this point of view, it's very interesting to observe how a global format migrates upon the triangle of the worlds that I have described. The novelty of reality TV is primarily its capacity to migrate on this mapping of these three worlds.

When a new format appears on the market, it is up to the producer to propose the labels that are suitable for it. To do so, the channel builds itself up as a reliable person by playing on the constitutive gesture of the selfhood: the promise. He makes what I call a *pragmatic promise*, built on different means of communication: the press conferences by the channel's president, press releases, the trailers and, even, the credits. This promise is a proposal of meaning that conditions the public debates about a program and its first meaning. In the case of *Big Brother* and its descendants, the pragmatic promise was to allow the identity of every contestant to express itself – having asked them to be them-selves, which can be read as an incentive to express *selfhood*. This promise worked so well that a lot of intellectuals considered that it was the best documentary ever seen about French youth. It appears that the strategy of communication was first and foremost "to sell" the program, saying that viewers could have never seen anything more real since it was broadcast 24 hours a day. But this strategy generates a lot of criticism. For instance, it was said that the contestants were in jail, worse, in a concentration camp. Rather than argue against these criticisms, M6, the channel that broadcast *Loft Story*, avoids the subject on which it is attacked (the real world), and begins a shifting to the ludic world. Indeed, the television marketing benefits from the fact that television genres are a sort of quicksand. Presenting the program from the ludic angle allows the de-dramatization of the debate and makes the program less objectionable. The president of M6's board of directors, Thomas Valentin, was in charge of this delicate mission. He claimed: "It is a game. It is not reality." This strategy slide shows the extent to which the so-called identity of a channel is a lure, since it badly resists the con-stituent criterion of selfhood, which is the preservation of oneself, and respect for the given word.

Is being a contestant work?

This strategy based upon the malleability of the genre is not peculiar to *Big Brother*; it characterizes reality TV in general. It aims at making a program pass for what it is not in order to take economic or other advantage of it. At least twice in France legal proceedings opposed actors from the audiovisual commu-nication and the show's producers. The first time was when the Court had to decide if *Pop Stars* was a documentary or not, and was allowed or not to receive subsidies put aside for this genre. The second when the contestants of *Temptation Island* (now in its eighth season) sued the producer in order to negotiate their status in the program. This case fundamentally questions the status of reality television, and attempts to eventually condemn it.

Its pragmatic promise to the audience locates it clearly on the reality side: the program would be the narrative of an experiment lived by the contestants. According to the producers, the program aims to show "individuals' everyday life" to whom it "is simply asked to be themselves." Taken this way, *Temptation Island* is in continuity with *Big Brother*: reality TV would be the place where people would simply be who they are. Uttered by a producer who introduces himself as a person, this order is indeed an incentive to the candidates to let them express what they consider subjectively as their *self*. So, it would achieve the ideal of the Age of the Enlightenment philosopher, Jean-Jacques Rousseau, that of a relationship between human beings based not on *seeming*, but on *being*, in a transparent society, contrary to that of the political world. Here is how the host introduces the show: "During 12 days and 12 nights, couples are going to be able to measure the strengths and the weaknesses of their love. But especially to answer this question: 'Am I with the right person? Is there another one somewhere else?'" In the present day when rites of passage have almost disappeared from society, *Temptation Island* accredits the idea that sexual and sentimental maturity must go through the rites set up by the program: that the couples have a passionate relation or that one of its members be fickle, it is necessary to live this experiment of temptation and if she/he leaves it victorious, it will be for life. According to the producer, television would make the young adult mature, because of the experience that it allows her or him to live.

Now it is exactly by challenging this initial promise of representing the candidates' selfhood that some contestants turned against the producers. In France, a contestant brought a lawsuit against the producers, claiming that it was in no way an enriching adventure for the couple, but only a job,[5] since he played a role that he was asked to play, instead of being himself. For their defense, the producer used the malleability of the genre and argued that it was only a game, moreover regulated by a "regulation" and not by a contract.

> The GLEM company maintains that the program's concept, which consists in a questioning of each of the contestants on his or her feelings towards her or his partner after agreeable activities such as sailing (catamaran and jet-ski), bungee jumping, bathing, horseback riding, fishing, massage sessions, involvement in the evening parties, dinners alone together, in an exotic and magnificent location in company of bachelors, infers only entertainment excluding any manual, artistic or intellectual work, that in compensation the participants only have to follow some simple rules [...] to agree to be filmed in the *ludic* moments, to answer the interviews in order to share their feelings and to respect the rituals of the program.

As we see, the reference to reality is suddenly underestimated to the benefit of the entertainment and ludic moments. To oppose these arguments, the contestants' lawyers tried both to pull *Temptation Island* out from the entertainment sphere, from the ludic world, and to bring it back towards reality, while keeping fiction on the horizon.

First argument against entertainment: the surveillance. "The intrusion of cameras in private life, even under an agreement, does not count as simple entertainment." The fact that everything is filmed, that "the concept of the program led the shooting teams to follow the participants permanently" shows their dependence with regard to the producer, whatever be the nature of the filmed activities and, notably, their ludic character. In other words, the apparatus of surveillance is more decisive in the qualification of the program than what it shows.

The second argument against the idea that *Temptation Island* is entertainment is that for the contestants, the ludic activities are minor; they are nothing but a compensation for their not very enviable fate; it is only for the viewers that these activities are entertainment.

Hence this conclusion: for the contestants, it is not entertainment. Insofar as the regulation demands a permanent availability of the participants for the shooting, under a ban to leave the site or to communicate with the outside world, it is work, understood here as a relation of subordination to an employer and defined by the execution of tasks under its authority.

What kind of work? On this point, the ruling is much less clear. It notes that the plaintiff "in order to satisfy the concept of the program, at certain moments he was advised on the analysis of his behavior and was obliged to *rehearse some of the filmed scenes.*" For example, the producers – as skillful film directors – occasionally conditioned the contestants' reactions by giving them false information concerning their partner; they made them replay some of their lines to obtain a more live or credible result. The participant is not far from being an actor. But the judge can't go as far as saying this, not wanting to assimilate the participants with the status of artists who are covered by collective agreements. So they note that the participant was not engaged "as a dramatic, lyric, choreographic or variety artist or as a cabaret artist, a stuntman, a puppeteer, a choir artist" and that he "did not play a role, being personally implied." Nevertheless, the border between reality and fiction is subtle, because the judge acknowledges that what is filmed does not much have to do with "real" life, but that at the same time it is not possible to use the word "fiction": "If the reality as lived was not that of everyday life because of the context and the formatted circumstances, the creation of fiction is absent."

If law stops at this point, the media analyst can go further. When an individual is encouraged to act out certain reactions, when he reacts to situations entirely worked out by the production, when he has to rehearse some of the scenes, as a broadcast collection of howlers testifies, he is not far from being an actor, and, actually, he approaches the territory of fiction. Doesn't he become almost a brother to an actor from the improvisation leagues who acts on any theme that is requested? The ruling is not far from recognizing this, while observing that this category of actor does not come under the collective agreement of the artists-actors. In fact, French Internal Revenue took this further by delivering a notice of reassessment to a candidate from *Les Colocataires (The Co-lodgers)*, a show about fourteen female and male 20 year olds living in two closely situated houses, under the pretext that his income didn't come from a game but was generated by his position as a film-actor.

If the status of fiction is questionable, one thing is sure: the control of the storytelling by the producer and his choice to always tell the same story, whatever the raw material of the improvisation. In other words, while they claimed to let the contestants express their selfhood, they reduced them to characters, condemned to always be the same, and to illustrate this sameness necessary to their storytelling. To support this assertion, it is necessary to go farther than the observation of the shooting and to confront the initial promise of showing an experiment around couples with the result that is the program.

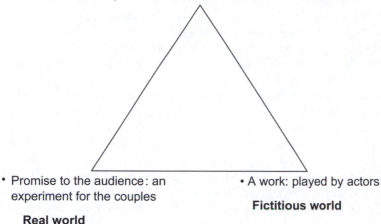

Ludic world

• The plea by the channel at the trial: an entertainment

• Promise to the audience: an
  experiment for the couples

Real world

• A work: played by actors

Fictitious world

Figure 3.2 The three "worlds" (b)

Adults made childish

Sponsored by Manix condoms, unsuitable for children under the age of 10, *Temptation Island* shows adults aged 20, 23, 25 or 28 and is supposed to address that adult group. Nevertheless, as soon as you watch the program, you notice that, in this particular case, the natural age does not correspond with the cultural age. If, according to the sociologists, the entrance to grown-up life does not take place any more at a definite age but between the years 18 and 29, it is clear that the participants are not all close to this stage and that they are sometimes closer to adolescence or childhood. Especially since the program has recourse to many devices of "infantilization" which hijack it from this explicit promise and conform it to an unmodifiable format written by the producers, whatever events the participants may live.

What is being adult, indeed? It is to be responsible for one's own narrative, a relevant feature of selfhood. "I am what I tell about myself," Ricœur says. How to be autonomous when everything is done, on the contrary, to transform the contestants into objects, and not into children endowed with freedom? The program's system is based on a double bind: be yourself, but do what we tell you to do.

First indication of this deprivation of autonomy: the campfire test consists of showing a participant images of her/his "fiancé"/"fiancée," generally her/him in a seduction scene with a "temptress," and in presenting this scene as emblematic of the reality that she/he lives in. The contestant is put in a position where he cannot criticize the images because he cannot put them in context. Images are seen as transparent. The editing is considered reliable and is based on the same device as the media manipulation against which the reality television was supposed to be built. Manipulation of events is a way of maintaining them in a child's status and of dispossessing them of their selfhood. Indeed, unlike that of the adult who exists by her/his narrative, "the narrative identity of the child depends wholly on her/his parents," since "it is the adult who structures time, space and the social environment for him."[6]

The second clue which strengthens the idea that the age of life staged by these programs is childhood is the fact that the scenes chosen in editing show certain contestants whose aim is less to be adult than *to grow*, which is obviously the aim of a child. Evidence of this is Lindsay, a contestant who says that his fiancée likes to tell him to "do this, do that, pick up your socks, go and wash your hands, that would be nice," even when he makes it clear that he was going to do it! Sometimes, he does not regret Joanna's attitude, but her method: "If she wants me to *grow up* she must stop holding my hand, if she takes off the bicycle's training wheels I'm going to learn to cycle alone." On her side, Joanna confirms: Lindsay is like a child and she's the mother: "I know that he is not going to manage to do certain things alone. Maybe the fact that I take too much care of him *as a mother* makes him slow to progress … he came to the show just to *grow* a little." The candidate does not rectify what could seem a slip of the tongue; she uses the same words as her "fiancé": it is not a question of being adult or of behaving as such, but only of *growing*[7] … The logical conclusion of these comments: the candidate hasn't yet achieved an adult's maturity, any more than his teammates; he lives in the immaturity of a "young person."

Third clue: the staging of a "relational morality" (Olivier Galland), for which "the consequences of the actions are less envisaged according to their intrinsic result (you must do this or that) than according to the concrete and direct effect which they can have on the others and particularly those whom we see most confidentially."[8] The other exists, and it is one of the features of the immaturity staged by the reality television there, only at a glance. Far from being determined by themselves, the candidates are all in the heteronomy: they cannot become the autonomous narrator of their story. The big preoccupation of the inhabitants of *Temptation Island* is to know if the family or friendly circle of acquaintances thinks that they are made to be with their fiancé/fiancée. So, the true preoccupation of the children-candidates is to look for the approval of the relatives. We are very far from the adolescent revolt.

The manufacturing of these formats attempts to adapt the conclusions of the sociologists who see "adolescents" in today's youth: retarded, hedonist and irresponsible thirty-year olds who multiply regressive behavior. If the behavior reveals the lack of maturity of the contestants, the apparatus aims to reduce them to a child's status, it makes them childish. An analysis of the program illustrates that, independently of the actual identity of the participants "living" before the cameras, the different episodes of the show all depict the same story, that of a group of people who have reached the age of majority, struggling with leaving childhood behind, and experiencing difficulty in growing and becoming autonomous.

As a result, the audience ratings become more understandable. If the most receptive audience to these programs is the 15–24-year-old group and also women, it is because they have all the qualities for federating the children and their mother. To young people it provides the comfort of identification, by showing that the difficulties to be gone through to reach adulthood are universally shared. To the mothers, they bring this reassurance: the children still need them.

This realistic reading which accepts the promise that the program talks first of all about reality, is not the only possible one. Some ground-work investigation reveals other uses. The first one is purely fictitious and consists of following the program as a soap opera. The viewer's pleasure is a weekly meeting up again with characters whose fate he wants to know about but without questioning the reality of what they're living. The pleasure looked for is close to fiction, and is situated in the simple stories that are told, which are at any rate close to popular novels.

The second is purely ludic. It generally draws together communities of young spectators who watch the program together, and whose pleasure, in this case, is to laugh at those who are on the screen and to make fun of them. The program then moves across to the ludic world.

What conclusions can be drawn from these approaches to *Temptation Island?*

First of all, it shows that the categorization of a program is not only a theoretical question, but that it has an economic, social and philosophical impact. From the economic point of view, the fact that TF1 was condemned for covering up work to pay more than 25 000 Euros to a contestant is a worrying legal decision for the broadcaster, because the lawyer has 130 other plaintiffs waiting.

From the social point of view, the belief in a channel's promises is variable. Their acceptance depends very widely on the age and of the identification of an existential questioning. The ones who identify their mental age adhere to the show without questioning it, whereas those who have the capacity to stand back from themselves and observe the work carried out by the media on the raw footage can take a tongue-in-cheek pleasure.

From the philosophical point of view, it's the status of the anonymous viewer that is transformed. While reality television was based on the promise to give her/him the floor to break away from the smooth and polished talking of experts and politicians, we are seeing a professionalization of today's candidates, which suggests that the border-line between the ordinary man and the artist-actor is becoming thinner and thinner.

Isn't the fact that a New York Reality TV School has recently opened a supplementary sign? This is the mission it announces: "The mission of The

New York Reality TV School is to train and develop non-actors, and actors, through the spectrum of experiences a reality TV contestant/actor will face: from the audition, to the many interviews you'll go through and the actual show."[9] This, I believe, is evidence that today's Reality TV is built on the ruins of the sincerity and the authenticity which were the selling points of earlier reality television.

What is reality television the symptom of?

This desire to learn how to be in real television programs brings us back to the point which I brought up in my introduction: the remarkable concomitance between the massive votes for the second season of *Loft Story* in France and the presence of right-wing Jean-Marie Le Pen in the second tour of the French presidential elections in 2002. I do not claim that there is a relation of cause and effect between these two events, as the upholders of the Frankfurt School endeavor to do, accusing television of creating a lot of trouble. But can't one see a symptom in this concomitance? While televiewers were voting massively for insignificant people, the presidential elections showed record abstention and enabled the success of the hardest populism protester since the Second World War. Isn't this a sign that the citizen imagines that TV, and especially reality TV, is an alternative to traditional mediations (parliamentary debates), to legitimate educational institutions and to information circuits? And isn't it also the hope of those who sign up with a Reality Television School? The behavior of the candidates and of the public before or after the programs contributes arguments in favor of this hypothesis.

In August 2008, for example, a candidate from the eighth season of *Temptation Island* considered that her appearance in media had a political mission. Dany, her first name, claimed that she does not want to be mediatized because of any egocentricity, but "to denounce the exodus of middle classes from her department, the Alpes-Maritimes," adding that she's waiting for "a debate with those in power." It's frequent to hear on radio, after the broadcast of an episode of *Temptation Island* or a similar program, a candidate saying that France must re-establish the truth about her/his couple, while forgetting that even if programs like these have record ratings, they hardly reach more than three million people. The confusion between the number of viewers and the people of France is nearly as constant as the one that identifies French people to the voters in an election, whatever be the percentage of abstentions.

The feeling that the candidates have that they represent the citizen better than the politicians or the elite is also confirmed by the public's attitude to programs such as *Star Academy* or *La Nouvelle Star (American Idol)* created to promote the anonymous. On April 11, 2007, three of *The New Star*'s budding singers, Martine, Vincent and Michel, were voted out by the public even though the jury had considered them the best. Worse, those that the musical talent experts had considered disastrous stayed on. The experts were once again squashed as if a crisis of the media representativeness was followed by a crisis of political representativeness. Anyway, the point is that the criteria taken into account by the musical experts, the "jury," are not the ones of the public: if the professionals judge according to vocal qualities, the public is rather less interested by that. The fans come to listen to their singers, with their encouragement panels prepared in advance, and this even before listening to the performances by their candidates. Sometimes, on these placards, the name of a region, a city or a department is added to the first name. And more and more frequently we see the public voting for a singer's local roots than for his vocal qualities. If this strengthens the divorce from the "experts," the public is even more satisfied. The public prefers bad singers who represent their community to a good singer deprived of a strong link with those whom he represents, with the result that their personal identity becomes a carrier of a wider identity, that of a community that they believe they represent.

Another cue of this kind of social revenge, which this revolt against the elite underlies, can be spotted in the treatment which reality television reserves for "people." At the same time as the quarter of an hour of celebrity that they demand as due, reality television viewers are delighted that the celebrities spend a bad quarter of an hour. By putting celebrities in prosaic situations, by asking them to exercise the common gestures of people from the countryside, *The Simple Life* provides by proxy a popular vengeance: the stars are deposed from Olympe, decreased, and undergo daily work as a punishment. The success of this program ensues from the fun made of the television starlets, who, in this particular case, embody an easy life, reserved for someone. Current commercial channels agree with this report tinged with irony which curtly formulates the "people" magazine *Public* about the stars: *they are like us.* Britney Spears? Like us, because she stained her skirt! Drew Barrymore? Like us, because she scratched her ankle while buying frozen food! Paris Hilton? Like us, because she puts her finger in her mouth …

The cult of the anonymous and the cult of the celebrities celebrated by private channels are two faces of the same coin. The presence of the human being without quality on the screen reassures the televiewer on the sudden transformation that her/his life could have thanks to the wave of a magic wand given by fairy television, in the same way as the devaluation of the celebrities, which is done to remind the viewer that they are human as he is.

All these topics come finally under *protesting populism*, defined by Taguieff as the ongoing fight of Little Man against Big Man, of individuals crushed by the system, on a background of the institutions' decline.[10] With their promise of showing individuals being themselves 24 hours out of 24, the producers of *Big Brother* (or of *Loft Story* in France) pretended that they were showing the viewer, in a limpid way, a world itself transparent and, as a result, they flattered "the antipolitical imagination of populism […] entirely centred on a refusal of the mediations, considered useless, even harmful."[11] And they backed up the launching of these programs with multiple declarations, in which they underlined that, for the first time, television gave the floor to "real people," and no more to experts of all kinds, artists or intellectuals. So, this idea that the elite was rotten, in particular the political elite, explains at the same time the high abstention figures of young voters during the French 2002 elections as it explains the attraction of other voters for the extreme-right leader whose speeches all developed this theme.

The French people's distrust of politics comes from their feeling of forced choices: required to choose among lists of candidates who appear remote to them, they do not feel represented. Above all, because politicians have three crippling defects for the people questioned: they are insincere because they want to please the voters, they "aren't like us," and they belong to the world of the powerful and the well-to-do, in short, "they are not only foreign to the citizens' everyday life, but more generally to their 'community'"[12] (the success of the program reaching its paroxysm the day of the election of the outgoing or, rather, the outcasts). In these contexts, the success of the first reality TV show, *Loft Story*, is definitely the symptom of political distrust, which is itself the "sign of a crisis."[13] In many aspects, the program remedied the defects attributed to politicians: first by showing people without any specific qualities; then by asking them to be themselves and by insisting they be sincere; finally, by making their fate dependent on the viewers' vote. The producers so successfully popularized the idea that they gave the floor to "real people" – an idea very close to the populist political speeches – that most of the presidential election candidates used very similar idioms in 2007. In this respect, there is nothing more significant than candidate Nicolas Sarkozy's last speech, the week before his election, claiming to represent "all those without rank, all those unknown people, all those ordinary people whose voices are not heard" and to whom he will give the right of speech.[14] He used exactly the words the producers had used to praise the merits of TV reality, promising to represent "real people" while doing for them what politics didn't know how to do: give a chance to the humble by casting them into the universe of the stars.

Reality TV was thus the instrument for the transformation of populism into TV populism. But if the demagogic promise of banishing the elite from the screen to make space for real people and of giving contestants the opportunity to express their selfhood may seduce at first, we are at present witnessing a "boomerang effect": contestants, reduced to the sameness of prebuilt characters, feel in a powerful position, as do viewers, and, like creatures escaped from their creators, they turn against those who allowed them to speak, and this includes legal action. Being on television becomes a job which everyone feels free to undertake. If reality TV evolves in this direction, it will definitely lose what made it successful: the promise of another world, more limpid than that of politics and media.

Notes

1 I thank warmly Thom R. Balme, J.-L. Marie and Olivier Rozenberg, "Les motifs de la confiance (et de la défiance) politique" and Davidson Noton, who revised and corrected my translation.

2 Paul Ricœur, *Soi-même comme un autre*, Paris: Sequel, coll. Points, 1995, 144; transl. *Oneself as Another*, University of Chicago Press.
3 Ibid., 147.
4 Ibid., 149.
5 In 2005, appeal February 2008. New trials are scheduled. There are more than 100 plaintiffs.
6 Éric Dechavanne et Pierre-Henri Tavoillot, *Philosophie des Âges de la Vie*, Grasset, 2007, 340.
7 This example is taken from the 2007 season, but other similar ones can be found in 2008.
8 My translation. Olivier Galland, "Individualisation des mœurs et choix culturels," *Politiques publiques et équipements culturels*, O. Donnat and Toila (dir.), Paris: Presses de Sciences-po, 87–100, quoted by Éric Dechavanne et Pierre-Henri Tavoillot.
9 http://www.newyorkrealitytelevisionschool.com/realitytelevision-instructors.htm.
10 *L'Illusion Populiste*, Paris: Flammarion, coll. Champs, 2007.
11 Ibid., 16.
12 These data are drawn from: R. Balme, J.-L. Marie and Olivier Rozenberg, "Les motifs de la confiance (et de la défiance) politique: Intérêt, connaissance et conviction dans les formes du raisonnement politique," *Revue Internationale de Politique Comparée*, 10, no. 3, 2003.
13 R. Balme, J.-L. Marie and Olivier Rozenberg, "Les motifs de la confiance (et de la défiance) politique," 460.
14 29 April 2007.

Chapter 4

Just be yourself – only more so
Ordinary celebrity in the era of self-service television

Laura Grindstaff

Introduction

While hosting the 2000 Emmy Awards on US television, comic actor Gary Shandling quipped petulantly, "I don't like this reality television. Real people should not be on television; it's for people like us, people who have trained and studied to appear to be real." Shandling got a laugh in part because the joke rightly referenced the historic rise in the representation of "real" or "ordinary" people on television, both in the US and across the globe. It also referenced an emerging tension between professional and amateur domains of media participation. Now, a decade later, the statement appears anachronistic as the various sub-genres subsumed by the term "reality TV" have formed a large and seemingly stable part of the global television industry.

Academic scholarship on reality programming has grown in tandem with the genre itself.[1] Much of this work focuses on broad questions of political economy, studies of fandom/consumption as accessed online, or textual readings of individual programs – particularly in relation to nationalism and/or neo-liberalism on the one hand and identity politics on the other. Sustained ethnographic inquiry is relatively rare, due at least partly to the fragmented and dispersed nature of media production and consumption in the "new media" era.

With an eye to this gap, I draw on insights gained from my ethnographic study of daytime talk shows in the late 1990s in order to make sense of some new research on the MTV reality series *Sorority Life*. Specifically, I use the case of *Sorority Life* to explore the meaning of "ordinary celebrity" as it unfolds in the reality television context. Increasingly, I have come to think of reality programming as a form of "self-service television"[2] in which producers construct the necessary conditions of performance and real-people participants serve themselves (more or less successfully) to these performances. The result is "ordinary" – or "self-serve" – celebrity. My aim here is to use the concept of ordinary celebrity to consider what media exposure means to, and how it operates for, so-called ordinary people, with an eye to its gendered, classed, and racialized dimensions. Inspired by but not limited to ethnographic evidence, I explore the cultural "work" being done by self-service television and the implications of this work for rethinking the connection between "celebrity" and the performance of everyday life.

Self-service TV: setting the scene

Reality programming, for whatever else it does, signals the increasing visibility of "ordinary" people as characters/performers across the media landscape. While this no doubt represents a certain democratization of the media insofar as constructions of ordinariness now join constructions of religious, political, economic, and/or culture authority as the basis for celebrity,[3] the increasing visibility of ordinariness on television also protects the value-hierarchy that distinguishes between ordinary and celebrity categories in the first place. To paraphrase Nick Couldry, the passage of non-mediated "ordinary" persona to mediated "celebrity" persona is one of the master frames of reality TV; that this passage is seen as a laudable achievement reinforces the hierarchy between the two categories.[4]

Generally speaking, the talk-show guests and reality TV participants that I interviewed understood quite well that television exposure was an escape from, not an affirmation of, their ordinary status. What is perhaps less clear are the ways in which "ordinary celebrity" – the incorporation of ordinary people into the celebrity framework – works ultimately to reproduce the frame via internal stratification. Scholars interested in the political economy of media have rightly pointed out the ways in which professional actors have suffered from the ascendance of flexible modes of production in which the unpaid, nonunion, widely-available labor of "ordinary" people generates new avenues of profitability and control for media institutions.[5] At the same time, however, the circulation (and therefore exchange value) of cheaply-produced ordinary celebrity is inherently limited because the vast majority of reality TV participants lack the accumulated intertextual capital that "real" actors have.[6] Indeed, as Sue Collins argues, ordinary celebrity – or what she calls "dispensable celebrity" – upholds the higher value of "real" celebrity by protecting it from "clutter," sustaining scarcity as a measure of value.[7]

It is precisely ordinary celebrity as a distinct stratum in the larger system of celebrity that interests me as an ethnographer. Ordinary celebrity is both a cause and consequence of what I call "self-service television," exemplified by older genres such as daytime talk shows as well as the more recent upswing in reality programming. Self-service television affords the opportunity for acquiring celebrity cafeteria-style; it enables ordinary people to walk in and serve themselves to celebrity status without the bother of extensive training, formal credentials, or even much in the way of talent. It is a form of "pre-made" television in which the scaffolding for a successful performance is constructed by producers (and other production staff) out of particular contexts of performance rather than the content of scripts, rehearsals, etc. In the research that I've done, ordinary celebrity requires self-service television and self-service television produces ordinary celebrity.

I witnessed (and participated in) the construction of ordinary celebrity in considerable detail during my year-long foray into the world of US daytime talk shows, first as an intern and then as a production assistant. And I have written about the ways in which the use of ordinary people – particularly of the sort appearing on shows like Jerry Springer, where "ordinary" has little to do with "average" or "representative" – puts tremendous pressure on producers to erect the conditions of possibility for a dramatic performance before a guest ever sets foot on stage.[8] For "soft-core" topics, producers orchestrate scenarios designed to evoke public expressions of joy, sorrow, or remorse, whereas "hard-core" topics necessitate conditions of possibility that support the dramatization of conflict – usually by bringing into direct confrontation guests on opposing sides of an issue. Central to the production of both versions of the "money shot" is the expenditure of emotional labor on the part of producers; producers must manage their own emotions (trying to feel enough or trying not to feel too much) in order to manage the emotions of guests: this means persuading guests to participate, keeping them committed to participating, and shaping their on-stage performances.[9]

The various genres of reality programming, including quiz shows, gamedocs, docusoaps, emergency rescue shows, etc., are also forms of self-service television whose success depends upon the construction of particular performative contexts that require emotional labor from production staff. However, different genres marshal and deploy these resources in different ways. Whereas talk shows draw upon a theatrical mode of performance (complete with stage and studio audience), docusoaps such as *Sorority Life* evince a more observational mode in which performances unfold over time in a more naturalistic setting. In this latter scenario, the conditions of possibility that provide the grounding for successful performances (and the making of ordinary celebrity) are co-produced between producers and participants to a greater degree. And the burden of emotion-work is also dispersed, not just to participants but also to "below the line" production staff, particularly camera crews.

In the next section, I draw on my research with *Sorority Life* participants to detail the experience of performing oneself on television and the production practices that enable these performances. I focus on the ways in which participants sometimes collude with, sometimes oppose, the aims of production staff, and the tensions and conflicts that arise between different categories of participants. In effect, I aim to illuminate how self-service television works "on the ground" from the perspective of participants, the constituency most underrepresented in current scholarship on reality programming. And while the cases I draw upon are based in the US, the insights they give rise to may well transcend national borders. As Mark Andrejevic and others have argued, reality shows are particularly well suited to global media production because they combine local talent and forms of viewer participation with customizable transnational formats at a fraction of the cost of traditional dramatic programming.[10]

Playing oneself

Sorority Life (along with its companion show, *Fraternity Life*) aired on MTV for several seasons between 2002 and 2006, with each successive series showcasing a different sorority/fraternity at a different college; at this point, it's unclear whether additional series are in the works. *Sorority Life* was never as popular as its model and predecessor, *The Real World*, but the original series filmed at UC Davis was clearly popular enough to replicate, garnering roughly two million viewers per episode.[11] The premise of the show is simple: put six "ordinary" college girls in a house and follow along as they pledge an "ordinary" sorority, mixing observation footage with interviews. Because I teach at UC Davis, I knew one of the students chosen to star in the series, and, through her, was able to interview 12 participants: five of the six "stars" who lived under surveillance in the Pledge House and seven sorority sisters. In the first season, the sorority in question was Sigma Alpha Epsilon Pi – "Sigma" for short – a small Jewish sorority not affiliated with the National Panhellenic Conference (NPC) and thus not bound by the NPC's prohibition on media exposure. While the opening episodes intimated that the Jewish identity of the sorority might become a hook for generating drama (would the sisters of Sigma accept non-Jewish pledges?), the matter of Sigma's Jewish orientation was dropped and never surfaced again largely because, according to the sisters I interviewed, the sorority membership refused to foreground it.

As with *The Real World*, the dramatic interest of *Sorority Life* stems from watching specific personalities interact on camera. Unlike game-based reality shows wherein participants compete for a prize or reward according to specified rules, *Sorority Life* invites participants to simply "live their lives" in front of the camera as they go about a "normal" 10-week term at college – which just happens to include rushing and pledging a sorority. Consequently, the potential for drama has to be built into specific contexts of interaction as well as into the larger set of conditions under which the pledge process unfolds. Whether they realized it or not, in choosing Sigma as the featured sorority, producers both hurt and helped the dramatic potential of the series. On the one hand, because the sorority was small and relatively low-key, it did not have a social calendar filled with parties and "girls gone wild" events; on the other hand, its very rejection of the stereotypical sorority girl image introduced a certain level of conflict between the sorority and its pledges because at least some of the pledges were invested in playing up that image (as were producers and other production staff). Dramatic potential was also embedded in the very choice of subject matter – life in a sorority. MTV did not, for obvious reasons, choose to focus on a chess club or knitters' circle.

Given the dramatic potential embedded in the topic, the very decision to take part in an MTV reality show was a matter of some contention within the Sigma membership. Although critics are quick to assume that participants are unconditionally eager to be on TV, this assumption obscures the extended deliberative process that, in this case, took place even before filming began. As with many of the talk show guests I interviewed, some of the sorority sisters had reservations about appearing on TV; they recognized that it simultaneously represented an opportunity (for conveying a message, for highlighting the community-service orientation of their organization, of which they were proud) and a risk (of being misrepresented or thwarted in their goals). The issue of stereotypes figured centrally in the debate among members. All were aware of the sorority girl image – shallow, narcissistic, preoccupied with parties and boys – and of the potential overlap between this image and that of Jewish girls as clannish, self-absorbed, and exclusive. Whether they liked it or not, the sisterhood felt a "burden of representation"[12] and this led some members to be wary of television exposure. By contrast, those wanting to participate argued that here was a golden opportunity to prove the stereotype wrong; they could show the whole country – indeed, the world – that Sigma was a different, and special, organization. According to my interviewees, no one lobbied to participate solely for the excitement of being on TV or wanting media celebrity, although these motivations were understood to play an important role for most of those in favor.

In the end, the membership took a vote and those wishing to participate in the series won by a narrow margin. What the sisters did not fully understand at the time was that the series would focus primarily on the pledges living in the MTV Pledge House, and the sisters' ability to convey anything much about Sigma itself would be limited. They also failed to anticipate the degree to which MTV's involvement would significantly change the pool of young women who opted to pledge as well as the pledge process itself. Key here was the fact that only a subset of six women from the entire pledge class was selected to live in the Pledge House, and the six were chosen by producers (not the sisters) as much for their "camera friendly" qualities as their interest in Sigma or the Jewish community.

Although conditions favored producers, they were far from perfect. In order for producers to appoint six "characters" to the Pledge House, the type of girl that they needed had to rush the sorority and be accepted by the existing membership as pledges in the first place. Fortunately for producers, the sisterhood accepted everyone unconditionally in an effort to avoid the appearance of exclusivity. Nevertheless, as I learned from my interviews, Sigma's low profile on campus meant that the pool of young women rushing the sorority was relatively small, and producers' attempts to augment the pool by recruiting at local bars and nightclubs were hampered by the fact that (a) the town had few such establishments and (b) the students who frequented them were typically beyond the age of joining sororities. Unlike *The Real World*, which attracts tens of thousands of hopeful applicants annually, the inaugural *Sorority Life* series had no track record and producers had fewer options for securing "talent," meaning fewer options for finding young women with the requisite qualities to entertain audiences: out-going, good-looking (according to narrow Euro-centric standards), and willing to cultivate an interesting (= dramatic) "character" in front of the cameras.

Generally speaking, and not surprisingly, the women appointed by producers to the Pledge House tended to possess these qualities to a greater extent than did the "regular" pledges. Convincing the "right" pledges to live in the House was no easy matter, however. Three of the six required considerable persuasion from producers: they received pleading phone calls, text messages, and in-person house calls, with frequent reminders of the material benefits awaiting them should they opt in (free computers, ipods, clothing, cosmetics, etc., not to mention free rent for the 10 weeks of filming). They required persuasion because, while viewing the prospect of being on TV as a rare and exciting adventure, they questioned the wisdom of attending college under 24/7 surveillance. The remaining three pledges appointed to the House had fewer qualms, but not for uniform reasons (more on this later).

The context of production was thus complex, with some elements clearly working in favor of eliciting drama (differing agendas among different groups) and some elements working against that mandate (a limited pool of participants, and less than total commitment from some). Once filming began, there was also the matter of the cameras and their influence. The cameras added an important if under-appreciated dimension to the overall scaffolding of the performative context out of which participants crafted their performances. Reality TV executives are oft-quoted dismissing the influence of the cameras on participants' behavior, insisting that after a while everyone forgets they are there. Yet none of the pledges I interviewed who lived under constant surveillance claimed to forget about the cameras; rather, the four who got the most coverage said they gradually grew used to having them around, which is a different matter. The cameras became familiar fixtures rather than fading into the background. In other words, the cameras were a recognized part of the alternative "reality" constructed for participants, just as was the Pledge House itself, its inhabitants, and all the emotions and interactions that developed. It was only because of the cameras that any of it existed at all. Thus to speak of reality programming as "re-presenting the real," or mis-representing the real, as some scholars and critics are wont to do, is misleading. A reality show like *Sorority Life* does not re-present anything other than the outcome of its own production process, because it does not simply take a pre-existing reality and transform or alter it; rather, the various activities, practices, and technologies of production actively construct for real what participants experience. And then, beyond this, there is a second-register packaging of that reality intended for television and internet audiences.

For the existing membership of Sigma, the presence of MTV cameras had profound effects. First, it ensured that the group of young women who rushed the sorority looked and acted unlike any group from previous years: on the whole it was older, blonder, more interested in partying, less knowledgeable about Judaism, and less interested in community service. Indeed, only two of the six identified as Jewish. Most were already in their third year of college and had made no move to join a sorority before. There was only one woman of color in the group: Jessica, a Latina student. The surveillance-format of the series also necessitated the creation of the Pledge House in which only a small sub-set of the pledges were allowed to live, which created resentment on the part of the pledges left out and meant that the sisters had two separate groups to oversee. Managing the resentment of the "regular" pledges toward the "special" girls in the Pledge House became a major preoccupation of the sorority leadership and required considerable emotion-work – which was never shown on television, because footage of "the regulars" was of little interest to MTV. If the regulars wanted to be on camera, they had to visit the girls in the House or tag along with them wherever they chose to go. Significantly, then, "ordinariness" itself took on hierarchical terms reflecting the degree of likelihood of being filmed, with the pledges in the House on the "worthy-of-being filmed" side of the divide.

For the six pledges living in the House, the cameras and their crews were not simply abstract forces with the power to determine one's televisual worthiness but were also omnipresent shadow participants in virtually every interaction. In addition to the stationary surveillance systems installed in the House, there was always at least one camera crew on duty, consisting of a male camera operator, a male sound person, and a (male or female) producer and/or assistant producer. Thus one never simply had a conversation with one's roommate; one had a conversation with one's roommate and the mostly-male camera crew. One never lay on the couch, alone, reading a book for a class assignment; one read a book with a camera crew looking on. The girls were forbidden from openly acknowledging the crews, yet the crews were always there, watching and waiting for something to happen. When it did not, crew members expressed their disappointment in subtle ways: sighing, yawning, or rolling their eyes – subtle forms of emotion management designed to prompt a response from the girls to "be interesting."

Being interesting and at the same time having to act "as if" the cameras weren't there required emotion-work from the girls in turn, since it required thinking about how one would "normally" act in the situation and trying to act like this way, but at the same time heightening the normality so as to fulfill the expectations of the production staff to entertain audiences. One pledge in particular felt constant pressure to "not be boring." She said she was always racking her brain for something witty or amusing to say or do. She experienced this as highly stressful and attributed her excessive drinking and partying during the course of the filming to the pressure she felt to always be "on" for the cameras. Alcohol was her crutch, she told me, because it relaxed her, allowing her to care less about monitoring her own behavior; this in turn accomplished her goal of pleasing the producers because it gave them the "girls gone wild" image they desired. In hindsight, this pledge recognized the complicated gendered dynamic at work here, in which she delivered a party-girl performance largely out of a desire to be the good girl who did what others expected of her.

Of course, it is also a notable gender dynamic when the "girls gone wild" image is one of the most familiar and readily available scripts for a young woman to enact when the pressure is on to perform. Cattiness, competitiveness, and back-stabbing among women also have cultural resonance, and these behaviors, too, were well represented on the show among certain pledges and even certain sorority sisters. Indeed, the cultural cliché is the foundation of ordinary celebrity in the era of self-service television. The context of production helps to set the scene and construct particular roles for participants to inhabit; to ensure that participants take up these roles with relative confidence in the absence of formal training, scripts, or rehearsals, the roles have to be easily assumed. Other scholars have recognized this, of course. As Alison Hearn puts it, "much like donning Mickey Mouse ears, becoming part of the immersive television experience involves adopting a 'persona' consistent with its dictates: the jock, the vixen, the asshole, the gay guy, the rich bitch, the grizzled vet, the buddy."[13] Now we can add "the sorority girl." And while more could be said about the specific case of *Sorority Life*, the larger point to underscore is that the contexts of production – including normative cultural scripts about gender, race, class, and sexuality – structure the content of performances in key ways, and this structuring is fundamental to the success of self-service television and one of its key outcomes: ordinary celebrity.

The politics of "ordinary" celebrity

Every episode of *Sorority Life* series opens with the following musical refrain: "Who wants to be ordinary, in a crazy, mixed up world? I don't care what they're sayin' as long as I'm your girl." The lyrics from which the refrain is taken tell the story of a misfit, "alternative" girl who is misunderstood by all but the one who loves her. Chosen no doubt for its explicit reference to "ordinariness," the refrain conveys the idea that being ordinary is over-rated, and that one needn't be ordinary to be loved and accepted. It's an interesting choice for the series, because reality TV is precisely about celebrating "ordinary" people while at the same time offering an escape from that ordinariness via the celebrity frame. Being ordinary is, indeed, over-rated, when one could be an ordinary celebrity instead. But contrary to the song, being an ordinary celebrity on *Sorority Life* has little to do with embracing an "alternative" identity.

Rather predictably, when the series aired on MTV, the "ordinariness" depicted was entirely consistent with the normative image of sorority girls that the members of Sigma wanted to avoid. With hundreds of hours of footage shot and only 13 half-hour episodes slated for broadcast, "ordinariness" had to be conveyed in very broad strokes. Overall, the series showcased a great deal of partying (two of the pledges celebrated their twenty-first birthdays on the show), and considerable bickering, including one bar scene in which a pledge accuses a sorority sister of acting "slutty" and gets slapped in the face. Scenes of the sisters and pledges getting along were relatively rare, as were scenes of the women studying, doing community service, or hosting philanthropic sorority activities – despite the fact that all of these activities occurred while the cameras rolled.

On the one hand, given the dramatic requirements of reality TV, one could legitimately wonder, what did Sigma expect? On the other hand, as I have tried to demonstrate, the conditions of possibility that get forged during the production process are complex and not nearly so easy to interpret when they unfold around you as when you examine them after the fact. Moreover, once the members of Sigma had voted to allow MTV into their lives, they were caught in a double-bind that worked to producers' advantage: if they refused to accept as pledges the girls who were rushing the sorority solely because of MTV's presence (rather than the sorority's identity and mission), they risked reinforcing the stereotype of their organization as cliquish; if they accepted those girls as pledges, they risked losing control of who represented Sigma to the broader public and reinforcing a different stereotype – that of the typical "wild" sorority girl. Either way, MTV had a potential hook for fulfilling the mandate of reality television for dramatic action built on stock characters engaged in interpersonal conflict.

Certainly some of the pledges under surveillance in the House facilitated this mandate, at times unwittingly but for the most part with a kind of self-reflexive knowledge about what constituted a "good" versus "bad" performance. Like the ordinary guests of the daytime talk shows I have written about in the past, the pledges who starred in *Sorority Life* were not naïve about the dramatic requirements of the show. Having grown up with *The Real World* and being familiar with a wide range of reality shows, they understood they were to play a heightened version of themselves. There were differences among them, however, as to what it meant, exactly, "to be oneself, only more so," in front of the cameras. The presence of cameras tends to provoke an affective response in people, either attracting or repelling them: some accept the offer to construct new versions of the self within the parameters at stake; some reject or resist this offer because the parameters fail to mesh with the sense of self they already possess. In the case of *Sorority Life*, all of the characters who got significant airtime – five of the six women in the Pledge House along with certain members of the sisterhood – could be categorized in a very general way as seekers rather than avoiders of the camera's gaze. But some were seeking more eagerly than others, and what they sought cannot uniformly be characterized as a desire for celebrity or fame.

In fact, one of the pledges, Jessica, had motivations much like those of the sorority leadership in that she wanted to use the show as a vehicle for achieving a social goal. The only Mexican-American student to rush the sorority, Jessica wanted to participate – and lobbied hard to be the sixth pledge in the House when the original choice fell through – in order to increase the visibility of Latinas on national television and represent them with dignity. She was well aware of the risks that visibility posed given the media's penchant for caricature. Moreover, her racial/ethnic otherness was compounded by her larger physical size; she knew that her inclusion would serve as a visual counterpoint to the whiteness and thinness of the other girls. But she wanted to participate anyway, she told me, because she wanted to give Latina viewers someone "real" with whom to identify. (This explains her careful behavior on the show, which online fans interpreted as boring and which relegated her largely to the background of events.) The other five pledges in the House, perhaps not surprisingly, had less noble aspirations. Being white and middle class – and therefore "free" to represent no one but themselves – they were motivated primarily by curiosity and a sense of personal adventure. They recognized that appearing on national television was not an affirmation of their ordinary life, it was a unique, once-in-a-lifetime event. Yet only two of the five said that they entertained half-serious hopes for using their television debut specifically as a springboard for "real," that is, ongoing, celebrity. (These were the three pledges, then, mentioned earlier – Jessica and the two hoping for "real" celebrity – who needed no persuasion from producers to live under surveillance in the Pledge House.) What this illustrates is that wanting to be on TV may be bound up with social identity categories (in this case, race/ethnicity) and the commitments and obligations they produce rather than, or in addition to, more individual desires. Moreover, what individuals desire may be the excitement and adventure of being part of the process that produces ordinary celebrity rather than celebrity or fame per se.

This complex layering of motivations was at work in the world of daytime talk shows that I studied. There, however, the lesser status of the genre, the lower-class status of guests, and the more explosive nature of their on-stage performances evoked stronger moral condemnation on the part of critics and a sharper distinction between legitimate ("classy") and illegitimate ("trashy") reasons for participating. For producers and critics alike, the more closely a guest's motives approximated those of "experts" on television – that is, the more they were oriented toward championing a cause, promoting an organization, or educating the public about an issue or event – the "classier" they were said to be. It was the "trashy" guest who had an axe to grind, a score to settle, or who simply wanted "mere exposure." Indeed, the willingness of such guests to deliver the money shot for no apparent reason other than exposure was considered proof of their inherent "trashiness." But after many months of working with, and interviewing, such guests, I concluded that America's poor and working classes want much the same thing as everybody else: to be noticed, to feel like they matter in the world, to participate in public discourse in a locally meaningful way.[14] Given the centrality of television in their lives but their limited options for getting on TV, assuming the role of talk-show guest was one of the few avenues for fulfilling this desire. It didn't much matter that the portrayal was unflattering, for the larger goal was validation, to be part of the discourse and part of the scene. Unlike their "classy" expert-like counterparts, "trashy" guests oriented to the ritual rather than the transmission function of media in which being part of the process itself matters more than any specific communicative outcome.[15] If there was a communicative dimension operating, the communication was "I exist" rather than "here's what I think" – the talking body rather than the talking head.

The *Sorority Life* participants could be characterized by a similar trashy-trashy binary except that the desire for "mere exposure" was not the purview of the poor and disenfranchised. The binary should be understood as an analytic device, however, not an objective empirical measure. With *Sorority Life* as with daytime talk shows, the broad distinction between transmission and ritual dimensions of media participation belies the messiness of participants' agendas and the impure nature of their desires: few of the young women I interviewed could be said to have possessed "purely" communicative or "purely" ritualistic motivations. Rather, they had a general inclination one way or another (either to educate the public or to experience the production of celebrity) but, for most, these inclinations were conceptually impure, incorporating elements of each orientation. Moreover, participants may have been less than entirely truthful about – or even cognizant of – their "true" orientations; specifically, they may have underplayed the allure of ordinary celebrity in their conversations with each other and with me, given the stigma often attached to this allure.

Indeed, it is easy enough to understand why people seek out media exposure to advance a cause they believe in, to sell a product or idea, or to achieve "real," ongoing fame. More opaque is the willingness to live one's personal life in public in exchange for a brief interlude of ordinary celebrity. If the desire for ritual connection is an underlying factor, it's worth considering the cultural "work" being done by ordinary celebrity such that a sense of connection as well as individuation is achieved. The idea that television and other media foster a sense of social belonging for audiences is certainly not new, despite contrasting claims that the media isolate and alienate individuals. As Couldry points out, it is through the media that people "gain access to what is marked off as social from the merely individual ... the media are [one] place we look for the reality we call 'social.'"[16] The question is how dispensable, self-serve celebrity functions for participants to simultaneously elevate and connect them to others.

One answer may lie in the middle-ground status of ordinary celebrity itself, located somewhere between "real" ordinariness and "real" celebrity. Self-service television does represent a certain democratization of celebrity in the sense that none of the young women I interviewed would have appeared as "characters" on national television had it not been for the rise of reality TV. At the same time, to reiterate a point made earlier, the concept of ordinary celebrity does not eliminate the value hierarchy on which "real" celebrity depends; rather, it reproduces and protects this hierarchy while supplying television producers and executives with cheap, dispensable alternatives for generating profits. Ordinary celebrity constructs a sense of self that connects simultaneously to those "below" – ordinary, everyday people – and those "above" – stars with accumulated intertexual capital. Residing at the peak of the value hierarchy, "real" celebrity cordons off the individual into a special category (even while fostering audience identification); ordinary celebrity marks the individual as special but not categorically "outside" or "beyond" the everyday. If, as P. David Marshall has observed, celebrity is "a discourse of the self" that moves the representation of individuality outside the text and into the "extra-ordinary everyday,"[17] self-serve celebrity qualifies this extra-ordinariness in key ways and potentially offers greater opportunity for ritual connection.

Another factor to consider is the degree to which "the performative" has become a central force in public discourse generally. Drawing on a wide range of scholarship in anthropology, sociology, and performance studies, Jeffrey Alexander argues that, in complex, modern societies, performance is a key mode of cultural expression, so much so that we are better served by the concept of a public stage than a public sphere.[18] According to Alexander, performance is the successor to ritual: its aim is to "create … the emotional connection of audience with actor and text and thereby to create the conditions for projecting cultural meaning from performance to audience."[19] Cultural texts are performed to convey meaning to others and "fusion" between text and audience is the hallmark of performative success. "Fusion" thus refers to the process of eliciting a sense of authenticity.

Historically, the development of the social role of actor, as distinct from ritual performer, was tied to a shift in ritual content from the sacred to the mundane in the context of early state-formation and the transition from religious to secular authority. According to Alexander, the incorporation of secular concerns into the sacred realm via performance introduced symbolic dynamics into everyday life and reconfigured culture in a more socially-oriented and dramaturgical way. Throughout the world's civilizations, Alexander tells us, ritual moved toward theater in tandem with growing social complexity. With the formal institutionalization of theater, fusion between text and audience remained the goal of performance but was more difficult to achieve because the elements of performance became separate and independently variable: writers, actors, directors, critics, and audiences each made distinct contributions. As Alexander notes, the defusion of performative elements creates self-consciousness about the artificiality of the process of performance. This is why professional actors typically receive extensive training: enacting a script written by someone else for an audience you've never met is not the same as "performing the self" in an everyday dramaturgical sense. Of course, performing the self in an everyday dramaturgical sense is no guarantee of authenticity, either. Authenticity is a function of cultural meaning, not of a particular performance type.

Reality TV, with its claims to raw, unscripted action, does not move us from defusion back to fusion necessarily. But fusion is certainly the goal of reality programming: by promising access to the "real" via the symbolic action of ordinary people without the mediating effects of scripts, rehearsals, etc., reality TV, in effect, attempts to re-fuse the elements of performance by collapsing the conceptual distinctions between actor and role (the actor plays herself) and between actor and audience (both are "ordinary" people). The authenticity of the performance is presumed to stem from the shared social location of those on- and off-screen outside the official production of professional celebrity.

In this sense, the production of ordinary celebrity through self-service television could represent yet another iteration in the gradual process whereby performance moves from the sacred to the mundane. Just as actors entered the "sacred" space of ritual performance in the development of early social drama, so are ordinary people infiltrating the "sacred" spaces of professional theatrical performance. Perhaps this is to be expected. As social power becomes more pluralized, the means of making and distributing cultural representations becomes more accessible.[20] The rise of new media arguably accelerates this process; self-mediation via blogs, video-logs, webcams, and social networking sites such as MySpace and Facebook lend credence to Alexander's assertion that in contemporary, complex societies, symbolic action takes on an overtly performative cast. The proliferating opportunities for "playing oneself" compete with but do not displace the more established discourses of celebrity in circulation; they offer new sites for identity construction that combine the sacred and the mundane. Self-serve celebrity creates what Andreas Kitzmann calls "an economy of recognition," in which the ordinary, "private" self undergoes a mutation "by virtue of being coupled with the very public spaces of performance, celebrity, and commercial media."[21]

This is not to romanticize the ordinary celebrities of reality TV, but to move explanations of their participation from psychological to sociological ground. Nor is it to imply that the rise of self-service television is a progressive development. As Turner notes, there is no necessary connection between demographic changes in the patterns of access to media and a progressive or democratic politics: semiotic participation is not political self-determination.[22] That being said, self-service television is an increasingly salient part of public discourse, and to adequately understand it one has to temper the "sacred" realm of theory with the empirically mundane. Paying attention to what participants say about their experience is less about uncovering the "truth" of ordinary celebrity and more about complicating our understanding of the social and cultural processes upon which its viability depends.

Notes

1 See James Friedman, ed., *Reality Squared: Televisual Discourse on the Real* (Rutgers University Press, 2002); Sam Brenton and Reuban Cohen, *Shooting People: Adventures in Reality TV* (London/New York: Verso, 2003); Mark Andrejevic, *Reality TV: The Work of Being Watched* (Lanham, MD: Rowman and Littlefield Publishers, 2004); Susan Murray and Laurie Ouellette, eds, *Reality TV: Remaking Television Culture* (New York University Press, 2004); Ernest Mathijs and Janet Jones, *Big Brother International: Formats, Critics, and Publics* (London/New York: Wallflower Press, 2004); Su Holmes and Deborah Jermyn, *Understanding Reality Television* (London/New York: Routledge, 2004); Annette Hill, *Reality TV: Audiences and Factual Television* (London/New York: Routledge, 2005).
2 Laura Grindstaff, "Self-Serve Celebrity: The Production of Ordinariness and the Ordinariness of Production in Reality Television," in *Production Studies: Cultural Studies of Media Industries*, eds Vicki Mayer, Amanda Lotz, and John Thornton Caldwell (New York/London: Routledge, 2009).

3 See Leo Braudy, *The World in a Frame: What We See in Films, 25th Anniversary Edition* (University of Chicago Press, 2002); Nick Couldry, *Media Rituals: A Critical Approach* (London: Routledge, 2003).

4 Couldry, *Media Rituals: A Critical Approach*; Nick Couldry, "Playing for Celebrity: *Big Brother* as Ritual Event," *Television & New Media* 3, no. 3 (2002): 283–93.

5 Chad Raphael, "Political Economy of Reali-TV," *Jump Cut* 41 (1997): 102–9; Graeme Turner, "Celebrity, the Tabloid, and the Democratic Public Sphere," in *The Celebrity Culture Reader*, ed. P. David Marshall (New York/London: Routledge, 2006): 487–500.

6 Sue Collins, "Making the Most out of 15 Minutes: Reality TV's Dispensable Celebrity," *Television & New Media* 9, no. 2 (2008): 87–110.

7 Collins, "Making the Most out of 15 Minutes: Reality TV's Dispensable Celebrity."

8 Laura Grindstaff, *The Money Shot: Trash, Class, and the Making of TV Talk Shows* (University of Chicago Press, 2002).

9 The concepts of "emotion work" and "emotional labor" stem from the work of sociologist Arlie Russell Hochschild; in particular, see Arlie Hochschild, *The Managed Heart: The Commercialization of Human Feeling* (University of Chicago Press, 1983).

10 Mark Andrejevic, *Reality TV: The Work of Being Watched* (Lanham, MD: Rowman and Littlefield Publishers, 2004); Ernest Mathijs and Janet Jones, eds, *Big Brother International: Formats, Critics & Publics* (London/NewYork: Wallflower Press, 2004).

11 Spencer Morgan, "Viewers Rush to MTV's Sorority Life," *New York Daily News* Online Edition, www.nydailynews.com/entertainment/index.html

12 Ella Shohat and Robert Stam, *Unthinking Eurocentrism: Multiculturalism and the Media* (London/New York: Routledge, 1994).

13 Alison Hearn, "'John, a 20-year-old Boston native with a great sense of humor': on the spectacularization of the 'self' and incorporation of identity in the age of reality television," in *The Celebrity Culture Reader*, ed. P. David Marshall (London/New York: Routledge, 2006): 621.

14 Grindstaff, *The Money Shot: Trash, Class, and the Making of TV Talk Shows*.

15 For an explication of "ritual" and "transmission" functions of media, see James Carey, *Communication as Culture* (New York: Unwin Hyman, 1989).

16 Couldry, "Playing for Celebrity: *Big Brother* as Ritual Event," 284; see also Roger Silverstone, *The Message of Television: Myth and Narrative in Contemporary Culture* (London: Heinemann Educational Books, 1981); Daniel Dayan and Elihu Katz, *Media Events: The Live Broadcasting of History* (Cambridge: Harvard University Press, 1992).

17 P. David Marshall, *Celebrity and Power: Fame in Contemporary Culture* (Minneapolis: University of Minnesota Press, 1997); P. David Marshall, "New Media – New Self," in *The Celebrity Culture Reader*, ed. P. David Marshall (London/New York: Routledge, 2006): 634–44.

18 Jeffrey Alexander, "Cultural Pragmatics: Social Performance Between Ritual and Strategy," *Sociological Theory* 22, no. 4 (2004): 527–73.

19 Alexander, "Cultural Pragmatics: Social Performance Between Ritual and Strategy," 547.

20 Alexander, "Cultural Pragmatics"; see also Chris Rojek, *Celebrity* (Reaktion Books, 2001); Graeme Turner, *Understanding Celebrity* (Newbury Park, CA: Sage, 2004).

21 Andreas Kitzmann, *Saved From Oblivion: Documenting the Daily From Diaries to Web Cams* (New York: Peter Lang, 2004): 87.

22 Turner, *Understanding Celebrity*; Turner, "Celebrity, the Tabloid, and the Democratic Public Sphere."

Part 2

Laboring the self

Introduction

Adrienne Shaw

Don Slater defines neoliberalism as the condition in which "consumer choice became the obligatory pattern for all social relations and the template for civic dynamism and freedom."[1] He explains that "[t]he ideological miracle carried out by 1980s consumer culture was to tie this image of unhinged superficiality to the most profound, deep structural values and promises of modernity: personal freedom, economic progress, civic dynamism and political democracy."[2] Critics have often argued that reality television is a mediated version of this neoliberal order.[3] Lifestyle television programs in particular, which focus on teaching individuals how to improve everything from their diets to dress to décor, are the subject of much academic critique. Briefly reviewed, this position argues that "'lifestyle maximization' and the care of the self replaces the watch of the state as the mechanisms through which 'free' individuals are governed across daily life, and through which they come to govern themselves."[4]

We can extend this to assert that, as a genre, reality television is characteristic of a neoliberal epoch. In a 2001 article entitled "Global Media, Neoliberalism, and Imperialism," Robert McChesney opens by saying that "the current era in history is generally characterized as one of globalization, technological revolution, and democratization."[5] It is not much of a stretch to replace history in that sentence with reality television. Reality television, as addressed throughout this volume, is a popular meta-genre across the globe, integrates state-of-the-art surveillance and communication technology, and promotes the image (if not the reality) of a democratized relationship between audiences and the television industry. These three aspects help perpetuate what Mark Andrejevic has called the "myth of reality television": "[t]he myth … that audience members gain meaningful control over the content of television programming when that programming becomes 'real.'"[6] This is problematic in two regards. First, the "reality" presented is packaged by producers to appeal to audiences in certain ways and in particular global contexts. Second, audience participation hides the exploitation of audiences upon which the shows are dependent. This myth also obscures ideologies supporting neoliberalism embedded within the genre. According to Nick Couldry, if "reality TV is opaque and resistant to appropriate contextualization, then this is one further characteristic that it shares with the apparently consensual regime of neoliberalism."[7]

In this section authors Gareth Palmer, Tania Lewis and Helen Wood and Beverley Skeggs outline, interrogate and expand these critiques. They address reality television's role in the construction, governing and negotiation of the self. Gareth Palmer evokes neoliberal discourses in the disciplining of bodies in shows like *The Swan* and *Ten Years Younger*. Tania Lewis contextualizes the makeover show, by reassessing the neoliberal critique in relation to Singaporean programs. Helen Wood and Beverley Skeggs foreground a new conceptualization of the relationship between television texts and audiences. In doing so these chapters, particularly the latter two, explore how different global contexts and the audience–text relationship trouble the usual accounts of lifestyle television.

Prior to critiquing the critique, we will look at an essay in which it is furthered, Palmer's "Governing Bodies." His chapter begins by comparing the tradition of documentary to that of reality television, noting the classed dimensions of both, arguing that while documentaries are aimed at changing the institutions, reality television aims to change the individual. This builds on John Corner's work, which looks at the relationship between documentary and reality television and analyzes the value judgments which go in to distinguishing the two.[8] Palmer investigates this distinction more specifically in terms of how reality television works, via a foregrounding of class differences, to discipline bodies. He asserts that neoliberal discourses aimed at making individual citizens responsible for their bodies mask the social and institutional inequalities which negatively impact the health and well-being of those same working-class individuals addressed in the programs. He argues that reality television serves the "anxiety-industry," as it constructs a never complete, always changing self which must be consistently monitored and maintained.

This neoliberal critique has been used primarily in an Anglo-context but, as asserted elsewhere in this volume, we must interrogate any attempt to apply it globally. When reality television formats are exported world-wide, all productions are adapted to local contexts; theory should be no different. Adapting theoretical perspectives to specific situations is crucial. As Lisa Rofel asserts there is "a sense that neoliberalism is a universal set of principles from which derives, in deterministic fashion, a singular type of neoliberal subject."[9] Rofel reformulates this by arguing that while in the West the focus has been on a rational subject, in China the neoliberal subject is best understood as a desiring one. In a similar fashion, Tania Lewis looks at makeover television in Singapore. In "Globalizing Lifestyles?" she considers the implications of these shows, their focus on consumption, surveillance and individualism, in an Asian cultural environment. First, she traces the rise of the makeover genre in the US and the UK and the ideological and socio-cultural foundations of these programs. Lewis goes on to describe lifestyle programming in Singapore, which while locally produced draws on a variety of Asian and Western influences. She argues that these shows, though they demonstrate some of the neoliberal tendencies of Western makeover programs, must be looked at in terms of local cultural values.

While rethinking our theoretical framework, we must also reconsider our methodological approaches. Reality television programs, like soap operas and romance novels before them, have largely been analyzed as texts and critiqued for the gender and class norms they promote. Like those previously disparaged genres, however, few authors look at how audiences interpret these texts and what role audience readings play in mediating the dominant messages encoded in the programs. Helen Wood and Beverley Skeggs, in redressing this oversight, question how gender and class norms are perpetuated by lifestyle programs and how researchers conceptualize the relationship between audiences and texts. In "Reacting to Reality TV," they question the "text/audience" dichotomy often used in reception studies. They use a "text-in-action" approach to investigate how four different friendship groups of women from differing class and racial backgrounds watch lifestyle programs. Both their methods and results are reminiscent of Liebes and Katz's cross-cultural study of audiences watching *Dallas*, and as such add a great deal of nuance to the usual understanding of reality television's meanings.[10] Moreover, they move beyond the classic *Dallas* study by situating their respondents' readings in relation to power and offer a nuanced analysis of the process of audiences' meaning making. Wood and Skeggs demonstrate the complexity of the emotive responses of these women, arguing that the meaning which emerges in viewing the shows results from a series of dialogic moments.

Each of these essays addresses some of the issues raised throughout this book. Taken as a whole they cover a range of approaches to thinking about lifestyle programs. Moreover, they challenge us to question how we approach reality television. In focusing on lifestyle programs these chapters call into question the trend of assuming we can discuss reality television as an entity in and of itself. Likewise, by looking at a specific genre, they posit theoretical and methodological questions that can be applied to other reality television formats. How do the nuances to the neoliberal critique called for in non-Anglo contexts make us question the ways in which it has been used in Anglo-countries? What does it do to our understanding of the song contest genre if we look at the regional specificity of each program? How do we make sense of power in shows like *Big Brother* in ways which take into account audience interpretations? Some of these questions are addressed elsewhere in this volume, but all require further exploration.

Notes

1 Don Slater, *Consumer Culture and Modernity* (Cambridge, MA: Blackwell Publishers, 1997), p. 10.
2 Ibid., 11.
3 Laurie Ouellette, "Take Responsibility for Yourself: Judge Judy and the Neoliberal Citizen," in *Reality TV: Remaking Television Culture*, eds Susan Murray and Laurie

Ouellette (New York University Press, 2004); Nick Couldry, "Reality TV, or the Secret Theater of Neoliberalism," *Review of Education, Pedagogy & Cultural Studies* 30, no. 1 (2008): 3–13; Katherine Sender, "Queens for a Day: *Queer Eye for the Straight Guy* and the Neoliberal Project," *Critical Studies in Media Communication* 23, no. 2 (2006): 131–51.

4 Laurie Ouellette and James Hay, *Better Living through Reality TV: Television and Post-Welfare Citizenship* (Malden, MA: Blackwell Pub., 2008).

5 Robert McChesney, "Global Media, Neoliberalism, and Imperialism," *Monthly Review* from http://www.monthlyreview.org/301rwm.htm (accessed September 19, 2007).

6 Mark Andrejevic, *Reality TV: The Work of Being Watched*, Critical Media Studies (Lanham, MD: Rowman & Littlefield Publishers, 2004), p. 104.

7 Couldry, "Reality TV," p. 10.

8 John Corner, "Performing the Real: Documentary Diversions," in *Reality TV: Remaking Television Culture*, 2nd edn, eds Susan Murray and Laurie Ouellette (New York University Press, 2009).

9 Lisa Rofel, *Desiring China: Experiments in Neoliberalism, Sexuality, and Public Culture*, Perverse Modernities (Durham, NC: Duke University Press, 2007), p. 2.

10 Tamar Liebes and Elihu Katz, *The Export of Meaning: Cross-Cultural Readings of Dallas* (New York: Oxford University Press, 1990).

Chapter 5

Governing bodies

Gareth Palmer

As the most contemporary of television genres, reality television offers a bewildering variety of perspectives on modern life. But while the subjects vary wildly, reality television offers narratives which are driven by an anxiety/resolution dialectic in which always already destabilized viewers are offered temporary solutions to problems of identity and belonging. Reality television and in particular that variant known as "lifestyle" play an important part in maintaining the anxiety-industry – a complex mixture of psychological and social forces powered by the engines of consumerism. Reality television formats propose a flexible model of the self in which no stable identity can be found and whose only tenet is that change is always good. This self has two apparently distinct but actually inter-connected parts: the *consumer self* that is endlessly re-rooted in the busy market place of identities offered by lifestyle is connected to the *responsible citizen* charged with self-management under changing patterns of rule. Into this flux reality tel-evision offers the salvation of hoped-for change and the comfort of belonging while also reminding us that the conditions for this momentary ease are transi-tory and unstable. The result is a self always ready for anxiety. The aim of this chapter is to consider documentary and in particular reality television's role in the formation of these two models of the self and the ways in which they may impact on the body – that object at the very core of the anxiety-industry.

I begin by considering the class-related factors that inform documentary making. I then discuss the role that surveillance plays in new models of the self in reality television and in particular lifestyle television before considering how new forms of television foreground the value of discipline for work on the body. Reality television's strategies and modes of address will be examined to see how they invite us to negotiate our identity as consumer selves and responsible citizens.

Documentary begins

In the UK what we now know as documentary began as a public-spirited enquiry into citizenship. As encoded by its founders and taken up by personnel in large broadcasting institutions, documentary was a social project which eschewed the political in its quest to discover the real nature of contemporary society.[1] The means of production, exhibition and distribution have always rested in large broadcasters such as the BBC whose employees shaped documentary within institutional codes. The individuals developing public-service documentary as a practice and as a career have been predominantly middle-class figures, established university graduates educated in the liberal arts. From its very beginnings the situation of the working classes has been of interest to this group of documentary-makers. The former live at a remove from the producers, geographically, culturally, and socially. Perhaps inevitably they become subjects of an argument constructed by middle-class people elsewhere. For example, it is still documentary practice to re-write the experience of subjects so that it can be edited for maximum effect. The professionalization of the industry, its traditions and use of ethical codes, all ensure that a distance is placed between the producers and their subjects. In this way the sense-making properties of a class are enmeshed in working practices.

The fact that public-service documentary's investigations of the social have been successful and have in some circumstances changed the lives of their subjects helps explain the genre's privileged place in televisual discourse as a valuable enterprise. High ratings and industry accolades for BBC programs such as "Cathy Come Home," "The Secret Policeman" and "7 Up" all contribute to the genre's reputation. Documentary is further privileged when it helps articulate the always classed concerns of critics in other media such as the quality press who share their liberal-progressive discourse. Its regular place in the schedule, its protected status amongst executives, the oft-quoted history of the genre, being a training ground for the finest minds of the industry – all of this lends what Nichols calls the "discourses of sobriety" considerable gravitas.[2] This respect is best preserved by Public Service Broadcasters whose continuing funding in a market-driven climate ensures a tradition of trust.

As a genre public-service documentary proceeds on the basis that it is offering viewers an insight into the world "beyond." There is a depth model at work here. We are offered the language of hard-won expertise, the insight driven by a care and concern for the subject, the perspective of those with experience in putting the form together – in short the documentary helps us to place a situation in the widest possible context. Public-service documentary's value, status and prestige derives from its claims to objectivity, the rendering of situations for our gently directed judgment. The tradition lives on through BBC 4 – a public-service channel producing thoroughly researched documentaries at high cost for low ratings. The result is an expanded idea of citizenship – the liberal-democratic intention that inspired the founders of the genre but one that is directed from a position of class-privilege.

Documentary changes

It is useful to note that reality television made its first impact in Britain and America in the 1980s – that decade in which the market made significant inroads into the industry. The opening up of the spectrum in both countries to more channels and the deregulation of the old broadcasting model challenged all genres. Reality television destabilized documentary's depth claims in pursuit of a flattened out world where drama, impact, and relevance are paramount. Reality television might be described as the market's take on the cautious and balanced documentary. On the surface there are obvious similarities – the focus on real people as social actors in a brutal world. Even its rationale appears to be the same – to inform us in faintly objective codes. But a consideration of what drives reality television makes it clear that the material is being ordered for purposes very different from that of public-service documentary. At the heart of reality television is a market logic. Social life is offered here as a series of exciting mini-dramas. Ordered debate and argument are secondary to the task of attracting time-poor viewers flicking through multiple channels. One instructive difference between old and new forms of documentary practice is in their production bases. The documentary tradition at the BBC and formerly ITV meant learning a craft in an institution where the individual had long-term security. In such circumstances time could be devoted to researching a subject. Those working in reality television in the commercial sector are casualized employees with far less time and security.

Another relatively under-discussed subject concerns the different class bases of reality television workers. The increasing size and professionalization of the industry has led to a proliferation of courses in universities for a new generation of media workers who start work already familiar with the means of production, already media-savvy and perhaps disposed to see the material differently. In place of the gradualism that underscored public-service documentary approaches they consider subjects for their utility and impact in the "show." Both public-service documentary employees and reality television workers represent respectively old and new fractions of the middle class taking a view on the working class: the difference is that the new groups may be more insecure and thus their work may replicate their own relatively unstable world.

At the core of the story documentary tells about itself is the promise of effectivity. Documentary-makers of all strands uncover subjects suffering unjust treatment and their films are an attempt to make change within the system. In Britain and America publicly funded documentary cleaves to its social-democratic function of correcting imbalances that also inspire others. Awards, industry accolades, and critical attention help sustain the prestige of the form. Documentary strands are still promoted as appointments-to-view, opportunities for engagement with the real filtered through the middle-class sensibilities of well-educated film-makers. When critics attack such publicly funded work, the documentary's role in changing public opinion for the good is offered as proof of value to citizens. By contrast, reality television is a lower-value promiscuous genre taking its measure from current affairs at one end and light entertainment at the other. Indeed the latter's emphasis on prizes, ordinary people, the vulgar, the competitive, the tactless as well as its ritual elements all find a home in the genre. This choice of subjects may be why reality television has had such a critical reception in popular media. But as Corner has pointed out, "when audiences connect what they see with what they know, the reality TV 'elicits from viewers certain kinds of investment of self which other media cannot so easily generate, if at all.'"[3]

Public-service documentary stands back from the fray to offer a critical analysis of institutions. By contrast reality television seeks to prove its social value when it showcases the deployment of closed-circuit television (CCTV) in the fight against crime, for example. At all levels from the international to the local, crime programming featuring CCTV highlights the happy co-operation of the police. Reality television became a space for a unity of voices celebrating the advance in crime fighting that new surveillance technology represented.[4] Public-service documentary's critical perspectives are replaced by unthinking advocacy for the police. Gradually the collaboration and sharing of information by the police and the need to attract high ratings developed reality television as sometimes little more than a shocking "show and tell" of contemporary life. Running through this strand has been a focus on proofs – the inclusion of material is always excused on the grounds that it works. Effectivity is crucial here and all sorts of liberties are excused because of it.

Reality television offers itself as a vehicle through which consumers can maximize their value. Its focus on the surface of things, its refusal of depth, its celebrating of the ordinary all belie its roots in the market. The various identities it offers are as flexible and mutable as the image onscreen. The self you need to be can be achieved with just this or that investment. Reality television formats and in particular lifestyle, create a productive instability around the self which can never be finished. It offers a kaleidoscope of new routes to the self whose only core principle is change.

Public-service documentary offered an ordered frame built by experts. The language, the tactics, the discourses of sobriety and the weight of tradition all gave such documentary (and still give it) a faintly noble air. It belongs in the ordered distanced world of the traditional bourgeois whose class gives him or her perspective. Reality television seeks to derive maximum profit from exploiting a weakness for real-life rescue entertainment while also presenting itself as a great benefactor. For example, after showing scenes of carnage programs end with a helpline or a link to a charity. This gesture is like the faint shadow of responsibility excusing the cynical and wanton immersion in abandoned bodies. The sheer quantity of reality television, its lack of argument, its indiscretions, crudity, promiscuity, all make it lowbrow. It is all too clearly a product of the market – that phenomenon public-service documentary took a perspective *on* rather than was *of*. Reality television seems to be an unreflective product of the systems it shows and as a result it can never gain the class or prestige middle-class tastemakers bestow on cultural objects. But despite this, reality television calls forth a complex relationship between viewer and object. As Annette Hill has written, "the ability for audiences to see through reality TV and by that I mean critique as well as watch stories in reality programs, is fundamental to our understanding of the reality genre."[5] In a sense reality television's strategies have given birth to a more critical, questioning audience than that imagined by the makers of public service documentary.

Watching subjects

Reality television is very much connected to the urban environment inasmuch as it often derives materials from myriad moments of city life. What is peculiar to the form is the way in which these captured fragments of behavior are tied to lessons in conduct. It is instructive to note how surveillance played an important role in Western states in the 1980s in policing the behavior of the populace. The mass installation of CCTV in England and Wales made them the most watched pair of countries on the planet.[6] In the USA levels of surveillance increased exponentially after 9/11. A similar increase was attendant in the UK after the London bombings of 2005. This increase in technology is supported by stories, PR, advice, warnings etc., all reminding us of CCTV's value. As a result we are all expected to play our part in the project of vigilance undertaken by the Western states in response to the threat of terror from without and within. This is the background buzz of the anxiety industry. Our images are all captured by the millions of CCTV cameras whose development comes with the promise that it is making our environments safer. The populace are offered new roles and responsibilities by authorities like the police working with reality-television producers to fashion lessons in conduct.

The economic crash of 2008 and the more aggressive flows of capital have entailed more insecure conditions for all workers but it is working-class women, ethnic minorities, and the poor who are left most susceptible to changes in economic circumstances, who live more closely with risk, and whose "options" are more limited by holding less educational, symbolic and cultural capital. Job instability is now built into a class with less unionization, fewer than ever craft guilds or apprenticeship and less sense of themselves as a class. Indeed class consciousness must always be the enemy of a vigorous individualism focused on the consumer self. Working-class women, ethnic minorities and other sections of the poor are gaining the most attention and the most aggressive warnings from the surveillance technologies of various authorities. For example in the UK the Benefits Agency has undertaken a series of advertising campaigns to change the way the nation feels about welfare claimants. The current campaign pictures guilty bodies finally caught in a web of deceit with the openly threatening tagline "We're on to You." Viewers are invited to phone in and report those suspected of working two jobs, for example. In place of "dole" are welfare-to-work programs which suggest claimants redefine themselves as enterprising job-seekers. A number of other surveillance-themed media messages such as the warning that cameras will catch ticket cheats invite us to consider such technology as useful while we also have a vague sense that it may be a threat. In such a culture surveillance becomes second nature for people. The social is redefined as a series of markets in services and provisions that encourage rational choice/calculation and individual decision-making. The invitation to consider our identity as responsible people means shaping ourselves as self-monitoring and self-normalization subjects. Reality television is only one of the many technologies helping people to be responsibilized so that they may take charge of themselves. The self is now an enterprising project to be invested in and invested with.[7]

In this new climate welfare is both hard to come by and an object of shame. As Jack Bratich and other scholars have recently noted, lifestyle television is one of the few spaces left where the poor can legitimately make a claim.[8] Some of the most popular programs in the genre foreground the needy displaying their circumstances and begging for help. For example when *Extreme Makeover: Home Edition* is being transmitted, thousands of people write in requesting help. Pointedly their applications come on self-recorded video tape: they have attempted to depict their own bodies and circumstances as failing the standards pushed so remorselessly through consumer culture. Similarly in *Extreme Makeover* the overweight are usually lower-middle- or working-class women who picture themselves as pitiful and in need of the sort of spectacular help only the magic of television can give them. After we have seen their own self-surveillance coding them as open and needy their bodies can be awarded the privilege of transformation.

Watching bodies

Documentary has long had a fascination with the body. It has been suggested that the development of the documentary idea can be tied in to the desire of governmental authorities to regulate bodily conduct from its earliest beginnings in films sponsored by public bodies such as the Gas, Light and Coke Company behind *Housing Problems* in 1935, for example. However, reality television technology has enabled infinitely more intimate explorations of bodily conduct and regulation. The bodies of those minorities that feature in reality television and Lifestyle programming are problem bodies for a variety of reasons linked principally to consumer culture and the new injunction to always present the self as an enterprising project. The first and most obvious cases of failure are the overweight. "The bad body is fat, slack, uncared for: it demonstrates a lazy and undisciplined self."[9] A failure to stay in (the correct) shape seems like a rejection of the discipline the rest of us are supposed to be enduring.

It is still largely the case that the majority of subjects selected for treatment are women and usually lower-middle-class or working-class women. This may be an acknowledgement that the audience is predominantly female but it also keys into the rationale of consumer culture to offer fashion and styling as long-standing solutions to the problems of self-worth. From the excesses of *The Swan* to the cruelties of *Ten Years Younger* the starting point is acknowledging the power of the norm – excess is un-feminine, greedy and not lady-like.[10] The double-bind of consumerism finds no expression here beyond mocking those trapped within it.

The managing of desire in a culture of commodities means balancing the work ethic against the need to be good (i.e. indulgent) consumers. The equation offered is quite simple: a change on the outside generates a favorable view from others which is in turn used as proof that the key to feeling better about oneself derives from others. The programs work to generate a consensus between audience, experts, and subject that being overweight is irresponsible. The formats are designed to encourage passionate reactions from the subjects themselves as well as friends, relatives, presenters and audiences live and at home. Gifted with the new common sense of responsible maintenance to the self, studio audiences and those at home are empowered to express their rage at departures from the norm. Perhaps there is also a fear in the audience when they may recognize themselves in the behavior or reported experience of those on stage and that slipping out of shape is just a snack away. As Susan Bordo points out, "The slender body codes the totalizing ideal of a well-managed self in which all is kept in order despite the contradictions of consumer culture."[11]

Lifestyle programming suggests that being overweight is a problem rooted not in class or the economy but is simply the result of faulty choices. In order to put the person on the right track strict measures have to be adopted. The principal instrument being used to change citizens in their own interest is discipline. Discipline via forms of surveillance is a technique that is given validation elsewhere in reality television. From the snooping presenters in *What Not to Wear* to the various house spies of BBC, daytime programming surveillance uncovers the "real" person behind the scenes. Having the truth about oneself revealed by surveillance and confessing to what cannot be denied (after all we viewers have the omniscience that comes from using surveillance and seeing all) is also a way of validating technology and method. With better use of surveillance twinned with the well-meaning discipline of experts there is every chance we can all improve.

In many programs people compete for the disciplinary trials of television in order to improve. The competition is presented as fierce and winning it is a matter of double prestige – for the emerging enterprising self and for the validation of the medium. The criteria for being selected are size and a willingness to change, to submit to discipline. But both class and gender are revealed in their decision to compete for treatment. Circumstances have left them quite literally helpless – they have no field of expertise and present themselves as victims desiring change and the body-ideal. Class also makes itself present when contestants loudly proclaim faulty diet choices and their inability to find the strength to change them. Our sympathy is elicited when some people demonstrate just enough awareness to know that they are "killing themselves" and "ruining their children's future." Home visits to families reveal that for the most part these are chaotic environments where the all-important element of order is missing. One new format (*Honey We're Killing The Kids*) even projects an onscreen fat future for the children of the wanton and slovenly. Furthermore, when contestants show themselves unfamiliar with the solutions and in particular the discipline being offered we are guided to think of them as people who have "let themselves go" in the way no middle-class person would. In short what we are asked to spectate upon is the ignorance of a class whose weight advertises their exclusion and inability to "fit in."

Class differences enacted

To meet the challenge that the working-class body represents is the etiquette of the middle class whose own position leads them to see such subjects as people who cannot "read" themselves. The project is not simply to change their shape but to help them see themselves as others do. This transmission of behavioral codes is a process that has a long tradition in popular media. Learning the significance of surface impressions is a skill in which the accomplished middle class excel. As we know from Bourdieu,

> Self-acceptance (the very definition of ease) rises with unselfconsciousness, the capacity to escape fascination with a self possessed by the gaze of others … it is understandable that middle-class women are disposed to sacrifice much time and effort to achieve the sense of meeting the social norms of self-presentation which is the precondition of forgetting oneself and the body for others.[12]

The dramatic apparatus of lifestyle is set up to elicit maximum drama from each transformation. A great deal of effort goes into presenting the individual as lacking not only the financial resources necessary for change but also the right environment. However complex the contestants might actually feel, the change is dramatized to look like a make or break, life or death crisis situation. Unlike their temporary allies in the "finished" middle class, by submitting to treatment individuals declare themselves in need of help and are thus self-defined as needing whatever the format requires. A common and very gendered/classed reaction to these cries for help is the simple one that a middle-class person would never be so "open." The program becomes a public reckoning of a seemingly fragile self legally bound up in the release form and played out across various media platforms. The mode of address adopted by the producers helps us to consider such openness as both naïve and vulgar. But it is worth noting that those subjects self-selecting for treatment are often women, sometimes ethnic minorities and almost always working-class people habituated to a high degree of surveillance and monitoring. In keeping with an increasingly managerial culture where "openness" is coded as honest, the contestants' willingness to change is recommended as a model of transparency. In a climate of encroaching surveillance it is difficult not to see the political significance of this idealized self-scrutiny especially when it is coupled with an emotional appreciation of discipline to find the "real self" on behalf of family and friends.

For the struggle to be worthwhile it has to be difficult. Change cannot be easy. Discipline has to be appreciated and valued. Thus in *The Biggest Loser* and *You are*

What You Eat new foods are tried with predictable and entertaining results such as rejection and disgust. Rebellion occurs and is put down without anything approaching liberal-democratic processes like negotiation. Meanwhile online dialogues away from the program focus on contestants' struggles. Groups that learn together, that support each other, are also valuable for the community as well as contributing to the drama that supplies the competitive element that underscores consumer capitalism. A long history of diet technologies still opera-tive through Weight Watchers, for example, is deliberately designed to form ideal relational communities in which people gain strength from one another. Online interactivity is defined as active involvement, a licensing of the entrepre-neurial instinct of the self to shape bodies-in-progress. This is of course guided by the consumerist discourses of the program.

It is not without significance that many body-change programs end where they begin: with the family. The family are treated to the big reveal as the moment of purest validation when all seems right, the moment when inside and outside meet. This works in dramatic terms but also reinforces the centrality of the family unit under capitalism as the ideal reproductive consuming machine. Transformation has worked but can only continue to do so if one understands mind and body (now happily aligned) as a perpetual self-project. Ideally self-discipline will have been learnt and entered into the character of the contestant who will now have a better relationship with the right commodities rather than being a slave to them. The change has come because discipline has been learnt as a way of taking responsibility for the self. The constantly articulated dream of class mobility that has dominated under capitalism is reinforced by sequences of newly efficient individuals regulating their food conduct. Eating choices are classed in these programs expressing a barely contained fear that the wrong choice will reveal the true class of the diner. What is being celebrated is not freedom from the system but successful integration into it in the name of empowerment for the self and for the family.

Classed bodies

I began by noting the class differences enacted in documentary practices: in short documentary's institutionalization meant that it developed as the province of the middle class recording the lives of others and suggesting solutions. In Lifestyle programming two middle-class fractions also focus on the lives of others – the established bourgeois represented in the UK by Nigella Lawson for example, and the new class of style-entrepreneurs such as Stacy London in WNTW (USA). Neither class fraction is interested in dialogue. Indeed armed with a new common sense both class fractions feel able to enforce dis-ciplinary procedures in the interests of the subject. In both cases middle-class premises never have to be examined because they have the finished minds and bodies of expertise, ever-vigilant and disciplined, perfected projects of the self.

Nothing distinguishes a modern-day new bourgeois more than a sensible and disciplined approach to his or her appetites. Thus acting from their own habitus they teach self-management to a class with the "wrong" understanding of their bodies and little time to demonstrate distinction. They have the time, the opportunity, and the inherited inclination to make a project of the body that takes the shape it does as a result of conscious effort. The very fact that they are seen onscreen to be (i) in shape; and (ii) possessed of the knowledge how to get into shape; and (iii) are an active part of television's magical apparatus means they are exempt from enquiry. Another example of the gap between classes is made apparent in the fact that the solutions recommended by middle-class experts are often very impractical. For example, the lifestyles of those who are to be treated may not be flexible enough to find exercise time given that they may have other pressing demands. "Finding time for yourself" is an option not always open to women or other members of the economically insecure class. The suggestion that one eat more fruit and vegetables may seem like common sense incarnate but this means eliminating old habits that may have become chemically engineered by the invitations of the advertising industry. It is not always possible for those living in crowded urban environments to find the time or opportunity to go beyond the local convenience store that will in turn be reluctant to store perishable goods. Public transport is being run down and those on tight budgets have to consider very carefully how they spend their money. Some of the food recommended requires an element of time and preparation that is not something often available to those living in a culture of necessity. Perhaps the greatest insensitivity is illustrated by suggesting viewers buy expensive branded products. Some food TV stars have a range of expensive food solutions tagged with the name of the show – thus adding massive publicity and making them profits and giving solutions a legitimacy the government will struggle to match. But making healthy foods one of your choices is also separating yourself out as an individual. As Bourdieu has established, the principle of conformity is one of the principal criteria of common taste.[13] Some may be reluctant to step out of line.

Working-class bodies take the shape they do historically as a result of labor patterns themselves shaped by their relation to the demands of capital. It is this inheritance we are dealing with in a world where the manufacturing base is in decline and there is less need of laboring bodies. The wondrous quick fix of television is unlikely to be able to engineer change in the structural elements of consumer culture despite the passionate entreaties of middle-class agents of discipline. While the rhetoric behind change programs is to help, what they are doing is inviting ethnic minorities and usually the women of the working class to internalize middle-class standards as more appropriate. Thus one by-product of lifestyle television from *Queer Eye for the Straight Guy* through to *What Not to Wear* is shared learning on the most appropriate diet, attire, table manner, etc. We are led to believe that we can all appear more middle class while of course having no other means to get them on that ladder of economic success.

It is interesting to note that manufacturers come in for no complaint in reality television. Indeed the manufacturer's willingness to label their products with the latest Health Authority injunctions (Calorific and Nutritional Numbers for example) is presented as part of the individual's solution. The advertising that goes around the show is now to be understood as temptations to be resisted or treats to be carefully calculated. No blame can be attached to manufacturers in a world where all the information required to make sensible choices is already out there. This might explain the WHO statement that supports, "creating an environment that empowers and encourages individuals and communities to make positive life-enhancing decisions on healthy diet and physical activity."[14]

The bodies we see on reality television are framed by larger debates about health under aggressive capitalism and an increasingly insecure public sector. Nowadays one's health is a question of one's own responsibility to the self. For example, the changing shape of health care in the UK has entailed a turning away from the welfare state and towards investments in privatized medicine. Health is now defined as the responsibility of the individual and then only secondly his or her immediate family. The community and the state have far less of a role to play as the empowered citizen is charged with their own care. In the UK some Health authorities are experimenting with devolved patient budgets in which individuals are invited to fix the parameters of their own care by making selections from treatment options within their own budgets. In a time when identity is more fluid than ever, new health discourses around the changing meaning of the self chime perfectly with lifestyle programming whose core principle is the endless potentiality of change. Improved health now stems not from a national system of care but from a more managerial perspective on the body. In lifestyle formats we are to disassociate ourselves and contemplate the body as a flexible instrument that can be changed by the correct use of the right tools. Health is now achieved through a combination of your own knowledge, a regulated autonomy, and the helpful gestures of the market. With so many channels for information and so many opportunities for the getting of this wisdom it is simply wrong to put the blame for any ill-effects elsewhere. Lifestyle is about choice and your problems are quite simply the result of unwise choices. "Medicine and public health have strong coercive elements in that they seek to shape and normalize human conduct in certain ways. Indeed in the contemporary western societies they have replaced religion as the central institution governing the conduct of human bodies."[15]

Conclusion

A wide range of governmental agencies are responsible for inviting participation in these models of the self. Health agencies, police forces, security firms and many others all seek to offer a regular identity that can easily be monitored. What documentary formats offer is an invitation to share in these identifications for our own good. Reality television may be best understood as a technology serving the anxiety-industry by promoting the notion that the correct forms of consumption will help purchase the body one needs and constant vigilance will produce a useful citizenship. Reality television showcases self-absorption in the self as a duty.

What has perhaps not been significantly discussed is the classed and gendered nature of this process. From public-service documentary with its patrician elite to new forms of reality television fashioned by rising middle-class fractions the bourgeoisie are still there recommending courses of action to modify the behavior of the lower orders. Documentary production is a profoundly classed process. Despite the passionate attempts of the onscreen "team" to help their subjects, the culture of necessity discussed by Bourdieu cannot suddenly be changed. The habitus of such groups are not formed in isolation but by economic and political circumstances, inherited traditions, family and friends.[16]

Those who have studied reality television viewers have found a "tremendously bargained relationship" between audiences and reality media.[17] But the terms of that bargain are informed by one's class position because the body bears its own history. Perhaps we can read that bargained relationship as an index of audience uncertainty when the power of the norm is so pervasive. The anxiety-industry thrives on people having degrees of uncertainty about what it is they are seeing and what they should be. In such a culture the call for difference is hard to make because dominant genres such as reality television call forth specific psychic investments underscored by the operations of consumer culture. People may indeed have complex relationships with the text but this should not detract our attention from the effort being made to bully anxious personalities into order "for their own good."

Reality television programs on health advocate a managerial approach to the body understood as a sign to be read both by the vigilant self and a world of watching eyes. Authenticity is to be found in the validation of others. But this can never rest. It needs constant maintenance. This self is both paralleled and supported in the work of the personal development movement. These new "experts of psy" identified by Rose as psychotherapists, counselors, nutritionists and other lifestyle-attuned professionals offer brave new identities for those prepared to "invest" in them.[18] But what is being sold in reality television is respectful subservience to market-tested expertise. Whatever methods, techniques and procedures offered, the ideal response is to accept them. All that one need aim for is a standardized individuality, an ordinary you in the crowd so that one no longer has to think about the self, no longer feels a painful sense of separation from the mass. The self-product is to be a happy, balanced, ordered, efficient citizen-consumer embracing the anonymity of normality. Accepting the wisdom of lifestyle increases your chance of finding the chimerical self that must remain forever elusive. In such a climate the anxiety-industry is sure to thrive.

Notes

1 Brian Winston, *Claiming the Real: The Documentary Film Revisited* (London: BFI Publishing, 1995).
2 Bill Nichols, *Representing Reality: Issues and Concepts in Documentary* (Bloomington and Indiana: Indiana University Press, 1991).
3 John Corner, *Television Form and Public Address* (London: Edward Arnold, 1995).
4 Gareth Palmer, *Discipline and Liberty* (Manchester: Manchester University Press, 2003).
5 Annette Hill, *Reality TV* (London: Routledge, 2005), 185.
6 Clive Norris and Gary Armstrong, *The Maximum Surveillance Society. The Rise of CCTV* (London: Berg, 1999).
7 Gareth Palmer, "Surveillance Technology in Light Entertainment of the 1990s: Scam shows, shaming and the body," *Salford Working Papers* 24 (1999).
8 Jack Bratich, "Programming Reality. Control Societies, New Subjects and the Power of Transformation," in *Makeover Television*, ed. D. Heller (New York: I.B. Tauris, 2006).
9 Susan Benson, "The Body, Health and Eating Disorders," in *Identity and Difference*, ed. Kathryn Woodward (London: Sage, 1997), 123.
10 Julie Doyle and Irmi Karl, "Shame on You: Cosmetic Surgery and Class Transformation is *10 Years Younger*," in *Uncovering Lifestyle Television*, ed. G. Palmer (London: Ashgate, 2008).
11 Susan Bordo, "Reading the Slender Body," in *Identity and Difference*, ed. K. Woodward (London: Sage, 1997), 194.
12 Pierre Bourdieu, *Distinction* (London: Routledge, 1989), 268.
13 Bourdieu, *Distinction*.
14 Brooke Groskopf, "The Failure of Bio-Power: Interrogating the Obesity Crisis," *Journal for the Arts, Sciences and Technology* 3, no 1 (2005): 43.
15 Deborah Lupton, *The Imperative of Health* (London: Sage, 1995), 5.
16 Bourdieu, *Distinction*.
17 Andy Ruddock, *Investigating Audiences* (London: Sage, 2007).
18 Nikolas Rose, *Governing the Soul* (London: Routledge, 1989).

Chapter 6

Globalizing lifestyles?

Makeover television in Singapore

Tania Lewis[1]

The past decade has seen an explosion of lifestyle makeover television shows with audiences being urged to "renovate" everything from their homes, bodies, and children to their pets, a process that has seen the emergence of an army of lifestyle gurus on television advising us on what not to eat and what not to wear. While critical academic attention has largely focused on blockbuster reality television formats like *Big Brother* and *Survivor*, more recently a growing body of scholarship has started to focus on the "lifestyle turn" on television and the rise of the makeover format.[2] To date much of the work on makeover television has focused on its role in the US and UK. However, in the past couple of years the lifestyle makeover show has become an increasingly global phenomenon with audiences around the world embracing everything from home renovation to plastic surgery makeover shows. This essay is concerned with examining the implications of the global dissemination of such modes of programming, associated as they are with ideologies of neoliberal individualism, self-surveillance and self-promotion, and with a strongly consumption-oriented aesthetic.[3] It emerges out of a pilot study I have been conducting with Dr Fran Martin at the University of Melbourne as a preliminary step in a larger transnational comparative study of lifestyle programming in Asia in which we seek to examine the role of lifestyle television in both shaping and reflecting broader shifts in social and cultural identity accompanying the rise of consumer-based modes of modernity.[4]

Although some significant work has been done on Western television as a pedagogical tool for teaching modernity,[5] extant studies explicitly discussing modernities outside "the West" have to date seldom approached television as an arena for the elaboration of hybridized forms of modern culture, citizenship and selfhood.[6] Lifestyle television, concerned as it is with instructing audiences in modern consumer and lifestyle practices, offers a privileged vantage point from which to survey current configurations and transformations of consumer culture and modernity in the Asia-Pacific region. While it can be seen on the one hand as a carrier of global ideologies around consumerist and neoliberal modes of selfhood, the genre also offers potential insights into local modernities as it tends to be particularly marked by its ties to the "national ordinary" through its focus on ordinary people and their lifestyles. What is of particular interest, then, is its double role as a global television genre associated with Anglo-American lifestyle-oriented consumer practices *and* as a local cultural and media form strongly shaped by national and local cultural contexts and concerns – as well as being marked by different nationally inflected industry histories and modes of reception.

While there has been little systematic research on lifestyle television in Asia, even a cursory glimpse across the region indicates that there are clear regional and national differences in the form, content, and cultural status of lifestyle and consumer advice television, pointing to the importance of localized, culturally specific research. Based on these observations, a crucial critical paradigm for the larger project that this essay emerges out of is that of multiple or comparative modernities, an influential strand of scholarship on non-Western modernities that has emerged from studies of postcoloniality and globalization in the humanities and social sciences over the past ten years (see for instance the work of Arjun Appadurai, Nestor Garcia Canclini, Marwan Kraidy, Aihwa Ong, Lisa Rofel, Dilip Parameshwar Gaonkar, and Lydia Liu). Focusing variously on "alternative," "other," and "hybrid" modernities, such an approach leads toward renewed attempts, in Ong's words, "to consider how non-Western societies themselves make modernities after their own fashion, in the remaking of rationality, capitalism and the nation in ways that borrow from but also transform Western universalizing forms."[7] Thus, while Holden and Scrase point to the ways in which popular media modes like television act as conduits for forms of "mediated modernity" across Asia,[8] a comparative modernities approach usefully extends this model by foregrounding how particular geo-cultural locations frame and specify locally pertinent processes of modernity.

In the Singaporean case study that follows, the emphasis is on both the recognizably "Western" elements of lifestyle television as well as the complex interplay of both globalizing and localizing elements at work in Singaporean lifestyle programming. The aim is thus to frame the lifestyle genre as exemplary of the multiplicity of culturally hybrid televisual modernities currently being worked out across the region.

The rise of the makeover show in the UK and US

Prior to discussing the role of lifestyle makeover television in Singapore I want to first briefly outline the rise of the format in the UK and US, before outlining the industrial, ideological and socio-cultural context out of which the makeover can be seen to emerge in the West. While the makeover format is often popularly associated with American television culture, the first successful makeover show to air on primetime television was the British home renovation-game show format, *Changing Rooms*[9] (broadcast on the BBC in 1996 and later sold into a number of international markets). Makeovers had previously featured on daytime television as segments on magazine programs and talk shows aimed at women. However, the 1990s saw the makeover expand into a full-length format and move into primetime schedules aimed at a broad audience including male viewers. Where daytime television makeovers had often focused on issues of personal style and fashion, the first successful makeover formats in the UK were shows oriented towards investing in and improving the home rather than the self.

By contrast, US television was somewhat slower to embrace the makeover show as a primetime format, focusing instead in the 1990s on a range of early reality-style formats from the low-budget, actuality-based television of the *COPS* variety to shows like MTV's *The Real World* (1992), which can be seen as a precursor to *Big Brother*. The first breakthrough makeover show on US network television was the surgical makeover program *Extreme Makeover* shown on the ABC which first aired in 2002 (although it should be noted that the cable channel TLC had already achieved high ratings in 2000 with *Trading Spaces*, a US adaptation of the BBC's *Changing Rooms*).

Since the emergence of these early primetime makeover shows, this mode of programming has proliferated and evolved with UK and US viewers now exposed to a range of sub-genres of the makeover. Focusing primarily on ordinary people (although occasionally dealing with wayward celebrities), everything from homes (*House Invaders*) and pets (*It's Me or the Dog*) to parental skills (*Supernanny*) and bodies (*How to Look Good Naked*) are now put under the spotlight and transformed – with the guidance of various life experts – under the gaze of the watching public. While there are important distinctions between what Kavka terms "the makeover cultures" of the UK and US, with the British particularly enamoured of domestically-based makeover shows and Americans with body makeovers,[10] today's makeover shows can be seen to be marked by a certain shared ethos and to emerge out of a (to a certain extent) shared political and social context. Before I go on to discuss lifestyle television in Singapore, I want to briefly focus on the ideological and socio-cultural connotations of the makeover.

The lifestyle turn

One explanation for the spread of makeover formats and reality television more broadly has been to see it as a side effect of global shifts within the television industry. In particular, the growing role of relatively cheap, "unscripted" television focused on ordinary people can be seen as an attempt to deal with an increasingly deregulated market and a fragmented audience, with free-to-air networks now competing with cable and satellite television for viewers' attention, offering audiences an abundance of programming choices.[11] The deregulation of the television industry around the world in the 1980s and 1990s and the emergence of a multi-channel environment has also produced a situation where the pressure for product has encouraged local producers to create programs that can potentially move across a range of markets.[12] The rise of reality and lifestyle makeover formats such as *Big Brother* and *Extreme Makeover* that can be sold around the world as pre-packaged program blueprints can thus be seen as an example of this globalization of product.

The success of the makeover format cannot however be purely reduced to a question of industry economics. The format's cross-cultural appeal is also linked to its unique blend of domestic melodrama, personal confession and aesthetic transformation, as well as its pedagogical dimensions – the fact that it offers audiences guidance in the realm of taste, consumption and lifestyle prac- tices whether in relation to tastefully updating one's home or "renovating" one's personal lifestyle. The rise of makeover television can also be linked with a number of wider socio-cultural developments, in particular the "lifestyling" of contemporary existence. Representing far more than just a convenient new way for the television industry to re-label popular advice programming, the concept of lifestyle has instead become one of the dominant frameworks through which we understand and organize contemporary everyday life. As David Bell and Joanne Hollows note in their book *Ordinary Lifestyles*,[13] while the term is used in a range of different contexts, from health to marketing, the notion of lifestyle is underpinned by a conception of identity that foregrounds personal choice and the malleable nature of the self. Rather than seeing selfhood as limited or con- strained by one's class, race or gender, today ordinary people are held up as being able to invent (and re-invent) their own life "biographies." The makeover show thus rather literally extends the DIY rubric to every aspect of one's life from home décor to selfhood.

The emphasis on an individualized, malleable self, alongside a broader focus on aesthetics and the art of living, also involves naturalizing consumption, with makeover television working "to alert viewers to the existence of more products and services for their utility in the endless project of the self."[14] What lifestyle programming "sells" to the audience here, however, are not just products but ways of living and being. Makeover television then is concerned not only with questions of individual style and self-presentation but also increasingly with the ways in which lifestyle choices are linked to broader concerns around selfhood and citizenship. Discussing the rise and role of what he terms "cultural citizen- ship," Toby Miller contends that there has been a growing convergence between civic culture and consumerism.[15] Within media culture this is evidenced by a privileging of discourses of individualized consumption, and in particular a life- style-oriented commercial culture focused on bettering the self through "ethico- aesthetic exercises."[16] Marking a broader shift away from traditional modes of organized civic culture and the rise of a personalized "lifestyle politics,"[17] the ethics and practices of selfhood and citizenship have become reduced to a series of commoditized cultural practices and lifestyle choices; or as Miller puts it, "'Good taste' becomes a sign of, and a means toward, better citizenship."[18]

An important critical approach that has sought to contextualize the rise of the lifestyle-oriented consumer-citizen can be found in Nikolas Rose's work.[19] Influ- enced by Foucault's conception of modern power and governance as being played out through the "freedoms" associated with liberal selfhood, Rose argues

that the rise of neoliberal governments in many nations in the 1980s (in particular the UK and US), alongside the emergence of a wider "enterprise culture,"
has seen a shift in the dominant paradigms through which we conceptualize
modern citizenship. In particular, the figure of the self-governing citizen, an
individual who is constructed as "enterprising" and self-directed, has become a
cultural dominant. This has occurred in the context of the state increasingly
seeking to devolve questions of social and political responsibility to the level of
the individual consumer-citizen, a situation shored up by a "therapeutic culture"
that pairs freedom and moral development with self-mastery and self-development.
Thus, in neoliberal settings, the personal, health and relationship advice
increasingly offered on lifestyle makeover shows like *The Biggest Loser*, for example, can be seen to be attempting to fill the gap left by the state as it passes on
responsibility for once public concerns like obesity onto the self-regulating
consumer-citizen.[20]

Overall, the makeover format can be seen to emerge out of and be marked by
a complex conjuncture of social, cultural, and economic factors. If the rise of
lifestyle television in the US and UK can be linked to these broader economic,
cultural and social shifts, the question then is to what extent these developments
can be applied to other cultural contexts? In his book, *Big Brother*, for instance,
Jonathan Bignell asks whether the transnational mobility of reality and makeover
television indicates the universalization of a specifically Western preoccupation
with "personal confession, modification, testing and the perfectibility of the
self."[21] Such a hypothesis is complicated by the fact that part of the reason for
the global success of makeover formats (as Bignell himself notes) is precisely their
ability to adapt to national contexts. Makeover programs offered up as format
"shells" have been shown to have considerable transnational mobility and sale-
ability,[22] as they are amenable to being readily indigenized through the use of
local presenters, lifestyle experts and members of the public and the instillation
of local concerns and values. Television formats and the process of local format
adaptation, then, represent sites marked by complex negotiations between globalizing forces and domestic concerns and contexts.[23] What follows is a discussion of how the lifestyle makeover format and its associated global ideological
baggage is (re)articulated to and localized via the lifestyle concerns and values
associated with Singapore and its distinctive mode of culturally hybridized
modernity.

"Oriental vogue" and "ethnic fusion": lifestyling Singapore

As noted, in recent years lifestyle makeover formats have not only "travelled"
extensively within linguistically and culturally congruous television territories,
they have also started to make an appearance in less culturally proximate sites
such as Asia. The emergence of new forms of consumer-oriented "middle classes" in the region[24] has seen the local adaptation of a range of Western-style
lifestyle shows. In China, for instance, the government-owned Beijing Television

Station has produced the magazine-style show *Jojo Good Living*, whose host has been compared by the *New York Times* to Martha Stewart.[25] Likewise in India, Sony Entertainment Television recently launched (in May 2008) *Naya Roop Nayi Zindagi*, a local version of *Extreme Makeover*; while Singapore, the object of focus for this essay, has produced a number of locally made makeover shows.

Unlike many of its Asian counterparts, Singapore – as an advanced capitalist, ex-British colony – already has a well-developed consumer and lifestyle oriented media culture. Advertising, radio, and print media in Singapore offer up a complex combination of "Western" and "Asian" lifestyle imagery and discourses while lifestyle television – often categorized as info-ed, infotainment or variety in Singapore – represents a significant proportion of programming on broadcast television. In contrast to the television industry in the Anglo-American context, where deregulation and privatization is the norm, however, broadcast television in Singapore is highly regulated, falling primarily under the jurisdiction of the state-owned collection of companies known as Mediacorp. Mediacorp thus operates all three Singaporean terrestrials – Channel 5 (English-language), Channel 8 (Chinese) and Channel U (Chinese) – as well as the TV12 specialty services: Suria for Malay audiences, Kids Central, Arts Central and the Tamil-language Vasantham Central.

While television broadcasting in Singapore is dominated by Chinese programming, a review of the evening schedule indicates that lifestyle television programs feature on most television channels. In January 2008, for instance, the 8–10 p.m. slot on Mediacorp's main Chinese channel,[26] Channel 8, featured Chinese-language shows like *Home Décor Survivor 3* (a home makeover show) and *Good Food Fun Cook* (a reality-style cooking show). Arts Central (which features a variety of mostly foreign, English-language programming often with Chinese subtitles) offered a regular 9–10 p.m. lifestyle slot including shows like *The Hairy Biker's Cookbook* (a UK cooking-travel show). The channel also aired a rather glossy, locally produced but strongly Western-inflected lifestyle show, *The Food Bachelor*, in which a group of attractive, ethnically diverse young men (chosen to reflect Singapore's multicultural community) with minimal cooking skills compete for the opportunity to host their own cooking show. The Malay channel Suria meanwhile offered two evening lifestyle shows, the D.I.Y. home décor show *ID Kreatif* and *Cari Menantu*, described as "a reality program that gives a spouse-to-be a crash marriage preparatory course." Primetime lifestyle programming however was featured relatively rarely on Vasantham Central, the Tamil-language channel (although more recently the channel has been screening a daytime beauty makeover show).[27] Thus, while lifestyle shows feature on all the Mediacorp channels, the majority of Singaporean lifestyle programs are made for Chinese audiences and hence the focus in this next section is primarily on Chinese formats.

On Chinese-language Singaporean television, the broad genre of lifestyle advice and info-tainment programming – food programming, travel shows, budget advice shows, etc. – consists mainly of local formats made for local audiences,[28] although the conventions and aesthetics of many of these shows draw from a range of international influences including US game shows, British lifestyle television, and Japanese variety shows. Makeover formats more specifically have also featured on primetime television, although like early forms of the makeover on UK and US television, these have often focused on beauty makeovers and have been aimed at female audiences (e.g., Channel 8's *Beautiful People* aired in 2003).[29] More recently though the makeover format has started to evolve and diversify on Singaporean television, targeting a broader audience through the emergence of Chinese-language shows like the eco-makeover program *Energy Savers* and the highly popular *Home Décor Survivor* series, which first aired in 2005 with the spin off *Junior Home Décor Survivor* coming in at number five in the top twenty television programs for the ratings period of March 2008.

One point to note here is that, aside from beauty shows, makeover shows focused on individual personal transformations have not featured so strongly in local lifestyle programming. Constrained by low budgets, an arguably more communitarian approach to lifestyle and a relative cultural reserve – amongst Chinese audience members at least – in relation to exposing oneself and one's lifestyle on television, the types of plastic surgery, behavioural and body makeover shows (such as *Extreme Makeover*, *Ladette to Lady* and *The Biggest Loser*) that have taken off more recently in the West are yet to emerge on Singaporean television.

The kinds of makeover shows that have started to become popular on primetime television are ones oriented towards renovating the home rather than the self. The *Home Décor Survivor* series for instance is a popular home show which borrows heavily from Anglo-American makeover formats, offering a kind of Chinese-Singaporean version of *Changing Rooms* with a touch of *Queer Eye for the Straight Guy* (albeit with the overtly gay elements and the personal makeover taken out). Featuring a competitive game show element, two teams each led by a young male host (comedian Mark Lee and Bryan Wong, known as Mediacorp's "hosting king") vie to makeover the interior space of two homes while staying within a budget of $6000. Like many Western home makeover formats, the show combines a class-inflected education in modernist taste, style and aesthetics (in one show there is a particular emphasis – highlighted by English words popping up on screen – on "modernism" and on creating spaces that are "funky" and "industrial looking"), with a focus both on DIY and thriftiness, and consumerism. Thus, the teams are seen creating one-off art works and wall stencils for the home interiors of the show's participants while home owners are also taken to various stores to buy furniture (with prices and the name and address of stores provided to the audience), with frequent adverts in the break for the show's sponsor, a homewares store.

While educating the audience in design and aesthetics, the overall tone of the program is one of youthful informality, with the young hosts and makeover team engaging throughout in cheeky banter and comic hi-jinks, presenting themselves and relating to each other in a manner that is distinctly "student-ish" as opposed to "respectable" or "serious." Thus the show offers a fairly soft and accessible form of pedagogy, modelling forms of middle-class cosmopolitan taste in ways that are clearly targeted toward "ordinary Singaporean youth": students and young families living in small, standardized government flats.

While the show borrows heavily from Anglo-American home makeover formats, it also draws upon the aesthetics and conventions of hybrid Japanese–Chinese variety television. In particular, the show has a comic, zany feel with pop-up coloured images and words exploding onto the screen accompanied by comic sound effects. The group presentation, slapstick humour, incessant cheeky cross-talk, "busy" screen aesthetic and dense soundscape contribute to an overall feel of *renao*, a positive term meaning "lively; busy; noisy; fun" that encapsulates the feel aspired to by much Chinese-language variety-style television.[30] Likewise, the content of the show blends European design tips and global cosmopolitan style with local concerns. The focus is mainly on renovating the small Housing Development Board flats in which most Singaporeans live with an emphasis on hybridizing modern design with traditional aesthetics; one episode is themed "Ethnic Fusion" with the team's goals being to blend ethnic Peranakan style with modern design while another focuses on "oriental vogue."

The program thus speaks to a young domestic Chinese-Singaporean audience while adopting a hybridized mode of address that is at once recognizably local but that also speaks to broader regional and transnational concerns. Thus the show generically draws from local, regional and transnational influences while the mode of pedagogy and aesthetic aspirationalism on display illustrates Harindranath's conception of the "transnational cosmopolitan elite" as a formation that cuts across national and East–West geo-cultural boundaries.[31]

Energy Savers, which aired in 2008 on Mediacorp 8 on Thursdays at 8.30 p.m., is another home makeover show of sorts, although one concerned with transforming the energy consumption of Singaporean households. Like *Home Décor Survivor* it adopts a reality-based, competitive game show format with the show's central "challenge" being for the twelve participating households to reduce their energy consumption by at least 10 per cent while thinking up "creative ways" for saving electricity along the way, with the best household winning $5,000. The show's male and female hosts are young attractive Singaporean personalities and like *Home Décor Survivor* the show's tone is highly comedic and playful with rapid comic voice-overs and the liberal use of pop-up images and words complete with "zany" sound effects to emphasize particular household tips or energy consumption issues.

However, while the show aims for a light variety-style feel its agenda is rather more educational than *Home Décor Survivor*; the hosts guide the audience through an audit of the households, noting the range of appliances they own and their current energy use and then offering suggestions for reducing energy consumption. The households on display here range from a young couple with a baby living in a Housing Development Board flat to larger, more affluent families living in freestanding houses suggesting the show is aimed at a rather larger cross-section of the Singaporean public than the more youthful audience of *Home Décor Survivor*.

While *Energy Savers* is similar in feel to other info-ed/variety shows on Singaporean television, the format's focus on reducing energy consumption aligns it with a range of recent lifestyle makeover shows coming out of the Anglo-American context from competitive weight-loss shows like *The Biggest Loser* to eco-makeover formats like Australia's *Eco-house Challenge* and *Carbon Cops*. While such shows are ostensibly entertainment-oriented makeover formats they can also be seen to promote neoliberal models of good consumer-citizenship in which community concerns such as obesity and the global oil crisis are treated as issues that can be dealt with at the level of individual consumer behavior and self-regulation.[32]

Such a show however also needs to be understood in the context of Singapore's rather distinctive mode of authoritarian capitalism. Possessing a neoliberal market alongside a strongly regulatory state, Singapore is marked by a form of neoliberalism rather different from its Western counterparts, one that as David Harvey notes blends capitalism with Confucianism, nationalism and a "cosmopolitan ethic suited to its current position in the world of international trade."[33] Singaporean entertainment-based television, while addressing consumers as self-governing citizens and consumers, is also strongly shaped by state dictates around cultural values (such as ensuring for example that hosts speak standardized Mandarin). While there has been a distinct pedagogical "turn" on Anglo-American lifestyle television, the bottom line for programmers in these settings (the BBC being somewhat of an exception) tends to be commercial and ratings driven. While such concerns are also important for Singaporean lifestyle television producers, the public educational elements of Singaporean shows are more overt; shows are often packaged in terms of their benefit to the community while lifestyle television producers often take into account government concerns and campaigns around lifestyle issues when they are creating lifestyle shows aimed at promoting good citizenship. A good example of this would be the 2007 infotainment-variety show, *The ABCs of Water*, an eight-part series aired on Wednesdays at 8.30 p.m. on Channel 8 hosted by two popular television personalities and sponsored by Singapore's Public Utilities Board in which "Television viewers learnt along with the celebrity contestants about how Singapore's reservoirs and waterways can be kept beautiful and clean, and what activities they can enjoy."

Another very popular form of lifestyle programming in Singapore which again speaks to the question of television's articulation to hybridizing formations of cultural modernity in Singapore is food television. Food programming has been a longstanding genre in a range of Asian television markets with the Japanese format *Iron Chef* even being exported to the US and remade as *Iron Chef America*. Alongside Japan, Anglo-American trends in lifestyle television have also arguably had an influence on the more recent rise in the region of the celebrity chef and entertainment-oriented cooking shows more generally, shows which, while not strictly speaking makeover shows, are marked by a "transformational aesthetic" and by a concern with teaching ordinary people about middle-class forms of taste and distinction.[34]

Typical of the kind of everyday lifestyle programming popular with Chinese-Singaporeans are cheap, down-home formats like *Good Food Fun Cook* (*GFFC*), aired in 2008 on Friday at 8 p.m. on Mediacorp 8. Targeted at housewives and showcasing the talents of celebrity chef Sam Leong, "the idol in the cooking world,"[35] and Quan Yi Feng, one of Singapore's top television hosts, *GFFC* brings "the kitchen out to the public," with episodes featuring Sam cooking in an open-air kitchen, haggling with vendors and mingling with locals at street markets.

As in *Home Décor Survivor* and *Energy Savers* the mode of address on the show is informal and zany and the feel aims for *renao*. The show has a highly populist agenda reflected in the way in which Sam and Quan Yi Feng interact with the ordinary members of the public who gather to watch and learn as they cook – people whose very ordinariness is framed to reflect the "aunties" that are the show's target audience. At the same time, like many Singaporean lifestyle programs, *GFFC* combines an entertainment-oriented approach to lifestyle with an educational agenda. Sam on the one hand is positioned as a man of the people – struggling with a very stilted Cantonese-inflected Mandarin, in distinction to the fluency of the Taiwan-born Quan Yi Feng – but at the same time, he is there to teach the audience about practical recipes, quality food, and style and aesthetics.[36] As the show's Senior Executive Producer, Tay Lay Tin, notes, "on *GFFC*, it's the first time we are educating the audience to say you can do this five star cuisine at home. The food is very simple but the presentation is upper class. Sam Leong is famous for this."

The show also teaches the audience about healthy food, with each episode focusing on one of thirteen themes, such as how to manage hair loss, how to look youthful, how to keep fit, etc. The show's research team thus includes a Chinese physician who helps choose healthy ingredients for the show's dishes and a research writer who, as Tay Lay Tin notes, makes "these issues simple, lighter ... more approachable for a general audience." *GFFC* combines a focus on taste and aesthetics (similar to *Home Décor Survivor*) with the kind of public educational focus apparent in shows like *Energy Savers*. The show initiates ordinary citizens into cosmopolitan forms of taste while at the same time addressing them as good healthy Chinese-Singaporean citizens.

In varied ways the three Chinese-Singaporean productions discussed can all be seen to position local audiences as reflexive cosmopolitan consumer-citizens negotiating Western, regionalist Chinese and local models of lifestyle consumption and social identity.[37] Through transforming the home *Home Décor Survivor* performs a complex hybridized cultural aesthetics tied to both global and Asian taste cultures but framed largely in consumerist terms. *Energy Savers* likewise speaks to both global and national-governmental concerns around thrift, responsible consumption and self-regulating modes of citizenship. *GFFC*, meanwhile, is a particularly localized and ordinary mode of lifestyle television – tied to local people and places, overtly addressed to "ordinary" (middle-aged, working-class, female) audience members, and offering practical how-to advice on simple, everyday home cooking. But here also we see a degree of cosmopolitan aspirationalism on display (again framed in highly localized ways) – played out in this instance through its concern with teaching audiences how to appreciate "five star cuisine" and the show's healthy agenda.

GFFC's consumer message (which ties aspirational taste to healthy lifestyles) can easily be read as affirming the simple spread of a global, neoliberal agenda of enterprising selfhood. But as I've suggested such modes of lifestyle consumption need to also be understood in relation to local and regional Chinese cultural values (for instance on *GFFC* Chinese traditions of medicinal food are an important focus of the show). Likewise the healthy, responsible model of selfhood promoted on such formats is articulated to a rather localized form of neoliberalism, here paradoxically reflecting the close regulatory relationship between the media and the Singapore government, which has been actively pushing a healthy lifestyle campaign through media sites such as television. While makeover shows like *Home Décor Survivor* and *Energy Savers* and lifestyle programs like *GFFC* all speak to a certain extent to the globalizing rubric of neoliberal "lifestyled" forms of identity, they nevertheless do so in ways that complicate universalistic models of lifestyle and modernity.

Conclusion

Despite claims about its impending demise, broadcast television is arguably playing an increasing role in shaping culture, identity and citizenship around the world. The media and entertainment sector in Asia for instance is one of the world's fastest growing industries, with television being by far the sector's dominant player. The rise of television in the region has occurred hand in hand with the liberalization of economic and, to a varied degree, state structures. One of the consequences of these processes has been the emergence of new forms of consumer-oriented middle classes with lifestyle aspirations that are shaped by national, regional and global influences.

Against this backdrop we have seen the emergence of a range of types of advice programming aimed at instructing audiences in consumption, taste and lifestyle. On lifestyle television, in particular, the homes and lives of ordinary people and celebrities are paraded as examples of ideal (or in the case of makeover shows, not-so-ideal) models of selfhood while lifestyle experts provide us with rules and guidelines for managing increasingly complex lives. Although not as prevalent as in the US and UK where a range of reality-style lifestyle makeover formats have flourished, the growth of home renovation shows and the celebrity chef phenomenon in sites like Singapore, for instance, marks the growing place of lifestyle-oriented modes of advice and consumption within Asian media culture. What does this global embrace of lifestyle formats tell us about local television markets and cultures? Does the transnational mobility of the makeover show mean that Anglo-American models of enterprising individualism and self-improvement are becoming hegemonic?

The Singapore case study presented here suggests that the notion of "lifestyle" needs to be understood not only in relation to global shifts in identity around consumer culture and late modernity but also articulated to specific geo-cultural contexts and local/regional modernities. As I've argued elsewhere, even in the case of ostensibly "Western" sites such as Australia, lifestyle advice culture and media is somewhat distinct from its UK and US counterparts.[38] Lifestyle programming, while on the one hand seemingly "selling" global models of lifestyles, taste and consumption, tends to be relentlessly tied to the familiar and the ordinary. The double-edged nature of these forms of programming is evident in Singaporean lifestyle shows, where the examples discussed display a complex and varied blending of local embeddedness and nostalgia for local and regional Chinese traditions with a global sensibility. On these shows, an emphasis on Chinese medicine and the health-giving properties of food sits cheek by jowl with the modelling of cosmopolitan middle-class taste and "five star cuisine"; advice on adapting Peranakan traditions next to a focus on modernist aesthetics.

This spectrum of variously hybrid cultures and taste formations – incorporating different mixes of the local, the national, and the transnational; different elements of that which is framed as "traditional" and that which is framed as "contemporary" – brings into focus the necessity of employing a multiple or alternative modernities model when discussing developments in transnational media culture. It also emphasizes the locally varied nature of modernity and lifestyle culture *within* specific sites, with contemporary culture in Singapore clearly internally differentiated along the axes of local/regional/global as well as traditional/modern. Along with these internally differentiated forms of syncretic modern culture come, too, transforming notions of selfhood as reflected, (re)constructed and disseminated via lifestyle television. A comprehensive consideration of the identities taught by this mode of programming is beyond the scope of this essay, and awaits detailed audience studies. But it would certainly be a mistake to assume that the forms of selfhood emerging through such media and their consumption will be merely "Western" or even "Westernized" in any simple sense. Instead, these forms of subjectivity and identification – like the French cuisine or the pop art design taught by the programs – are themselves likely to be significantly indigenized and "made-over" in their uptake in these specific cultural contexts.

Notes

1 I'd like to thank my co-researcher on the Asian lifestyle TV project Fran Martin for her valuable critical insights, many of which were drawn upon in this chapter.
2 David Bell and Joanne Hollows, eds, *Ordinary Lifestyles: Popular Media, Consumption and Taste* (Maidenhead, England: Open University Press, 2005); Charlotte Brunsdon, "Lifestyling Britain: The 8–9 Slot on British Television," *International Journal of Cultural*

Studies 6, no. 1 (2003): 5–23; Laurie Ouellette and James Hay, *Better Living through Television* (Malden, MA: Blackwell, 2008); Frances Bonner, *Ordinary Television: Analyzing Popular TV* (London: Sage, 2003); Tania Lewis, *Smart Living: Lifestyle Media and Popular Expertise* (New York: Peter Lang, 2008); Dana A. Heller, ed., *Makeover Television: Realities Remodelled, Reading Contemporary Television* (London: I.B. Tauris, 2007); Tania Lewis, ed., *TV Transformations: Revealing the Makeover Show* (London: Routledge, 2000); Toby Miller, *Makeover Nation: The United States of Reinvention* (Columbus: Ohio State University Press, 2008); Gareth Palmer, *Exposing Lifestyle Television: The Big Reveal* (Aldershot, England; Burlington, VT: Ashgate, 2008).

3 Alison Hearn, "Insecure: Narratives and Economies of the Branded Self in Transformation Television," in *TV Transformations*; Toby Miller, *Cultural Citizenship: Cosmopolitanism, Consumerism and Television in a Neoliberal Age* (Philadelphia: Temple University Press, 2007); Mark Andrejevic, *Reality TV: The Work of Being Watched* (Lanham, MD: Rowman & Littlefield, 2004).

4 As part of the pilot study for a larger project on lifestyle TV in the Asia-Pacific region, Dr Martin and I have been conducting research on lifestyle TV in Singapore and Taiwan. The aim for the larger study is to utilize a three-fold methodology involving industry, audience and program-based research. To date we have conducted an analysis of scheduling patterns, content-textual analysis of selected Chinese-language programs (which were translated from Mandarin to English by Dr Martin) and some in-country industry interviews (conducted in English by myself and Dr Martin).

5 John Hartley, *Uses of Television* (London: Routledge, 1999).

6 For exceptions to this see R. Ganguly-Scrase & T. J. Scrase, "Constructing Middle-class Culture: Globalization, Modernity and Indian Media" in T. J. M. Holden & T. Scrase, eds, *Medi@sia: Global media/tion in and out of context* (London: Routledge, 2006); M. Kraidy, *Hybridity, or the Cultural Logic of Globalization* (Philadelphia: Temple University Press, 2005); R. Harindranath, *Audience-Citizens: The Media, Public Knowledge, and Interpretive Practice* (New Delhi: Sage, 2009).

7 Aihwa Ong, "Anthropology,China,and Modernities: The Geopolitics of Cultural Knowledge," in *The Future of Anthropological Knowledge*, ed. H. Moore (London: Routledge, 1995), 64.

8 Todd Joseph Miles Holden and Timothy J. Scrase, eds, *Medi@Sia: Global Media/Tion in and out of Context* (London: Routledge, 2006).

9 *Changing Rooms* was the brain child of British lifestyle TV guru Peter Bazalgette, who also created groundbreaking lifestyle formats such as *Ready Steady Cook* and *Ground Force*. Bazalgette's TV production company eventually became part of Endemol UK, and as chairman of the company he introduced *Big Brother* to British television audiences.

10 Tania Lewis, "Changing Rooms, Biggest Losers and Backyard Blitzes: A History of Makeover Television in the United Kingdom, United States and Australia," in *TV Transformations: Revealing the Makeover Show*, ed. Tania Lewis (London: Routledge, 2009) 7–18; Misha Kavka, "Changing Properties: The Makeover Show Crosses the Atlantic," in *The Great American Makeover: Television, History, Nation*, ed. Dana Heller (New York: Palgrave Macmillan, 2006), 211–30.

11 Frances Bonner, *Ordinary Television: Analyzing Popular TV* (London: Sage, 2003); John Ellis, *Seeing Things: Television in the Age of Uncertainty* (London; New York: I.B. Tauris, 2000).

12 Albert Moran, *Copycat Television: Globalisation, Program Formats and Cultural Identity* (Luton: University of Luton Press, 1998); Silvio Waisbord, "McTV: Understanding the Global Popularity of Television Formats," *Television & New Media* 5, no. 4 (2004): 359–83.

13 Bell and Hollows, *Ordinary Lifestyles*.

14 Bonner, *Ordinary Television*, 104.

15 Miller, *Makeover Nation*.

16 Ibid., 11.
17 L. Bennett, "The Uncivic Culture: Communication, Identity, and the Rise of Lifestyle Politics," *PS: Political Science and Politics* 31, no. 4 (1998): 745.
18 Miller, *Makeover Nation*, 11.
19 Nikolas S. Rose, *Governing the Soul: The Shaping of the Private Self* (London: Routledge, 1989); Nikolas S. Rose, *Inventing Our Selves: Psychology, Power, and Personhood, Cambridge Studies in the History of Psychology* (Cambridge, England; New York: Cambridge University Press, 1996).
20 Ouellette and Hay, *Better Living through Television*.
21 Jonathan Bignell, *Big Brother: Reality TV in the Twenty-First Century* (Basingstoke, UK: Palgrave Macmillan, 2005), 40.
22 Waisbord, "McTV."
23 Moran, *Copycat Television*.
24 V.T. King, "The Middle Class in Southeast Asia: Diversities, Identities, Comparisons and the Vietnamese Case," *IJAPS* 4, no. 2 (2008): 73–109.
25 Janice Hua Xu, "Brand-New Lifestyle: Consumer-Oriented Programmes on Chinese Television," *Media Culture & Society* 29, no. 3 (2007): 363–76.
26 Mediacorp's other Chinese channel, Channel U, also has some lifestyle shows but these cater for more of a niche audience, addressing in particular university students and high school students with shows like *Campus Yummy Hunt* where the hosts head to different campuses to find the best and cheapest food outlets.
27 Vasantham Central also aired a primetime info-tainment style magazine show called *Naam* that included a short lifestyle feature providing the latest updates on fashion, hobbies, travel tips and interior design.
28 According to Tay Lay Tin, a Senior Executive Producer with Chinese Entertainment Productions, lifestyle TV audiences are primarily housewives supplemented by students at primetime. She argues that, given long work hours in Singapore, "workers" tend not catch programs in the 8–10 p.m. slot instead watching after 10 p.m. (a time slot dominated by news and documentaries). Interview with Tay Lay Tin, Senior Executive Producer, Chinese Entertainment Productions, Singapore, January 2008.
29 At the time of writing, a new full-length beauty show was being aired on Mediacorp 8 at 8.30 p.m. on Friday. *Follow Me to Glamour* is a reality style "outdoor game show" based around the search for suitable candidates to undergo beauty make-over sessions in public.
30 Thanks to Fran Martin for this observation.
31 R. Harindranath, "Reviving 'Cultural Imperialism'," in *Planet TV: A Global Television Reader*, eds Lisa Parks and Shanti Kumar (New York: New York University Press, 2003).
32 Tania Lewis, "Transforming Citizens: Green Politics and Ethical Consumption on Lifestyle Television," *Continuum: Journal of Media & Cultural Studies* 22, no. 2 (2008): 227–40.
33 David Harvey, *A Brief History of Neoliberalism* (Oxford; New York: Oxford University Press, 2005), 86.
34 Isabelle de Solier, "TV Dinners: Culinary Television, Education and Distinction," *Continuum: Journal of Media & Cultural Studies* 19, no. 4 (2005): 465–81.
35 Interview with Tay Lay Tin, Senior Executive Producer, Chinese Entertainment Productions, Singapore, January 2008.
36 Again, thanks to Fran Martin for these observations.
37 While Singaporean TV might be seen to legitimate global middle-class lifestyles, there are limits to the kinds of cosmopolitan lifestyles it will portray. For instance, featuring queer identified actors or hosts is a no go zone for Singapore TV (although it can feature camp hosts who are "read" by the audience as gay) as evidenced by the recent

case of a home makeover show that was fined for featuring a gay couple who wanted to transform their game room into a new nursery for their adopted baby. "Singapore government fines TV station for gay show" http://www.boston.com/news/nation/articles/2008/04/24/singapore_fines_tv_station_for_gay_show/

38 Tania Lewis, "Changing Rooms, Biggest Losers and Backyard Blitzes: A History of Makeover Television in the UK, US and Australia," in *TV Transformations*.

Chapter 7

Reacting to reality TV

The affective economy of an "extended social/public realm"

Helen Wood and Beverley Skeggs

Introduction

The endless mutation of reality television, the numerous sub-genres and variation in formats, has led some commentators to suggest that the term is no longer useful as a generic category,[1] whilst on the other hand Nick Couldry argues for maintaining the term because of its suggestiveness about the myth of the mediated center: "presenting itself as the privileged 'frame' through which we access the reality that *matters to us as social beings.*"[2] This difference of opinion represents a broader tension in our scholarship around whether television's textual-aesthetic or social-relational character should provide us with the dominant frame of reference. Taking our lead from Richard Johnson's observation that the textual/ social split in cultural research is inherently "phoney,"[3] this chapter addresses the social character of reality television as it meets its audience. We argue that the immediacy offered by the form draws out what *matters* to us in ways that intervene in the politics of social distinction. But we insist that it is best not to understand that relationship between television and identity via a text/reader dynamic in which audiences are interpellated and made subject to the text's dominant meaning system: a model which has ultimately reified and rendered static the categories of "text" and "reader."[4] Rather, we discuss the experiential aspects of being involved in reality television and explore how identity is evoked in the dynamic responses of our audiences. By addressing what *matters* to audiences in this way we begin to unpack how reality television intervenes in the affective economies of the UK's current socio-political realm.

Immediate sensation and audiences

Reality television's play with immediacy represents a triumph of the medium ultimately fulfilling its promise as a technology of intimacy.[5] Television's temporal and spatial organization of "liveness" means that it operates as a fiction of "presence" rather than as a medium of *re*-presentation.[6] Thus the affective aspects of television – the feelings of "being there" – help to account for how the real of reality television becomes meaningful. As Kavka points out: "The exposure of the internal cabling in a program like *Big Brother* suggests that view-ers find truth not in the transparency or erasure of the media frame, but rather in the social or inter-subjective truths that arise out of the frame of manipula-tion."[7] Therefore "reality" in any tangible sense relates more to a "structure of feeling," to deploy Raymond Williams's phrase, rather than to an objectively observable or external truth. But privileging the sensory experience of television disrupts expectations around text and meaning. For Jon Dovey, "the rhetorical structures whereby texts make generalized meaning through specific representa-tions are of less importance than the overall interactive relationships between audiences and texts that constitute public discourse space."[8] Anita Biressi and Heather Nunn suggest that reality television might be considered as an "exten-ded social/public realm."[9] Thus reality television offers us a frame of reference through which people and personhood (as audience *and* potential performers) are increasingly and normatively mediated.

The ideas outlined above are rather paradoxically drawn from observations on the nature of the text. Wood's earlier study, *Talking with Television*, is a talk show audience research project which argues that a text–reader relationship would import an unsatisfactory literary framework to texts that involve the dynamic business of un-scripted talk.[10] That research uses an interactive analysis to explain how talk shows are received as "communicative events," and similarly here an alternative framework is required to capture the intimate forms of con-nection that are apparently characteristic of reality television. We think that by investigating the workings of an extended social realm we can begin to theorize the role of television in social relationships, which is imperative given the increasing number of mediated "others" across televised space.

Writers engaged in the phenomenological aspects of the media have been asking us to bring down the barriers of thinking between mediated and social communication. For instance Paddy Scannell's work has called for a greater understanding of how media are ritually embedded in everyday life, detailing how broadcasting invests in forms of sociability and everydayness.[11] His emphasis upon communicative *action*, and not flatly on *text*, is really helpful, but as he moves away from traditional questions of representation, David Morley points out that "sociability is simply not the indivisible Good which Scannell assumes it to be."[12] For Nick Couldry the media's rituals operate as instruments of power[13] and we want to add to that debate by considering what part material inequality must play. Whilst sociability suggests inclusion it is also premised upon exclusion; experiencing media forms in late modernity must surely be uneven given the uneven processes of modernity and capitalist social relations.

Methodology

Our research[14] focused on self-transformation reality television programs in the UK between 2004 and 2007, and it is clear that national structures and values[15] shaped the output. British reality television is resolutely, spectacularly and unapologetically about class divisions. Predominantly focusing on class extremes such as the aristocrat teaching the abject underclass (*Ladette to Lady*, *What the Butler Saw*), it also pits the aspirational working class against the less respectable (*Wife Swap*), exposes the danger and pathology of the working-class mother (*Supernanny*), the danger of the working-class man (all the reality crime programs), and provides instructional advice for social mobility (*What Not to Wear* and all the lifestyle, home, gardening and property programs). The middle class, during the period of our research, were almost invisible as television participants (but not as experts), although currently visible on property programs. Reality television participants are usually working class,[16] selected to display their need for transformation, or abjection. Whilst many of the formats of the above programs are successfully globally franchised they always take on national inflections.

Our audience research involved three stages: interviewing, watching reality television with participants, and focus groups, conducted with forty women, middle and working class, white, Black and South Asian, settled and recent residents from four areas of South London.[17] Our research interviews provided information on how the women watched and used television and how it fitted into their lives more generally. We developed the "text-in-action" method[18] to explore the viewing experience itself, watching a self-selected "reality" program (from our range of ten) with participants (and sometimes their friends) and recording their immediate reactions alongside the television text. Finally, we convened focus groups taking up key themes from our interviews to explore how group opinions of reality television mobilized around popular public debates circulating about reality television at the time. This chapter concentrates on examples of the text-in-action sessions which capture immediate responses to reality television, a process we call immediation as television immanently mediates through women's social relations.

Moral authority and social distinction

In the text-in-action sessions we recorded viewers talking with television. Our data involves numerous paralinguistic affective responses – tuts, sighs, gasps and laughter, etc. – that we call "affective textual encounters" which can be seen in the following transcripts (in italics). These affective interventions are frequently followed by an "Oh my God" statement of astonishment which is then converted into a moral judgment. It is not surprising that when comparing recordings of viewers watching the same program, these heightened reactions came at the same moments in the text, often elicited by the editing of the program.

Elsewhere, we have discussed the "pursuit of care" evident in many of our audience's reactions to reality television, where viewers made concerted attempts to empathize with participants regardless of how negatively they were framed.[19] However, there were also key moments when our audience members assessed the "value" of participants on reality television through making moral judgments of their actions, which is what we might expect given the genre's emphasis upon exposing modes of behavior and ways of life. The popular press has written about reality television as a form of morality play, and Gay Hawkins refers to an "ethical turn" on television.[20] Others have explored the rampant govern-mentality across new television formats in terms of their neoliberal imperative to how one *should* live.[21] Whilst Annette Hill's audience research provides evidence that reality formats encourage viewers to judge good and bad conduct, the findings are interpreted around a relatively conservative consensus of "the family" and "responsibility." Whilst this is a start, it is also in danger of reproducing the idea that a universalized moral consensus exists outside of social inequality. As Andrew Sayer points out:

> Differences in the distribution of respect, contempt, envy, resentment or condescension and deference are partly a product of inequalities in eco-nomic distribution, not merely because wealth is often taken as an index of worth but because economic inequalities make objective differences to people in terms of their chances of achieving things that are likely to win conditional recognition.[22]

We found that moral reactions were made in socially differentiated ways because our participants had both uneven access to resources to establish moral authority and also radically different values about what constitutes "good" and "bad." The forms that respondents' reactions took also relate to socially differentiated types of emotional performances engendered through reality television's sense of "presentness" and its "structure of feeling."

Middle-class reactions: commentary and taste

Taste distinctions as well as knowledge about public debates of reality television were more likely to resource the authoritative positions taken by our middle-class participants, which also enabled us to see how different methods invoke perfor-mances of class.[23] As part of a broader cultural skill to hold the form at a dis-tance, they would often provide commentary during the "text-in-action" sessions. Ien Ang's audience work on *Dallas* describes how commentary can be used to control the object on which it reports.[24] Middle-class discourse operates with a "neutralizing distance" establishing a middle-of-the-road ideology and marks a distinction from those who let themselves get carried away.[25] When middle-class viewers *do* offer more heightened emotional responses they are often resourced by taste, and they regularly challenge the knowledge of TV experts. In the next example viewers are watching an episode of *Faking It* where Leeds bottle-factory worker Mick is mentored by extravagant London designer David to "pass" as a fashion designer.

Here we can see how Vish, Deirdre and Jemima defend the attractive parti-cipant, Mick. They attack David, the expert's, clothing (which is not that difficult

Table 7.1 Middle-class reactions: commentary and taste

Audio/visual marker	Program audio extract Faking It	Forest Hill viewers' comments[i]
13:17 David: to camera	It's becoming apparent that he doesn't know a lot about fashion or about designers he doesn't even particularly know what he likes, what does he like?	
Clothes on the rails	David: Marc Jacobs again that's a really famous designer that's a name that you really do have to learn. Mick: Marc Jacobs	-*What!* [loud] [*Laughter and outrage noises*] -*Ohh* poor thing -And he looks like a (buffoon)! -He probably does know what he likes it's just (?) and quite simple quite (?) -Yeah - not bright colors and -yeah
13:36 Mick to camera	Some of the stuff I saw today was ok some of the stuff was just completely off the wall you know unbelievable I can't believe that anybody would wear something like that and then I met David	-If the mentor had done some legwork he'd have taken him to some designers who are a bit more like that than (?) simple (?) because that's what his style is - but they just tried to choose somebody outrageous
David and Mick walking down London street	Mick: I didn't embarrass you too much today then? David: Not at all I never get embarrassed do you think I'd look like this if I got embarrassed	-They tend to look for really stark differences (?) -Mmm - I suppose -And on both sides really -you know a lot of people <u>are</u> interested in clothes why not choose one of them
Montage shots of London Streets		
14:05	Voice Over: London's Brick Lane, the heart of cutting edge fashion, and where Mick will be based for the next few weeks in his own studio.	-That's where erm Yasmin gets all her clothes from Brick Lane -Is it? Yeah but quite (?) It can be quite (frumpy) I find I get quite a few tops we go to the market when normally we shop
14:57 David and Mick in design studio	David: what you need to do now is to really start really looking at clothing, you know observe all the details then start utilizing them in your own design work Voice Over: For Mick to start designing his own range of clothes he needs to learn whole new production process David: it's important to think about the concept I want you to gather together a whole heap of things that are going to influence you … once you've gathered this research then the design starts	- the thing is he doesn't seem to realize that he doesn't look that well dressed himself he doesn't actually look like a very - he doesn't look like <u>anyone</u> that you would want to dress like - *No!* - you know you're not whereas there are people that do look really great aren't there. - really inspiring yeh - he looks sort of Boy George gone slightly wrong -[*Laughter*]

[i] Transcription conventions: <u>underline</u> for stress, CAPITALS for shouting, (in brackets) for inaudible or best guess.

as he is clearly eccentric) suggesting that he should have put in more effort, again critiquing the television production. They also show knowledge of the "set up" of the program: "they tend to look for stark differences." But what is significant here is that their authority is resourced by their own cultural knowledge of fashion. London's trendy Brick Lane neighborhood is familiar and ordinary to these viewers, in contrast to Mick's experience of the North of England. They say, "That's where Yasmin gets all her clothes from," where one of them gets "quite a few tops" and where "we go to the market" which allows them a platform from which they can call the expert fashion designer a "Boy George gone wrong."[26]

We do not want to imply that the middle-class groups were less "involved" in reality television, but that they were less likely to immanently connect to participants, which is perhaps not surprising given the over-representation of the working classes on many shows. There was a visible and tangible difference between the ways these connections were made in comparison to our other groups.

Asian women's reactions: cultural difference

The Clapham group of South Asian women were more likely to talk of reality television in terms of getting "tips," particularly on fashion and parenting. This type of response concurs with other audience research on lifestyle TV where advice and educative tips, particularly from the makeover, are collected but not necessarily acted upon.[27] The more recent migrants in our group tended to discuss aspects of reality and lifestyle in terms of learning about British Culture and more often chose to watch *Supernanny* and *What Not To Wear* in their text-in-action sessions. In the next extract Naheid and Lilly are watching an episode of *What Not To Wear* about making-over tired mothers.

We can see here the way in which the women are encouraged to criticize the participants on the TV program. The viewers say, "Why don't you do it yourself?" and "Have you not thought about getting a bigger size then?" as the TV participants hold up examples of the "failing" wardrobe, or squeeze into a pair of jeans that are too small. Notice how they are using the second-person pronoun addressing the participant directly as "you," clearly referencing the "presentness" of the experience. They begin to discuss their own experiences: "I used to work a lot then," and then resource their critique through cultural difference – "I must say Asian women are hardly ever fat unless they are educated and they don't do stuff." They are referring to their discussion about how breast feeding and having to work helps to keep off baby weight-gain. Ultimately Lilly starts with a moral comparison to herself – "When *I* had *my* babies" – but is cut off by a discussion of whether she would want to talk about breast feeding and working on tape. Their position of moral authority therefore is framed through cultural difference: tips and standards of honor and shame resourced many of the emotional reactions from our Clapham group.

Table 7.2 Asian women's reactions: cultural difference

Audio/visual marker	Audio program extract What Not To Wear	Clapham viewers' comments
02:43 Video tape of woman holding up a saggy nightie	Woman: …and not the sexiest thing to wear in the bedroom perfect for feeding the baby but no baby to feed so I don't know why I'm still wearing that	
cut to Trinny and Susannah on the couch	Susannah: It's all about sexiness isn't it they're so so aware of what's wrong but they don't know how to put it right. Trinny: yep	-But I think, if you know that, why don't you do it yourself? -Instead of getting sort of the telly to do it -yes -Okay I would (always wear sexy things)
VT Michalena trying on clothes with some of her stomach sticking out of her jeans	Michalena: the - there is gap there but that's how all me pants are look me bits	-Oh, my God [laughter]
Presenters shock edited over Michalena's VT Michalena shows how she dresses	hhhh [sharp intake of breath, squeal, experts look horrified] Michalena: I can manage to squeeze that in but it's not too painful I can just shuv that down there like that and then put me tops over Trinny: we know she's going down don't we	- Have you not thought of like getting a bigger size then? -Yeah?
Susannah: hand over mouth	Susannah: definitely [waves hand] Trinny: definitely	-Oh my god. -I think I've seen this I think
03:28	Trinny: Their biggest issue obviously is after they've given birth got back their weight and everything has redistributed in a way that their clothes don't fit them. If they've put it on their thighs it has to come off and that's why I find you do end up in that stretch trouser you wore when you were pregnant. (other VTs) Susannah: it's amazing how they all lose sight of the woman they were before they had children. …	-You know (Vy?) after she had a baby she was (?) -I know but she was breast feeding that helps -I used to work a lot though then - you used to -You were breast feeding -No: I put them (on the bottle) it was too hard -My- -Heh, heh, -No way! -Especially (?) two babies.
04:06	[Trinny and Susannah on telephone about the "winners"]	-So that's the thing with Asian women I must say they are hardly ever fat. (I think I know why.) Unless they are educated they know then maybe they don't do stuff -When I had my babies I also had - - this is on record - heh heh

Working-class reactions: emotional responses to mothering

The dominant resource for our Black and white working-class participants, viewers from Brockley and Addington, was with reference to the experience of motherhood. Half of the Addington group were non-working mothers, all but one of the Brockley group were either not working or working part time, and those that worked did so in the care industry or the service sector. This particular *Wife Swap* example is between a more affluent working-class aspirational mother who works as a legal secretary and a less affluent working-class mother of six children who stays at home.

Here the viewers prefer the less affluent wife, Kate, with six children, as more "normal"; they morally object to the apparent materialism of Tracy, noting "don't you think that's saying more about her?" when she talks of her fear of going to a wealthy home, and show no empathy for her crying to camera when faced with the prospect of looking after six children. The Brockley viewers in the extract below watching the same episode also take a dislike to Tracy's apparent aspirational airs and are outraged at her not getting home from work until her child has gone to bed. Notice how the image of the caravan as Tracy's new home in the swap provokes emotive responses from the viewers in both extracts.

In our data there are clearly moments when the viewers enter into the drama on television as they make emotive and often angry assessments of others on television. Our working-class participants make this emotional performance much more freely. In the last extract for Sonia at home, Tracy on television emerges as "nothing special," as all the viewers are outraged by her pretentiousness and lack of maternal care.

According to Sara Ahmed emotions work to align subjects with some others and against other others.[28] But here viewers are not straightforwardly more empathetic towards participants who are more "like them": relations of proximity work in a much more complex manner. In the last example Sonia's response is defiantly angry and in emotional schema anger typically follows from a moral violation that infringes upon the idea of the self, leading to a desire for retribution.[29] During the session Sonia tells us that she is also a legal secretary, having made difficult decisions about work and motherhood. In their work on the politics of affect, both Sara Ahmed and Elspeth Probyn suggest that there must be some contact or threat of contact in order for disgust, and the pulling away it involves, to take place.[30] The most emotive reactions came from working-class women watching *Wife Swap* whose intensity is generated from historical and class-specific investments in being "a good mother," which in the UK is a strongly class-contested category. Working-class mothers who often care for middle-class children are highly critical of those who do not look after their own offspring, whilst working-class mothers are subject to intense micro management by the state.[31]

Table 7.3 Working-class reactions: emotional responses to mothering (a)

Audio/visual marker	Program audio extract Wife Swap	Addington viewers' comments
04:14 Tracy packing clothes	Voice over: It's the day of the swap and both wives are getting ready to leave.	
Cut to image of caravan in the garden Cut to Tracy to camera	Because the Thomas house is so crammed full of kids Tracy will be staying in the family caravan. Voice over Tracy: I'm worried that I'm going to be going to a house totally above my level you know sort of multi million pound house or	
Trevor with shovel / Kate in caravan getting it ready	something going into this big house with nannies and a guy who's you know really <u>pompous</u> Kate: I hope she thinks this is nice Trevor: Well this is a five star hotel if <u>she</u> moans I'm goina 'av a	- Don't you think that's kind of saying more about <u>her?</u> - The other one seems more (.) normal - yeh
06.36 Tracy looking round the house looking stressed as she sees the number of children's beds Kate looking around the other house	Voice Over: Kate and Tracy get to explore their new homes before they meet the families	
Back to Tracy	Kate: It looks like there is only one child	
		-seems like definitely she's not actually for kids really
Back to Kate in child's bedroom Tracy to camera	Tracy: Its different from my house I think somebody's having a joke heh, heh, oh dear Oh what a diddy little bed	- She's more mater-, like for material things and like fancy jumpers - yeah
Kate walking down stairs Tracy crying	I'm a bit worried there seem to be a lot of cots and beds with children's the the that's six I've seen so far six children hmm that's an awful lot of children gosh I don't think I could do it [looks scared] Kate: going from one child to six is really hard I hope she's ok Tracy to camera: I don't think I can look after all these children, ok?	-Is she crying? - yeah, looks like it [dismissively]

Rachel Moseley suggests that in destabilizing the categories of viewer and participant, makeovers produce a potential dis-ease where the safest response is to retreat into a position of class- and taste-based superiority.[32] But that superiority can only be generated through material and cultural distinctions. *Wife*

Table 7.4 Working-class reactions: emotional responses to mothering (b)

Audio/visual marker	Program audio extract Wife Swap	Brockley viewers' comments
Tracy to camera	I'm an individual I've built up my career over the last twenty years or	
Cut to shot of Tracy going to work	whatever you know Charlotte's lovely and wonderful and I love her to bits but one	All: Laughter
Cut back to Tracy to camera Shot of Mark in warehouse Shot of Mark collecting Lottie	day she's going to fly the nest when she's eighteen or twenty and I want to have a life left. Voice over: As Tracy's work is 2 hours away Mark has a local job so that he can pick her up from nursery. They have a routine and having only one child works for them.	
Tracy and Mark to camera	Tracy: I've got friends who have more than one child and I've seen firsthand how it can affect your relationship Mark: yeh Tracy: and that really worried us because eh you know Mark is my rock and I don't want to lose that and Charlotte is my second rock and I don't want to lose her and I don't know how I could possible have enough love for another child.	-he picks her up, he picks her up that's right - You're only a bloody legal secretary do you know what I mean? -But she has to be there EARLY IN THE MORNING - yeh, but she think she's on the car<u>ee</u>r ladder I know cos I am a legal secretary - No but what it is - - She's only a bloody legal secretary that's what I'm saying - That is it, she's a PA and that's it what's up with that anyway - What, don't get home till baby's gone to bed!
04:23 Image of caravan in the garden – cut to Tracy to camera	Voice over: Tracy is going to stay in the family caravan Voice over Tracy: I'm really worried that I'm going to be in a house totally above my level you know sort of million pound house or something going into this big house with nannies and a guy who's you know pompous	Hmmm - See what I mean how does <u>she</u> know? All: laughter - People have this thing about a
Kate in caravan getting it ready	Kate: I hope she thinks this is nice	legal secretary and she's <u>nothing</u> special <u>nothing</u> special at all

Swap is not a makeover, and there are clearly generic differences which affect responses, but for Sonia there is no class-based or taste-based authority to take, unlike that offered to the middle classes watching *Faking It*, or the morally-culturally superior position taken by members of the Clapham group as they watch *What Not To Wear*. For our working-class participants the key resource, in the absence of other forms of capital, was generated through their prior investment in and intense attachment to motherhood. In this way we begin to see how reality television is shaped through an "affective economy" – a phrase used by Ahmed to insist that emotions are distributed across social as well as psychic fields.

Affect, pleasure and politics

Emotive responses to reality television are thus resourced through structurally differentiated access to forms of moral authority: potentially made more intense by an over-presence of the image for working-class women who recognize themselves in the over-representation of the working classes on reality television. Rather than these engagements representing a kind of "sociability," in Scannell's term, we might instead say that they represent a type of mediated "sociality." Nigel Thrift suggests that the increased engineering of affect is central to the political life of contemporary Euro-American life. This is largely explained through the rise of the mass media, the mediatization of politics, and the ubiquitousness of the screen, which enshrine a "performance principle" in which the reciting of emotion becomes an index of credibility.[33]

Thrift's work on non-representational theory is useful to the overall framework here, but it does not help explain how this new politics of performance enters into the material world in ways which intervene in inequality. In his later account of the "misanthropic city," he argues:

> Though it hardly needs saying, sociality does not have to be the same thing as liking others. It includes all kinds of acts of kindness and compassion, certainly, but equally there are all the signs of active dislike being actively pursued, not just or even primarily as outbreaks of violence (for example road rage or Saturday night fights) but more particularly as malign gossip, endless complaint, the full spectrum of jealousy, petty snobbery, personal deprecation, pointless authoritarianism, various forms of *Schadenfreude*, and all the other ritual *pleasures* of everyday life.[34]

Previous work in feminist media studies has established some of the ways in which the pleasures of culture are intricately tied to the politics of experience,[35] and in a similar fashion we argue that the politics of gender and class combine here to produce the affective pleasures of reality television viewing. In an early essay explaining working-class attachment to musical films, Richard Dyer argued that the affective sensibilities of the film texts – abundance, energy, transparency, intensity and community – were reveled in as direct responses to the social conditions of the time (the 1970s) – scarcity, exhaustion, dreariness, manipulation, fragmentation.[36] The musical generated an affective sensibility which was closely tied to a working-class sense of community. But the "utopian sensibility" of Dyer's argument was generated through a gap between material reality and the fantasy of the entertainment world, whereas for our working-class viewers in the case of *Wife Swap* the classed gap is closed by the immanence of the gendered form and the domestic verisimilitude of the settings. Here the proximity of reality television generates "misanthropy" as well as "community."

Potentially, therefore, Dyer's arguments about working-class community require reworking in the current neoliberal climate. Neoliberal policy emphasizes us all re-orienting ourselves around the labor market and the UK has seen numerous government initiatives to get mothers back to work. In 2006 the British government announced a multi-million-pound "parenting academy" because the working classes are considered not to be capable of parenting "properly" and there are now a number of "parenting orders" criminalizing poor parenting.[37] There is of course a longer history of blaming working-class mothers for the failure of the nation.[38] In which case affective pleasures perhaps *do* offer a solution to neoliberal governance where working-class mothers can, if momentarily, take the high moral ground, thereby making sense of their extreme emotive reactions in the viewing encounters.

Conclusion

This chapter has made some headway into researching audiences' affective relations with television in order to understand how reality television circulates in the current political climate in the UK in which class relations are experienced affectively as well as structurally. It will conclude by making two points. First, our methods, text-in-action and the affective textual encounter, reveal how television through reactive moments enters into sociality. This allows us to change focus from meaning-making made after the encounter and/or produced through cognized reflection to other forms of response. We showed how viewing is an immanent experience through which there is rarely a singular stable "reading" of a program, but rather a set of immediate affective moments through which our audiences experience and locate themselves in the unfolding drama. Thus we rely less on a text/reader distinction but more on the idea of an "extended social/public realm" where life is immediated (immanently mediated), experienced in significant and dynamic moments of connection. Second, this enables us to see how emotions work as forms of capital:[39] "Affect does not reside positively in the sign or commodity, but is produced only as an effect of its circulation."[40] Therefore these reactions cannot be read as encounters of "sociability" which suggests a neutral and horizontal set of relations with television. Rather, affective reactions and the scale of their intensities are strong clues to what really matters to us. Watching reality television engages us in taking moral positions that can only be resourced by the differentiated access that one has to authority. Given the (new) mediated relations of proximity, pleasure can be derived from the spaces in which we dramatize, perform and validate our own experience. Therefore, any sense of an "extended social/public realm" must take into account the way in which affective and material forces are brought to bear when reality television calls us into/onto the stage.

Notes

1 Su Holmes and Deborah Jermyn, *Understanding Reality TV* (London and New York: Routledge, 2004).
2 Nick Couldry, *Media Rituals: A Critical Approach* (London and New York: Routledge, 2003), 58 my emphasis.

3 Richard Johnson, "Reinventing Cultural Studies: Remembering for the best version." In *From Sociology to Cultural Studies: New Perspectives*, ed. Elisabeth Long (Oxford: Blackwell, 1997), 452–88.

4 Helen Wood, "The Mediated Conversational Floor: An Interactive Approach to Audience Reception Analysis," *Media, Culture and Society* 29,1 (2007):75–103.

5 Beverley Skeggs and Helen Wood, "The Labour of Transformation and Circuits of Value around Reality TV," *Continuum* 22,4 (2008):559–72; Misha Kavka, *Reality TV, Affect and Intimacy* (London: Palgrave, 2008).

6 Margaret Morse, *Virtualities: Television, Media Art and Cyberculture* (Indiana: Indiana University Press, 1998).

7 Misha Kavka, *Reality TV, Affect and Intimacy* (London: Palgrave, 2008), 5.

8 Jon Dovey, *Freakshow: First Person Media and Factual Television* (London: Pluto Press, 2000), 159.

9 Anita Biressi and Heather Nunn, *Reality TV: Realism and Revelation* (London: Wallflower Press, 2005).

10 Helen Wood, *Talking With Television: Women, Talk Shows and Modern Self-reflexivity* (Urbana: University of Illinois Press, 2009).

11 Paddy Scannell, *Radio, Television and Modern Public Life* (London: Sage, 1996).

12 David Morley, *Home Territories: Media, Mobility and Identity* (London: Routledge, 2000), 111.

13 Nick Couldry, *Media Rituals: A Critical Approach* (London and New York: Routledge, 2003).

14 Funded by the UK Economic and Social Research Council, "*Making Class and Self Through Televised Ethical Scenarios*" (Res-148-25-0040).

15 See Beverley Skeggs, *Class, Self, Culture* (London: Routledge, 2004) for the class shape of the contemporary British nation, and the way we defined class in the project.

16 See also Mimi White, "Investigating *Cheaters*," *The Communication Review* 9, 3 (July 2006): 221–40.

17 Addington: 10 white working-class (5 mothers, 5 not mothers), ages 18–72. Occupations mainly centre on care work and full-time mothering. Brockley: 6 black British working-class, 3 white working-class, 1 Maltese (only one not a mother) ages 26–68. Occupations in public sector and service sector administrative, caring and secretarial work. Clapham: Southern and British Asian, Asian, Pakistani, Bangladeshi, settled and recently arrived; trans-national class differences (7 mothers, 2 not mothers) ages 18–45. Two are highly educated professional women, one student, the rest full-time mothers or part-time helpers with husband's work. Forest Hill: 7 white, 3 self defined as mixed race, all self defined as middle class (3 mothers, 7 not mothers), ages 30–57. Occupations centre on public sector educational, art and psy-science work.

18 Helen Wood, "The Mediated Conversational Floor: An Interactive Approach to Audience Reception Analysis," *Media, Culture and Society* 29,1 (2007): 75–103.

19 Beverley Skeggs and Helen Wood, "The Labour of Transformation and Circuits of Value around Reality TV," *Continuum* 22,4 (2008): 559–72.

20 Gay Hawkins, "The Ethics of Television," *International Journal of Cultural Studies*, 4, 4 (2001): 412–26.

21 Gareth Palmer, *Discipline and Liberty: Television and Governance* (Manchester: Manchester University Press, 2003); Laurie Ouellette and James Hay, *Better Living Through Reality TV: Television and Post-Welfare Citizenship* (Malden, MA: Blackwell, 2008).

22 Andrew Sayer, *The Moral Significance of Class* (Cambridge: Cambridge University Press, 2006), 225.

23 Beverley Skeggs, Nancy Thumim, Helen Wood, "'Oh Goodness, I *am* Watching Reality TV': How Methods Make Class in Multi-Method Audience Research," *European Journal of Cultural Studies* 11,1 (2008): 5–24.

24 Ien Ang, *Watching Dallas: Soap Opera and the Melodramatic Imagination* (London and New York: Routledge, 1985).
25 Niko Besnier, "Language and Affect," *Annual Review of Anthropology* 1990: 418–51.
26 1990s British pop star famous for his outlandish and feminine clothing.
27 Annette Hill, *Reality TV: Audiences and Popular Factual Television* (London and New York: Routledge, 2005); Katherine Sender, *Makeover Television and its Audiences* (New York: New York University Press, forthcoming).
28 Sara Ahmed, "Affective Economies," *Social Text* 2,2 (2004): 117–39.
29 George Lakoff and Z. Kovesces, "The Cognitive Model of Anger Inherent in American English." In *Cultural Models in Language and Thought*, edited by D. Holland and N. Quinn (Cambridge: Cambridge University Press, 1987).
30 Sara Ahmed, *The Cultural Politics of Emotion* (London and New York: Routledge, 2004); Elspeth Probyn, *Blush* (London and New York: Routledge, 2005).
31 Beverley Skeggs, *Formations of Class and Gender: Becoming Respectable* (London: Sage, 1997).
32 Rachel Moseley, "Makeover Takeover on British Television," *Screen* 41, 3 (2000): 299–314.
33 Nigel Thrift, "Intensities of Feeling: Towards a Spatial Politics of Affect," *Geografisker Annaler*, 86 series b, *Human Geography*, 1 (2004): 75–103.
34 Nigel Thrift, *Non-Representational Theory: Space, Politics, Affect* (London and New York: Routledge, 2008), 208, my emphasis.
35 Ien Ang, *Watching Dallas* (London and New York: Routledge, 1985); Dorothy Hobson, *Crossroads: The Drama of a Soap Opera* (London: Methuen); Janice Radway, *Reading the Romance: Women, Patriarchy and Popular Literature* (Chapel Hill: University of North Carolina Press, 1984).
36 Richard Dyer, "Entertainment and Utopia," *Movie*, 24, Spring (1977).
37 See also Val Gillies, "Raising the Meritocracy: Parenting and the Individualisation of Social Class," *Sociology* 39,5 (2005): 835–55.
38 Steph Lawler, *Mothering the Self: Mothers, Daughters, Subjects* (London and New York, Routledge, 2000).
39 See Diane Reay, "Gendering Bourdieu's Concept of Capitals: Emotional Capital, Women and Social Class." In *Feminism after Bourdieu*, edited by L. Adkins and B. Skeggs (Oxford: Blackwell, 2004).
40 Sara Ahmed, "Affective Economies," *Social Text* 2,2 (2004): 120.

Part 3

Performing the nation

Introduction

Oren Livio

Like the more celebrated cases of Mark Twain, God, and the capitalist mode of production, initial reports of the nation-state's death appear to have been greatly exaggerated. If the twenty-first century was projected, with Panglossian naïveté, to be one of neoliberal hyperglobalization, with globalization dynamics predicted to lead to the decline and eventual disappearance (or irrelevance) of the nation-state and its immersion in (or replacement by) transnational economic forces and organizations, then the continued, and often intensified, power of nation-centered configurations, identifications, and impulses has made it apparent that this prophecy was far off the mark. At the same time, ignoring the significant transformations in the principles according to which social and economic affairs are carried out on the global and local stages is no less misguided. Indeed, rather than extinguishing the nation-state or reducing its influence substantially, globalization appears to have radically altered both the functions fulfilled by nation-states in the new world order and the ways in which these functions are carried out. While the importance of these transformations has been recognized, it seems that at this stage, communication scholarship is still struggling to develop the appropriate conceptual tools to study them systematically. It is the complexities of such thinking about the new roles of the nation-state in the specific context of reality television, and the possibilities inhered within this genre for the development of such conceptual tools, that the three essays in this section attempt to address.

Reality television is particularly fecund territory for expanding traditional ways of thinking about the nation-state, as the genre embodies many of the tensions and ambivalences surrounding globalization and its organizing logic, projects an image of democratic involvement and participation that is associated with the political mechanisms of the nation-state, and is inextricably linked to the advent of new media technologies that are associated with the nation-state's reduced control over the production and circulation of cultural content. All three essays in this section engage with these issues to different extents, and in combination, their carefully situated, nuanced analyses cover a wide spectrum of possibilities regarding reality television's relation to the construction of national identity, which reveals both commonalities and disparities across the different local contexts analyzed: from the similar dominance of market-based logics in all three examined cases, through the differences arising from the inevitable discrepancies between producer intentions, textual manifestations, and audience reactions, to the range of spaces opened up in different countries for both socio-cultural stagnation and potential radical change.

Highlighting the role of the market in the production of national identities, Zala Volčič and Mark Andrejevic employ the concept of "commercial nationalism" to examine the ways in which contemporary constructions and imaginings of nationhood are imbricated in, filtered through, and transformed by the forces of commercialization. Focusing on *That's Me*, a *Big Brother*-style Balkan reality show that explicitly attempted to promote peaceful, market-driven coexistence in a region still recovering from the wars of the 1990s, Volčič and Andrejevic demonstrate how the show's contents in fact often functioned as a catalyst for online fans to indulge in public displays of intolerance that were grounded in traditional nationalistic sentiment and ethnic stereotyping. Revealing the intricate and often contradictory nature of globalization processes and their interactions with local identities, the discourse surrounding *That's Me* illustrates how the logic of the market may simultaneously mobilize both utopian visions of post-national harmony (as promoted by the show's producers) and resurgent forms of nationalistic animosities (as practiced by the show's audience).

Further complicating this issue, Fabienne Darling-Wolf's case study of the discourse of the French *Star Academy* draws attention to the ways in which the negotiation of local cultural identities is concurrently situated against both the platform of the nation-state and the larger-scale context of the global scene. On the one hand, *Star Academy* is an archetypical illustration of the sensitive tailoring of global reality TV formats by show producers so that they appeal to local tastes: the show is steeped in references to what are perceived as traditional aspects of French culture, and is invested in reducing the complex realities of the modern-day French socio-cultural environment to an idealized, integrated version of a post-racial, multicultural France that is rooted in neoliberal values promoting hard work and the illusion of equal opportunity. On the other hand, this negotiation is itself defined in relation to the global, by asserting France's prime cultural position in the competitive global market, emphasizing its role as the leader of an imagined global francophone community, and selectively excising from this community those nations that might remind viewers of France's uncomfortable colonial past. Darling-Wolf's analysis thus demonstrates reality television's capacity for the construction of national identities grounded both in territorially-based conceptualizations of geopolitical space and in linguistic and culturally-based conceptualizations of tribal space that transcend the physical boundaries of the nation-state; more importantly, the analysis shows how the construction of these conceptualizations is situated within, and reproduces, the unequal power relations that characterize both the nation-state and the global system in which it is embedded.

Turning his lens toward audience reactions to, and interactions with, the third season of *Indian Idol* within the Northeastern Indian state of Meghalaya, Aswin Punathambekar presents a cautiously more optimistic view that illustrates the ways in which active engagement with reality television may not only simulate, reflect, or exacerbate longstanding socio-cultural and political tensions, stereo-types, and power relations, but may also take part in their reconfiguration by transcending traditional ethnic, religious, spatial, and linguistic fault lines. Focusing on the mobilization of fan support for local contestant Amit Paul, Punathambekar suggests that the complex dynamics of reality television, and in particular the new forms of interactivity and participatory culture arising from its reliance on mobile media technologies and practices, have led to the formation of fluid, transient "mobile publics" that define themselves based not on the con-ventional ethnic alignments associated with the nation-state, but on a variety of civically-oriented terms that may potentially be less exclusionary. Rather than representing a fundamentally Durkheimian ritual for the performance and reaf-firmation of the socio-cultural status quo, reality television and its associated mobile publics may, in this view, enable new, prospectively transformational modes of cultural and political expression.

How might these variations in the possibilities offered by reality television in different national contexts be thought, so that the necessary recognition of complexity and the crucial awareness of changing cultural contours not be reduced to an altogether unhelpful vision of complete disorder or anarchy? The three essays avoid this potential pitfall by carefully situating their claims – as well as the new conceptual tools they offer – in ways that implicitly reveal their shared theoretical foundations, with variations and differences thus being reflec-tive of significant underlying factors that are brought to light in the analysis. Thus, for example, Punathambekar's relatively optimistic view regarding the emancipatory potentials facilitated by reality television through the creation of "mobile publics" is grounded both in awareness of the fact that these publics are only one instance of changing relations in Northeast India that have been going on for several years, and in the recognition that traditional ethnic cleavages receded into the background only in the presence of the shared economic and cultural marginalization experienced by citizens of different ethnicities, religions, and languages that rendered identification with a similarly marginalized con-testant more likely. Reality television, in this view, is not some fundamentally different entity than that portrayed by Volčič and Andrejevic or Darling-Wolf, but rather reveals for us a range of possibilities along a continuum that are shaped by different socio-cultural realities.

Likewise, the significance of new media technologies in people's interactions with televisual texts – referred to in all three essays, but with rather different consequences – can be considered in relation to the different forms of agency engendered by different modes of regulation and control in different societies. If the nation-states of early modernity were consolidated to a large degree through their control over information and industrial technologies, then decreased control over these technologies in contemporary societies, and the accompanying increase in people's abilities to participate in the socio-cultural sphere, are one characteristic of the transformed roles and functions of the nation-state. In these circumstances, what appear to be completely different reactions by audiences in different countries may in fact be adjusted forms of negotiation and resistance targeted at differently perceived mechanisms of regulation and control: from resistance to the top-down attempt to implement market-driven peace and harmony in the states of former Yugoslavia, to resistance to the continued economic and cultural marginalization of Northeast India by the central government.

The three essays in this section cannot answer any of these questions definitively, but they open up significant spaces for contemplating reality television's relation to the nation-state, along with its inherent ruptures and contradictions, and the roles played by different agents in the active construction of national and global identities. The difficulties in reconciling their positions notwithstanding, these essays cannot – and, unlike many of the real world reality contestants they refer to, should not – be voted off.

Chapter 8

Commercial nationalism on Balkan reality TV

Zala Volčič and Mark Andrejevic

Introduction

This chapter focuses on the role played by nationalism in the pan-Balkan reality show *To Sam Ja (That's Me)*. The program is a "transnational" reality show that attempts to re-connect and integrate the former Yugoslav republics after the wars. Of interest to this chapter is the way the show, caught up in the shifting currents of post-socialist nationalism, channels these into what might be described as a form of commercial nationalism.

Towards the end of the 1980s and the early 1990s, when the nationalisms of all the republics of the former Yugoslavia escalated, each community re-activated or re-created national television systems in order to reinforce a sense of national identity and difference. At the same time, however, the same nations experienced the growth of commercial broadcasting in the new post-socialist era. All seven new former Yugoslav nation-states, Slovenia, Croatia, Bosnia and Herzegovina, Serbia, Kosovo, Montenegro and Macedonia, have gone or continue to go through the process of transition from a centralized, socialist, state-run economy to a privatized, market-driven one. Politically, these new nation-states are also still involved in the project of national identity building, since few of the republics had the historical experience of being an independent nation-state. The new government broadcasting outlets in newly independent states focus on consolidating national identity and fostering socio-economic development. In this regard, they recall, albeit in dramatically reconfigured form, the nation-building project of Yugoslav state broadcasting, before the late 1980s, which had pursued the vexed project of building Yugoslav unity by downplaying a sense of national and ethnic belonging to its constituent republics.

Television in the Balkans remains a central stage on which national identity is portrayed, represented, and shaped, although the landscape is being dramatically transformed by the advent of commercial broadcasting.[1] Amidst the different ways in which cultures connect and overlap in the Balkan region, national culture has emerged as a preeminent frame of reference.[2] Verdery insists on the importance of state broadcasting in the Balkan region in crafting the ways in which the nation operates as "a symbol," a "sorting device" and a "tool of classification." She argues that the nation maintains its importance as "an aspect of the political and symbolic/ideological order and also of the world of social interaction and feeling."[3] These nation-states are attempting to make themselves over, in other words, so as to fit within the Western elite club of countries. Even as these nations seek to participate in the formation of a pan-European sense of shared identity, they are working to create bulwarks of nationalism.[4]

As in the rest of Europe, the main trend in television production in the Balkans is commercialization, with entertainment pervading all formats. The most flourishing rise in prime-time television has been reality TV, which at first started to broadcast formats such as "docu-soaps" (*The Osbournes*), reality game shows (*Big Brother*), quiz shows (*Who Wants to be a Millionaire?*), and other hybrid reality shows (for example, *Hell's Kitchen*). Later, the local production of reality television shows followed. Each new nation-state in the region produces numerous reality shows. For example, in Slovenia (less than two million population), between 2003 and 2007, seven original reality shows were created. To local producers, the reality show represents an attractive genre since it promises interactivity, convergence, and the multi-platform integration of the internet, television and mobile phones. Similarly different international organizations, such as State Department, have attempted to finance reality TV programs after the wars with an aim to spread "democracy, tolerance, and multiculturalism" in the region.[5] At the same time, reality formats have been proliferating on the new commercial channels, and have incorporated elements of the forms of nationalism previously associated with state broadcasting. As Erjavec and Volčič[6] point out in their analysis of nationalist sentiments in Balkan reality TV – when young participants compete against each other in *Pop Idol*, they become like brand names for their nation-states: commercially produced symbols meant to mobilize national support for increased ratings.[7]

Our main goal here is to explore the relationship between *That's Me*'s commercial format, its promise of overcoming outdated, pre-capitalist forms of ethnic tension, and the forms of nationalism that characterized the show's reception. On the basis of in-depth interviews with cast members, producers, and text analysis of the listservs we explore how this show promotes a vision of nationhood that runs along commercial lines. First, however, we analyze, while using the concept of commercial nationalism, the tensions characteristic of the cultural forms that promulgate commercial nationalism: on the one hand the liberation promised by the market, on the other, the way in which this freedom is enlisted by nationalist forces and harnessed to commercial goals.

Mapping commercial nationalism

After the fall of communism and after the wars, new commercial imperatives contributed to a twofold process whereby politics was, at least in part, transposed into the realm of entertainment and entertainment came to function politically. We invoke the term "commercial nationalism" to designate transformations in the ideological forms which enable the reproduction of a concept of nation. Specifically, commercial nationalism refers to the way in which nationalist appeals migrate from the realm of political propaganda to commercial appeal: that is, the appeal to nationalism as a means of increasing ratings, popularity, and sales. As Seo (2008) has argued, commercial nationalism represents the process whereby the commercial sector comes to adopt or embrace nationalist imperatives, thereby distributing the responsibility for their reproduction in ways that are no longer under the full control of the state.[8] As in the Chinese context discussed by Seo, there is a tight relationship between the entrepreneurial and political class – and one that tends to run in the opposite direction from the flow of power in Western capitalist democracies.[9] The entrepreneurial class is, in important ways, dependent upon the political class, and often owes its economic position to its political connections. In this regard, it is not particularly surprising that commercial broadcasters might adopt nationalist imperatives and rely upon their connections in the state and regulatory apparatuses to do so.

Nationalism has been explained in terms of ethnies,[10] waves of industrialization,[11] print capitalism,[12] or culture, identity and discourse.[13] However, the commercial production of national identities has been largely ignored – except in the somewhat narrow form of national "branding" as a tool for marketing and tourism.[14] Thanks to the processes of economic and cultural globalization, the state's political legitimacy to control a territory, to exert power over its inhabitants, and to insure obedience from them has been declining, or, more accurately, it has adjusted to the rise of global capital. Furthermore, the economic and political interconnectedness of contemporary nation-states has fostered an altered and fragmented notion of the state as an entity that is undergoing fundamental structural changes. At a time when global capitalism and global media have been perceived as tools which can unsettle the very meaning of the nation-state, the mass media are still considered and used by the state as either instruments to promote national integration, loci for public debates about national issues, or a commercial industry in need of control. In the Balkans globalization is combined with the emergence of neoliberal political and economic transformations that "marketize" state forms of governance and transpose nationalist ideological formations into a commercial register. This creates a particular situation – one in which nationalism entails corporate thinking, and combines patriotic emotional ideas with marketing goals, integrating commercial and national appeals: using the affective appeal of national identification, prejudices, and stereotypes to sell.

The notion of commercial nationalism then helps us to understand not only, for example, the processes of nation branding associated with foreign-investments and tourism (marketing to other nationalities) but also the marketing of nationalism to domestic audiences. Citizens are addressed not simply as consumers; rather, they are positioned and produced as *nationalist(ic)* consumers. They are socialized in new forms of national belonging that rely upon the dynamic of consumption: national belonging is not just the locus of a particular form of imaginary identification, but of reiterated practices of consumption. In this regard we might talk about an ideological practice that need not rely on the same mechanism of imaginary identification associated with state-sponsored national propaganda. The model of commercial nationalism fits neatly with the participatory promise of the interactive era – and echoes its logic: the invitation to participate not just in marketing to oneself, but to "propagandizing" oneself. The logic of the market reinforces the mobilization of nationalism not as a top-down imposition but as the reflection of the aggregated desires of individual consumers. In this regard, we might think of commercial nationalism as a "neo-liberal" form of ideological identification: a kind of propagandizing "at a distance." Rather than the state imposing nationalist ideals, these ideals are incorporated into the appeal of commercial products, and hence portrayed as the reflection of a "bottom-up" demand. Having to turn up for a state-sponsored parade and demonstrate one's commitment to the nation is a form of state-sponsored nationalism that recalls the era of socialism. Tuning in to a commercial TV show that boosts its ratings through appeals to nationalist sentiment as an entertaining experience to be consumed takes some of the "top-down" pressure off the process and invokes individualized modes of consumer desire rather than collective affiliation to a centralized state apparatus. We might describe commercial nationalism not just as the marketization, but also as the "reflexiviza-tion" of state-sponsored nationalism. If the latter, as Žižek suggests, relies on a certain (ironic) distancing from official state ideology, commercial nationalism makes this distancing explicit.[15] To paraphrase Žižek's paraphrase of the fetish-istic disavowal ("I know very well that things are one way, but nevertheless I continue to act as if they are not"), commercial nationalism allows us to make fun of state-sponsored forms of nationalism while simultaneously reinforcing them in our consumption practices: we know very well that nationalism is an ideological formation, nevertheless, we end up replicating it in our acts of consumption.

Balkan style makeover

We continue here with a political example that wasn't a reality TV show, but that, in the wake of the recent spate of makeover formats, certainly resonated with the genre. It was a televised event that epitomizes the emerging and unique blend of nationalism and pop culture characteristic of the post-political form of "commercial nationalism" in the Balkan media. We are referring to the televised arrest of Radovan Karadžić in July 2008: he is accused of genocide and crimes against humanity for his role in ethnic cleansing during the Bosnian war in the 1990s, including the killings of thousands of Bosnian Muslims at Srebrenica. According to the Serbian radical party, he is "the greatest Serbian hero," but former UN ambassador Richard Holbrooke calls him "a European Osama bin Laden."[16] Karadžić was forced to step down as president of RS in 1996 after the Dayton Agreement, and later went into hiding for thirteen years.

Karadžić was captured as Dragan Dabić on July 21 2008 in Belgrade, where he had cultivated a long white beard and was practicing alternative medicine as a kind of new-age slash orthodox healer. In his new identity, he went from being a brutal nationalist political leader to serving as a regular health magazine contributor and giving spiritual lectures. Masquerading as an expert in so-called *human quantum energy*, the fugitive was so confident in his disguise he even had his own website, and would give out business cards during alternative medicine lectures he organized in Serbia, but also in Croatia and Austria.

Karadžić is reported to have frequently played the Serbian *gusle* – a one-stringed instrument – in the bar *Luda Kuca* (which, interestingly, means *Crazy House*), while singing songs under a photo of himself as Karadžić. The striking aspect of this image is its sheer audacity – the confidence that Karadžić placed in his own makeover, and in those who were supporting him behind the scenes. He was a leader who had gotten away with mass murder – and perhaps the magnitude of this escape contributed to a sense of his own invulnerability.

Karadžić's makeover was a kind of a Balkan-style makeover – low tech and effective. He created a second exaggerated image by inverting his defining features. The media local and international alike mostly focused on his transformations and his secret private life. There was an enormous amount of trivial rubbish circulating in the media, for example, how he treated erection problems, and how he "practiced orgies in his Belgrade apartment that included men and women. There was a huge collection of personal hard core pornographic tapes found in his apartment, undoubtedly proving Karadžić's bisexual orientation ... "[17] An implicit nationalistic discourse was characteristic for most of the Serbian media coverage of his arrest. For example, the mainstream media used "the strategy of denial" while largely ignoring the themes and social actors that would connect Serbia with Karadžić and his war crimes and that would represent the country in a negative light.

The media fascination with Karadžić can be viewed against the background of what had by then become a staple of popular programming: the makeover reality format. As a number of theorists have argued, most importantly Palmer,[18] the makeover as a genre has an important role to play in the neoliberal era that emphasizes the entrepreneurialization of the self, constant self-training and retraining. As Rose puts it, the model of the "efficient" and self-responsible citizen within the context of neoliberal governance strategies is that of the "entrepreneur of him- or herself" who conducts "his or her life, and that of his or her family, as a kind of enterprise, seeking to enhance and capitalize on existence itself through calculated acts and investments."[19] In the Balkan region, the "triumph" of (neo)liberalism in the 1990s has been accompanied by the faith in an individual only. An emphasis is on the (rational) individual (individualism) as an actor prior to the existence of any community, or society. Anything "collective" started to be questioned and, consequently, criticized, while encouraging/expecting citizens to care for themselves as *individuals* only.

The notion of the makeover had already served as a readily available media frame for the coverage of the hunt for Saddam Hussein, as evidenced by ABC News' interview segment with a plastic surgeon devoted to the question of whether the overthrown ruler might have obtained a "new face."[20]

But the frame has a particular salience for post-socialist Yugoslavia, a country in which political leaders and power brokers had to rapidly reinvent themselves, their commitments, their politics, and their rhetoric to adapt to the sudden and vexed transition to the era of post-Yugoslav capitalism. As is well known, the change in political systems did not result in a wholesale change in political leadership, but rather in a hasty series of makeovers: former party insiders transformed themselves into ardent post-communist, capitalist and/or nationalist opportunists. The commitment was to the capture of power – not to a particular political ideology, and in this regard, the most successful were those who were most able to remake themselves – including Slobodan Milosović.

Karadžić is a psychiatrist by profession, and was not only a ruthless political and military leader, but also a poet. Karadžić's poetry is described as "a psychic landscape of eerie and illogical violence" and as embodying a "paramilitary surrealism."[21] Perhaps the most fascinating aspect of Karadžić's makeover was the slippage from one apparent extreme to another – from brutal nationalist leader-poet to charismatic new-age charlatan. It was a short step from the opportunistic mobilization of hate and fear by lyrical nationalist gibberish to the mobilization of fear and hope by a garbled pastiche of mysticism, pseudo-science, and orthodox Christianity. Consider for example the opening lines of Karadžić's Serbian language web site, which describe the theory of human quantum energy as an effective remedy for physical and psychological disorders alike:

> We are energetic beings … Numerous energetic processes in us, on which all the functions of our body depend, are caused by the energy of the higher source (cosmic energy, prana, mana, organic energy, quantum energy, the Holy Spirit). They flow in us and around us and they are our highest good and the source of health and our well being.[22]

It's hard not to discern in this formulation, the strains of new-age self-empowerment rhetoric that characterize such self-actualization movements as *EST* and its descendant, *The Forum*.[23] Nor is it difficult to trace the affinities between the maximization of our vital bodily processes envisioned by human quantum energy and the heady if garbled pseudo-spiritualism of Karadžić's nationalist poetry:

> People nothing is forbidden in my faith
> There is loving and drinking
> And looking at the Sun for as long as you want
> And this godhead forbids you nothing
> Oh obey my call brethren people crowd …[24]

If there is a thematic difference between these two formulations – the lyrical/ nationalist and the mystical/therapeutic – it is the shift from the collective to the individual: from an address directed toward what Karadžić invokes as "my people" – the "brethren people crowd" and the self-actualizing individual. Perhaps it is not too tenuous here to align this shift with that from a vestigial socialist nationalism to post-socialist, commercial nationalism, and neoliberalism. Karadžić has adapted to the structural economic and political shift. In both cases, however, it is hard not to sense his ongoing scorn for those whom, in the earlier poem, he describes as "amorphous dough" – the audience whom he sets out to remake according to the dictates of his brand of charisma, either in the form of nationalist leader or new-age guru.

What does the spectacle of Karadžić's makeover have to do with the forms of reality-based entertainment that are the subject of this chapter? What is suggestive about his case is the way in which it reveals links between a free market version of individual self-actualization and a suppressed form of primordial ethnic belonging. This is the paradox of the Karadžić case: that the seemingly ungrounded or "worldless" form of spirituality dedicated to the enterpreneurialization of the self in a disenchanted, neoliberal world, whose only defining bond is that of the marketplace and the need to maximize one's personal assets emerges against the background of its apparent opposite: a sense of deeply enchanted ethnic belonging. It is not an unfamiliar paradox: the market's dissolution of all that is "solid" – its form of corrosive liberation from tradition, history, and so on, creates the space for the emergence of newly invented forms of "deep tradition." The passionate attachment to these bulwarks that present themselves as refuge against the very storm that created them is not so much a return to tradition as it is the mobilization of nostalgia by the market.

We find a similar conjunction in the US: the neoliberal capital of the world and also the most deeply religious – and fundamentalist – of developed nations.[25] The conjunction of the corrosive freedom of the market which dissolves historical attachments with resurgent nationalist fundamentalism, although contextually unique in the Balkan case, is a familiar formation. If Karadžić embodies it, we can also find it in the paradox of *That's Me* – a show nominally devoted to the representative makeover of the citizenry – an attempt to leave behind a socialist past and embrace the amnesiac satisfactions of the history-free world of consumer capitalism.

That's Me: evoking the national "we"

Reality show *That's Me* is a *Big Brother*-style reality show produced after the Yugoslav wars in Macedonia for three seasons from 2004 to 2006. It featured several cast members from former Yugoslav republics living together in a house in Skopje, while being involved in a variety of challenges. *That's Me* was accompanied by months of media hype, involving different aggressive promotional strategies, such as billboards, spots on televisions, and articles in magazines. The show's producer describes it as an attempt to foster peace and harmony in a region still recovering from the 1990s wars. The goal of *That's Me* was to symbolically negotiate the tensions that still dominate the region, and in doing so, to mobilize the commercial appeal of nostalgia for Tito's socialist Yugoslavia. Some scholars see the show as a part of a phenomenon called *Yugo-nostalgia* – a commercially exploited sentiment that celebrates the longing for an idyllic Yugoslav past. *Yugo-nostalgia* has come to characterize diverse events, spaces, identities, and media representations, including films, television series, and music as well as consumer goods and tourist travel packages that invoke fond memories of the Yugoslav era.[26] However, the producer, Zoran Ristoski, himself a successful businessman, strongly disagreed while claiming that "we want to go beyond political troubles, and we want to forget. We are not Yugo-nostalgic, we don't care about the past. All we want is a free-market … places where people can come and have fun … like shopping malls."

Indeed, the recurring message of the show's producers is that underneath their disparate histories, there is common ground between members of formerly hostile groups: they are unified by the desire to enjoy the benefits of the new consumerism: to party and purchase, and leave behind the age-old hatreds of the former Yugoslavia. At the same time, as we shall see, the show served as a catalyst for nationalist sentiments centered around reaffirming individual nation-states at the expense of pan-Slavic/pan-Balkan solidarity. It also provided raw material for the re-construction of ethnic stereotypes. We have, in short, a very similar constellation to that evidenced in the makeover spectacle of Karadžić: the linkage between the consumerist therapeutic ethos of post-socialist neoliberalism and the embrace of ethnic nationalism and fundamentalism.

Conceived and produced in Macedonia, *That's Me* was a regional hit. Despite the multiple languages (Slovenian, Croatian, Serbian [Serbo-Croatian], Macedonian, Albanian), the show used neither subtitles nor dubbing. The assumption was that former Yugoslavs, despite their current differences and new national identities, would share Yugoslav cultural languages.

That's Me was broadcast on both public channels and the satellite channel of the public broadcaster in Macedonia, as well as on commercial television stations in several former Yugoslav republics including Serbia, Bosnia, Croatia and Slovenia.[27] Because it was carried by the satellite channel MKTV SAT the show was accessible to former Yugoslav diaspora. The show succeeded in attracting an international audience, with callers to the evening show from across Europe, the US, and Australia. The evening installment of *That's Me* showcased feedback from this international audience, running crawls comprised of telephone and text messages from viewers around the world.

The ratings were high: according to the producer, Zoran Ristoski, the show had more than 5.6 million viewers on average. Although international market research shows that *Big Brother* formats are usually most popular with a younger demographic (in the 16–44 age range),[28] this was not the case with *That's Me*. Audience research showed that it was the 40–49 age group that watched the show most (25 per cent), followed by the 50–70 age group (21 per cent), and then the 10–19 demographic (18 per cent).[29] That the show appealed to an older demographic has proven effective – the show became popular throughout the region. This needs to be explained further – perhaps, the peculiarity of Yugoslav cultural identity, together with the social and cultural memories of life in Yugoslavia, still strongly influence the social and private lives of a specific generation of former Yugoslavs (born roughly between 1960 and 1980) who live inside or outside of the territory of their former homeland. Namely, over the period of almost forty years (1945 to mid-1980s), the territorial space of SFR Yugoslavia signified a cultural location within which customs, rituals, stories, beliefs, myths, and other significant practices of everyday life came to form a mental space within which the sense of historical togetherness started to develop.[30] This emergence of the sense of belonging resulted in formation of Yugoslav cultural identity; that, however, was not strong enough to survive the rise of ethnic nationalisms, as evidenced by vicious wars and also, ironically, by the reactions and responses to the show.

The show also had an interactive website, which producer Zoran Ristoski claimed drew 1.5 million visitors over the course of the show.[31] As in the case of other reality formats the show generated an active online response. Perhaps, predictably, much of the online bulletin board activity on two of the most popular Web sites, the official site and a fan-produced one, expressed support for favorite cast members and critiques of their companions. As in the case, for example, of international sports contests, where national identities are expressed, the show tended to pit nations against one another by proxy – the cast members came to stand as representatives for the aspirations and character of their respective nations.[32] According to Polley, "A national team can, in media and popular discourse, take on the guise of the nation itself."[33] Rowe writes that the media can use "great sporting occasions as festivals of nationhood ..."[34] Events such as the Super Bowl in the US, the Olympics and the soccer World Cup, encourage the commercial type of nationalism – the one that, similarly to reality shows, promotes a specific kind of commercial-nationalistic type of identity.

Much of the online activity focused on instances of conflict and love in the *That's Me* house – incidents that tended to bring out the strongest nationalist responses. Most conflicts in the house were played out at the personal, individual level – however, they were taken up in the online responses as exemplifying stereotypical national roles within the former Yugoslav context.[35] For example, the Serbs were defined as being hospitable, strong-willed, proud, yet violent, and by their obsession with history, the victimhood, the paranoia, and the cruel warrior ethos. Slav Macedonians usually enjoyed the stereotype of being emotional, lazy, relaxed, and unreliable, while Montenegrins were seen as passionate, corrupt, disorganized, indolent and sloppy. Slovenes were seen as being cold, arrogant, Germanic, inward-looking, industrious, introverted, and provincial. Similarly, Albanians were positioned as cowards, traitors, fake, and having no "real history" and Croats were understood as irresponsible, jealous, untrustworthy, and backstabbers. These stereotypes continue to be used and exploited in different ways by different social actors within the region,[36] and were also played out in reactions to the show. For example, one of the first incidents happened between an Albanian Muslim participant Admir and the Macedonian Orthodox cast member Drago. The conflict started with an escalating exchange of nationalistic statements and culminated with Admir's threatened plan to stab Drago while he was sleeping. To compound threat with insult Admir showed Drago his genitals – an incident that generated both widespread publicity and debates about decency rules governing broadcasting in Macedonia. The rest of the participants attempted to de-escalate the confrontation, but avoided more in-depth discussion of the incident, which nevertheless confirmed the Serb cast member's stated mistrust of Muslims. One of the participants said that "I am very tolerant, you know … but this was wrong, what happened. It seems to me that it is about religion … the Christians are kind of more peaceful … also, more kind of … civil to each other …"

Not surprisingly, the stabbing threat sparked interest on the internet listservs devoted to the show – interest that manifested itself in much more blatant stereotyping under the cover of anonymity. Self-identified "Slovenec" claimed that "all you do down there is killing each other. You have always been better at killing each other than at work." Another post argued that "a war against the Muslim terrorists is the only real way to go about and win the war against terrorism. We should not only show them our [genitalia] … we should go about and use it, as a weapon." "Stancar" invoked a Bosnian military leader known for his ferocity to his enemies during the war, "Islamic terrorists … you are all like Naser Oric … look at this … they kill us all – when we sleep … they even proudly say they will kill us all … The Albanians and Bosniaks, they are all the same … they kill us in reality, and on reality TV!"

The occasional flare-ups of nationalism and ethnic tension on the show were echoed and amplified in the anonymous free-for-all on the listservs. The voting process whereby cast members were selected to remain in the house tended to provoke nationalist competition and rhetoric on all sides, but often with distinct anti-Muslim overtones. As one post addressing the Croatian cast members put it, "Sydney and all the Croats are with you." Other posts continued this exchange: "It's in the national interest to vote for Serbs, if you are a Serb. Let's show them all who the winner always is", or "Love has home in sLOVEnia."

These posts tended to articulate ongoing prejudices with current political claims and conspiracies, as in the case of one contributor who identified himself only as a "Proud Serb": "Do you really want to know what's going on? Muslims in Bosnia, Kosovo, and Macedonia are connecting with Syria, Iran, Yemen, and Saudi Arabia … they are all coming … forget peace and democracy … if we don't stop them, we will be burnt."

Voting for "ethnic" candidates was seen as a badge of patriotism, a clear indication of national belonging. Often the messages served to comment on contemporary political disputes over borders and the postwar settlements. Again the assertion of nationalist sentiments can be captured by a few selected posts: "There was no war in Slovenia because Slovenes were always cowards, fearful farts …"; "Slovenes have a moral obligation to get more coast from Croatia, and also access to the sea. Don't you see? Croats have stolen the Slovene territory, they robbed Slovenes of their historical right to proudly enjoy the Adriatic coast …"; "Croats are a nation of traitors and whores, who suck up to whoever seems more powerful and whoever will give them the most personal gain"; "Macedonians will never enter EU, never. You are too lazy for Europe … you cannot work efficiently, but just want to shop … can't you see?"; or "Bosnian? Bosniak? That's not a national identity … that's some falsified thing. You are all just suppressed Turks – and should go back to Turkey, and practice Islam there."

If the goal of the house was to model peaceful coexistence, the apparent appeal to online fans was a pretext for indulging in public but anonymous displays of intolerance that reinforced the ethnic tensions fomented during the wars of the 1990s. Although many different forms of exclusion and intolerance were manifested in the online commentaries, the one that featured most prominently was the nationalist one (complete with its sexist overtones). Apart from the manifest and diverse vulgarity of some of the commentaries, the debates had little direct connection to the content of the show itself. Rather the show served as a jumping off point for a full-fledged dive into ethnic and nationalist stereotyping.

This was in contrast to the stated intentions of the Macedonian producer and director, Zoran Ristoski who insisted that the show was, from the start, based on the goal of providing a celebration of "our common South Slavic identity, and to learn from each other." At the same time, it was not hard to anticipate that national loyalties would help draw viewers and maintain their interest in what amounted to a competition to see which of the various nationalities would win the show.

If the show's participants for the most part avoided expressing overtly confrontational nationalistic statements, the voting process (with text-messaging included!) elicited them: it resuscitated the old stereotypes and resulted in the exclusion of cast members on the basis of nationalist themes. Many of the viewers did not take the show as an opportunity to break down ethnic stereotypes, but rather to emphasize them.

Discussion and conclusion

Drawing on the example of *That's Me*, we wanted to offer a preliminary attempt to trace the rise of commercial nationalism in the post-socialist Balkans. Nationalism remains a major force in the Balkans. Abu-Lughod argues that "it is the nation that is still the crucial frame for the workings of, and imaginative responses to, all sorts of processes."[37] Two main trends, in particular, constitute the pillars of Balkan television at present: first, the focus on national levels of television programming in terms of production and consumption, that pushes for the need to reassess the viability of the notion of nation-state; and second, the contradictory presence of globalization that gives vent to nationalism and mass commodity consumption at the same time. Abu-Lughod, while rethinking the nexus consumer-citizen, argues that both capitalism and mass commodity consumption "are not necessarily antithetical to national identity formation."[38] Citing Karadžić's poetry, Slavoj Žižek goes a step further. He describes the combination of resurgent nationalist fundamentalism with the corrosive freedom of the market which dissolves historical attachments as characteristic of what he calls "postmodern nationalism," in which "passionate ethnic attachment," far from serving as a return to core traditional values, "functions instead as a liberating call: 'You may! You may violate the stern regulations of peaceful coexistence in a tolerant liberal society! You may drink and eat whatever you want! You may flout political correctness ...'"[39]

The bulletin board posts about *That's Me* are devoted to this injunction, at least insofar as they might be described as an empathic and vigorous exercise in defying political correctness by venting nationalist, racist, and religionist sentiments. If Žižek is right, and if the example of *That's Me* might be interpreted as confirming his interpretation, perhaps some wariness is in order toward claims that ethnic tensions in the region will give way to neoliberal economic reforms and the emergence of a full-fledged consumer society. This hope is much the same as Ristoski's vision of *That's Me* writ large: that, with the rise of a post-socialist market economy, the pleasures of consumer society will allow former antagonists to shed their hatred and recognize their shared commitment to shopping and popular culture. It is a vision that is well established in the political and diplomatic spheres – and is enshrined in the common-sense assumptions of neoliberalism. As one account predicts, for example:

> Both Serbia and Kosovo will see increasing prosperity, which will in turn displace the bitterness of the last thirty years ... accession to the EU will reduce organized crime in both places. Kosovo will begin producing food and continue lobbying rich countries to take its unskilled labour, while Serbia will attract foreign investment in manufacture, property, banking, and eventually agriculture. There will be broad agreement about the two things it's easy for Serbs and Kosovo Albanians to agree on: the ills of communism and the virtue of markets.[40]

By contrast, Žižek's more pessimistic analysis and the example of the *That's Me* boards suggests that the logic of the market might well open up spaces for the flourishing of multiplying forms of ethnic and nationalist sentiment. Indeed, the arrival of free markets in the region has so far done little to lessen such tensions. The proliferation of local versions of neoliberalism, the glocalization of market reform, does not necessarily bring about the liberal version of the end of history and the advent of perpetual peace amidst endless free-market competition. On the contrary, the response to shows like *That's Me* augurs the emergence of new forms of commercial nationalism, in which nationalist identifications are freed up from the commitments of international politics and mobilized by economic entities as means of attracting and mobilizing audiences by appealing to sentiments banished from the political sphere proper.

Notes

1 In thinking about ways in which global media today influence different national cultural media, Iordanova suggests that we hold on to the concept of *the Balkans* as a region within Europe with a common cultural denominator. This then allows us to name and critique important transnational issues, such as the way in which emergent forms of nationalism are played out on television screens. See Dina Iordanova, *The Cinema of the Balkans* (London & New York: Wallflower Press, 2006).
2 Different empires/cultures have conquered the Balkans: Latino-Venetian-Catholic-Mediterranean, Austro-Hungarian, German-Mitteleuropean, Greco-Byzantine, Russo-Slavic-Orthodox, Turkish-Arabic-Oriental.
3 Katherine Verdery, "Whither 'nation' and 'nationalism'?" *Daedalus*, 122 (3) (1993): 37–46.
4 Zala Volčič, "Yugo-nostalgia: Cultural Memory and Media in the former Yugoslavia," *Critical Studies of Mass Communication* 24 (1) (2007): 21–38.
5 For example, a State-Department sponsored reality TV program involving Serbian and Albanian youth. The young people, split up into two ethnically-mixed teams, were involved in different work-projects in Montenegro. The program, according to its producers, "seeks to promote tolerance, cooperation and utilize conflict resolution skills through fun, yet challenging, activities," http://podgorica.usembassy.gov/balkan_youth_promote.html
6 Karmen Erjavec and Zala Volčič, "Rehabilitating Milošević: Posthumous Coverage of the Milošević Regime in Serbian Newspapers," *Social Semiotics*, 1470-1219, 19 (2), 2009: 125–47.
7 Vesna Sopar, "The *Big Brother* of the Balkans," *Southeast European Media Journal* (2005), http://www.mediaonline.ba/en/?ID=350[March 2008].
8 Jungmin Seo, "Manufacturing Nationalism in China: Political Economy of Businesses," paper presented at *ISA*, 2008.
9 Ibid.
10 Anthony D. Smith, *The Ethnic Origins of Nations* (London: Basil Blackwell, 1986).
11 Ernest Gellner, *Nations and Nationalism* (Oxford: Blackwell, 1983).
12 Benedict Anderson, *Imagined Communities* (London/New York: Verso, 1996).
13 Craig Calhoun, *Nationalism* (Minneapolis: University of Minnesota Press, 1997).
14 Craig Calhoun & Richard Sennett, *Practicing Culture* (New York: Routledge, 2007); Nadia Kaneva, "Meet the 'New' Europeans: EU Accession and the Branding of Bulgaria," *Advertising & Society Review* 8 (4) (2007): 15–24.
15 Slavoj Žižek, *Mapping Ideology* (London: Verso, 1994).
16 *Mladina*, 26 July, 2008.
17 *Politika*, 22 July, 2008.
18 Gareth Palmer, "'The New You': Class and Transformation in Lifestyle Television," in *Understanding Reality Television*, eds S. Homes and D. Jermyn (New York: Routledge, 2004), 173–90.
19 Nadi Rose, "The Politics of Life Itself," *Theory, Culture & Society*, 18 (6) (2001): 1–30.
20 Karmen Erjavec & Zala Volčič, "Rehabilitating Milošević: Posthumous Coverage of the Milošević Regime in Serbian Newspapers," *Social Semiotics*, op. cit.
21 Andrew Rubin, "The Executioner's Song," *Lingua Franca*, July/August 1995, p. 8.

22 Human Quantum Energy, http://www.psy-help-energy.com/
23 Scholars analyzing spiritual self-help discourse agree that spiritual self-help is an individualized voluntary enterprise. It is an undertaking to alter, reform or transform the self, or some "intrinsic" aspect of it, which is contingent upon a person's search for some external form of authoritative assistance. This self-help discourse attempts to instruct citizens in techniques of spiritual self-management. Such discourse may be understood as an instructional form of self-help in a post-communist, post-welfare state era when citizens are increasingly urged to take responsibility for developing the skills to successfully navigate a climate of reflexive risk. See H. M. Rimke, "Governing citizens through self-help literature," *Cultural Studies*, 14 (1) (2000): 61–78; G. Redden, "The new Agents: Personal transfiguration and radical privatization in New Age self-help," *Journal of Consumer Culture*, 2 (1) (2002): 33–52.
24 Slavoj Žižek, "The Military-Poetic Complex," *London Review of Books*, 14 August 2008, 17.
25 Tariq Ali, *The Clash of Fundamentalisms: Crusades, Jihads and Modernity* (New York: Verso, 2002).
26 Zala Volčič, "Yugo-nostalgia: Cultural Memory and Media in the former Yugoslavia," *Critical Studies of Mass Communication*, op. cit.
27 Vesna Sopar, "The *Big Brother* of the Balkans," *Southeast European Media Journal* (2005), http://www.mediaonline.ba/en/?ID=350 [March 2008].
28 Annette Hill, "*Big Brother*: The Real Audience," *Television & New Media*, 3 (1) (2002): 323–40.
29 Vesna Sopar, "The *Big Brother* of the Balkans," *Southeast European Media Journal* (2005), http://www.mediaonline.ba/en/?ID=350 [March 2008].
30 The ideological foundations of this new identity were in the socialist nature of the state and its emphasis on the collective struggles of South Slavs during the Second World War (People's Liberation Movement and the idea of "brotherhood and unity"), the uniqueness of the Yugoslav road to socialism (the central characteristic being the workers' self-management), and the international politics of nonalignment. These three elements started to create the so-called "Yugoslav road" to socialism, which became known in the West as "Titoism."
31 "Tisuće surfera na netu zbog *To Sam Ja*" [Thousands of surfers on the net because of *To Sam Ja*], *Večernji List* (2004), http://www.vecernji.hr/newsroom/scena/171303/index.do [December 2008].
32 Sean Jacobs, "Big Brother, Africa is watching," *Media, Culture & Society* 29(6) (2007): 851–68.
33 Martin Polley, *Moving the Goalposts: A History of Sport and Society Since 1945* (London: Routledge, 1998).
34 David Rowe, *Sport, Culture and the Media* (Buckingham: Open University Press, 1999).
35 Klem Krikšić, "Srp, čekić i tri velike Titove slike uzburkale duhove [Hammer, Sickle, and Tito's photos triggered controversial debates]," *Novi list*, 21 January 2005.
36 See more in Allan Dundes, *Cracking Jokes: Studies of Sick Humor Cycles & Stereotypes* (Berkeley, Calif.: Ten Speed Press, 1987). Also, see Mattijs van de Port, *Gypsies, Wars and Other Instances of the Wild: Civilisation and Its Discontents in a Serbian Town* (Amsterdam: Amsterdam University Press, 1998).
37 Lila Abu-Lughod, *Dramas of Nationhood. The Politics of Television in Egypt* (Chicago: University of Chicago Press, 2005).
38 Abu-Lughod, *Dramas of Nationhood*, 195.
39 Slavoj Žižek, "The Military-Poetic Complex," *London Review of Books*, 14 August 2008, 17.
40 Jeremy Harding, "A Man or a Girl's Blouse?" *London Review of Books*, 14 August 2008, 14–17.

Chapter 9

World citizens "à la française"

Star Academy and the negotiation of "French" identities

Fabienne Darling-Wolf

The invasion of reality television programs on the world-wide popular cultural scene is the logical fulfillment of processes of globalization with which international communication scholars have long been preoccupied. Indeed, the fact that the genre's attraction is predicated on its successful adaptation of global formats to local environments makes it the perfect exemplar of twenty-first-century transnational capitalism at its best – in all its glocalized, deterritorialized, indigenized and disjunctive messiness. As such, reality television texts provide a particularly fruitful terrain on which to explore transnational dynamics in relationship to various local environments and advance our understanding of the local "as the space where global forces become recognizable in form and practice as they are enmeshed in local human subjectivity and social agency."[1]

Employing the case of the adaptation of the Endemol *Star Academy* format to the French environment – the first in a series of such adaptations that would eventually spread through fifty nations – as a specific example, this essay proposes to tease out some of the "global-local articulations"[2] of reality television. Understanding *Star Academy* as a propositional text – i.e. as a text that is generating claims about the world – this analysis is particularly concerned with the implicitly propositional statements[3] the show is making about the local in relationship to the broad concept of "the global," as well as to other local environments. This concern leads to a set of more specific questions this work attempts to address: how and where do claims about the local and the global intersect in the text? In what ways do such claims relate to the format of reality television? What are the translocal dynamics at work in the text's engagement with the global? How are participants (and, by extension, viewers) positioned within the global environment?

But before these can be addressed, *Star Academy*'s impressive success must be placed within the broader context of reality television's recent explosion.

The context of reality TV

The product of a combination of deregulation policies, an increased fragmentation of television audiences, efforts on the part of traditional networks to reclaim their audience, and across-the-board increased commercial pressures, "Reality TV has come to permeate the popular zeitgeist, occupying lucrative time slots across the globe and a prominent place in the cultural imaginary."[4] Fusing elements from a global palette of available formats into highly hybrid unabashedly commercial texts, reality TV is often heralded – for better or for worse depending on the interlocutor – as having ushered in a new era of television programming.

Whether characterized as a debased genre catering to the lowest common denominator – "la télé-poubelle" as one French television executive put it[5] – or as a democratizing agent allowing for increased audience engagement, reality TV exhibits a number of attributes worth considering. First, as mentioned, the fact that reality television programs are adapted to local environments from highly global formats has interesting implications for international communication scholars, a point to which I will come back in a moment. Reality TV also represents a qualitative shift in the nature of its relationship to the varied popular cultural contexts in which it is produced and distributed. While all television texts have become increasingly intertextual in nature with the advance of the Internet and with concentration of ownership allowing for more cross-advertising, reality TV's success rests to a much greater extent on its ability to fully capitalize on the hypermediated environment surrounding it. Aside from the obvious addition of the interactive element provided by an intensified 24-hour web presence and the possibility of audience participation, reality TV has learned to create a broader cultural discourse through which it manages to impose "the terms used to discuss the products it proposes to the public."[6] In other words, reality TV has managed to commodify every element of the television experience: from participants' daily interactions, to the music, fashion, or food they produce and/or consume on the show, to viewers' votes through text-messaging. Even reality "is shaped and offered for sale like any other consumer product."[7]

Indeed, reality TV is further premised on "a self-conscious claim to the discourse of the real."[8] While distancing itself from the documentary tradition's concerns with veracity and the ethics of representation,[9] it claims the real through camera use, lack of narration, and the promise of authenticity. Most importantly, the "fiction réelle"[10] it constructs blurs and complicates the notion of reality by actively engaging viewers in its negotiation. The result is "a multi-layered viewing experience that hinges on culturally and politically complex notions of what is real and what is not."[11] Viewer participation is a central element of this process. Rather than pretending to straightforwardly "represent" reality, reality TV proposes to take viewers behind the curtain of its construction. Shows such as *Star Academy*, for example, are attractive not simply because of the intrinsic qualities of the performers they promote (which are, at best, questionable), but because of their focus on the apparatus of celebrity construction.

An additional source of pleasure in reality TV consumption stems from the audience's ability to deconstruct what is presented by producers as "real" through the recognition of processes of mise-en-scène, editing, and other forms of manipulation, as well as through the search for "authentic" moments that escape producers' control – as when candidates fail to perform in accordance with the mediated selves they (and/or producers) have carefully crafted. Online communication about the text provides an important forum for this act of deconstruction. Viewers might even manage to derail the process of reality construction as intended by producers, as when, for instance, voting for the clearly least talented but most sympathetic or "authentic" candidate.[12] Producers might acknowledge, in turn, the audience's savvy understanding of the format and its conventions and establish a "more 'knowing' relationship with the audience."[13]

This relationship, however, as with all hegemonic relationships, must be constantly re-negotiated. As producers move the back stage of television production to its front stage by revealing its artifices, they engage viewers in a never-ending game of receding mirrors – the new produced-for-television front stage has its own back stage that must be itself revealed, as in the numerous reality-TV bloopers shows that spring up around each format. Furthermore, all this is happening in the context of a broader cultural moment when the reality of "the real" is increasingly questioned and, some might argue, perceived as increasingly irrelevant.[14] A context, as Žižek puts it, in which we are made intensely aware of the fact that "'reality' itself is caught in the movement of our knowing of it."[15] A cultural context, also, where our discomfort with surveillance technologies has been dulled by the age of interactive media and its incursion on individuals' personal privacies. This broader context is an important backdrop to our understanding of reality TV's relationship to the global.

The global as "imagined reality"

Reality TV's engagement with "the real" intersects with its role in constructing localized versions of reality from global formats. Reality television must thus be considered both in relationship to its claims to a locally constructed reality and to the trans-national production context in which these representations are constructed.

On the broadest level, the extreme success of reality television in the first decade of the twenty-first century has engendered a subtle yet significant shift in global power relations. The move from selling "finished" and, consequently, significantly culturally marked media products – think of the global impact of *Dallas*, or *Sex and the City* – to selling more "culturally odorless" formats, has eroded the relative economic advantage of powerful nations, such as the United States, with the capital to develop extensive production facilities supported by a vast national market. As former head of Israeli television Yair Stern put it when describing the audiovisual landscape in his country, "it used to be all American TV series, like *Dallas* or the hospital show … *ER*. Now it's all reality TV formats" (personal conversation, October 21, 2008). The rise of the small Dutch company Endemol illustrates the fact that reality TV's low production costs have allowed for smaller players to start competing on the global market at a level previously unattainable to them.

Furthermore, in interesting contrast to the fluid negotiation taking place between producers and their savvy audiences around the format's clearly questionable assertion that it represents the unmediated reality of participants' experiences, the claims reality TV makes about the local are often couched in quasi-anthropological language. As Jost notes, reality television is often presented as a microcosm of society.[16] Thus the discourse surrounding the first season of *Loft Story* – France's equivalent of *Big Brother* – focused on the group of teenagers as representative, for better or for worse, of contemporary French youth. This claim is particularly intriguing considering the extent to which reality TV is embedded in global processes of production and distribution and trans-national flows of capital, as described above. Often, however, the global nature of reality television is swept aside to focus on its ability to localize, as when Kilborn argues that "broadcasting in nationally and regionally defined spaces still bears the clear imprint of specific traditions and preoccupations. *Nowhere is this more apparent than in the attitudes that broadcasters have displayed towards various types of factual/documentary material*"[17] (emphasis mine).

But, as Žižek reminds us, local traditions and national identities are ultimately defined in relationship to the global.[18] The webs of significance[19] that build the culture we experience as local are embedded in much larger global networks we are more subtly aware of.[20] This is particularly obvious in the case of reality TV. Thus, if, as Anderson[21] proposes, nations are best envisioned as imagined communities fostered by citizens' engagement with shared cultural texts, the global in reality TV might be similarly conceptualized as an "imagined reality" arising from consumers' awareness of the global nature of the format and its subtle nods to the transnational context of its creation and distribution. A reality not ostensibly "represented" by the localized text, yet lurking at its margins.

This construction of a global imagined reality in reality TV is significantly tied to its monitoring role in an environment where surveillance technology is increasingly tolerated, and, in many cases, embraced. A detailed analysis of this much discussed role[22] is beyond the scope of this essay, but suffice to say that the increased awareness of watching and being watched epitomized by reality TV also signals an increased awareness of a global process of surveillance. As Chinese boys in a dorm room and cranky old ladies crossing the street become instant transnational phenomena, the presence of a global watching audience is more and more difficult to ignore. While this development applies to various elements of media and technology consumption, the contrived emphasis in reality TV on the process of surveillance coupled with the global nature of its formats makes this context particularly obvious. Thus, if reality TV proposes to construct localized versions of "reality" it also produces more implicitly propositional statements about the nature of the larger global environment in which this reality takes shape. The following section illustrates this point through a case study of one reality TV show.

World citizens "à la française": negotiating the global in *Star Academy*

Owned by the Spanish branch of Endemol, *Star Academy* represents one of the most successful reality television formats to date. Started in France in October 2001, it has since been exported to some fifty different cultural environments, though never successfully to the United States. The show's huge success can be credited in part to its ingenious merging of two extremely popular reality television formats. The show combines *Big Brother*-like 45-minute daily broadcasts from the "academy," the school for music and dance where candidates live, with weekly two and a half hour "primes" – in the vein of *Pop Idol* in Britain or *American Idol* in the US – broadcast, as their name suggests, during prime time, and during which students perform live in front of judges and an international audience. The official website for the show also provides live footage of life at the academy for twenty-two hours out of every twenty-four-hour period. While the show started its eighth season in the fall of 2008, the bulk of the analysis for this essay is based on textual analyses of its seventh season.

An important context to understanding the popularity of *Star Academy* in France is the country's long history of game and variety shows. Particularly significant to the issues at hand is the fact that such shows have historically provided a space for national and cultural identity construction. For instance, the Eurovision Song Contest, famously won by ABBA in 1974 and broadcast throughout Europe without interruption since 1956, pits European countries against each other in its annual one-day competition. Similarly, *Jeux Sans Frontières* (Games Without Frontiers), broadcast for nine weeks every summer from 1965 to 1999, featured teams from different countries and crowned one nation its ultimate winner. While the global/local articulation in the more recent reality TV incarnations may be more subtle than in these earlier shows born out of an upbeat post-war effort to promote European unity through friendly competition,[23] reality television nevertheless continues to serve as a terrain on which national and cultural identities are negotiated and constructed in relationship to the global.

Localizing *Star Academy*: *France as a reconciled nation*

Most obviously, *Star Academy* illustrates the process of localization global reality formats undergo when adapted to local environments. Participants' daily life at the academy – housed in a castle in the Paris suburb of Damari-lés-Lys[24] – is steeped in references to what is likely to be interpreted by the audience as "traditional" aspects of French culture. This is particularly apparent in the shows' daily broadcasts that follow the candidates' every move as they study, eat, and sleep together (pun intended).

The organization of the school itself is, for instance, modeled after the French educational system. The complex process of selection of candidates for possible elimination on the Friday night "prime," with its system of averages and "repêchage" (retest), closely resembles the process of evaluation for the bacca-lauréat, the French national exam. Similarly, the way classes are organized around a set schedule, the grading system on a twenty-point scale, the emphasis on strong discipline, all mirror elements of life in a French lycée. *Star Academy*'s version of French education, however, is clearly an idealized "reality." As Jost explains, "[T]o parents who deplore the abdication of educational responsibility on the part of professors and to children who condemn the school system for teaching boring subjects, *Star Academy* offers the image of a reconciled school, where adults and adolescents work together to reach a common goal."[25]

But the school system is not the only element of the French cultural environment the show works to reconcile its audience with. *Star Academy* also constructs a world in which adult professors and the diverse cast of adolescents they teach are portrayed as sharing a common "French" cultural heritage celebrated through-out the daily broadcasts. This is accomplished in part by the physical presence on the show of various French cultural icons, ranging from artists who have been present on the French popular cultural scene for decades – Renaud, Michel Sardou, Johnny Hallyday – to relatively newer arrivals intended to appeal to a younger audience. When mixing with each other and with the young candidates, the presence of these artists in the *Star Academy* castle suggests that their appeal transcends generational differences. This suggestion is reinforced by the selection of songs to be interpreted by candidates throughout the week, often drawn from the repertoire of celebrated French singer/songwriters – Gilbert Becaud, Hughes Aufray, Yves Montand – and similarly offered as components of a cultural heritage shared across generations.

Various French customs and traditions are further alluded to in *Star Academy* as they are used to invigorate the otherwise rather dull reality of daily life. For instance, in the show's seventh season, one of the candidate's mother visited the castle in February to make the traditional crêpes in celebration of the Catholic Candlemas. Her exceptional intrusion into the otherwise autarkic life of the candidates not only served to break the monotony of school work, but also helped construct a vision of France as a culture in touch with its traditions.[26] Because each season of *Star Academy* runs for several months, such allusions to "traditional" aspects of French culture can be made repeatedly to remind viewers of this shared heritage.

The fact that the show's candidates are chosen to represent various areas of France further extends the reach of this imagined community to the country's entire map. As the candidates' regional diversity is made obvious in their online biographies, through allusions to their home towns or regions, and through regionally accented speech, audiences are reminded of the richness of France's diverse local cultures. Claims of geographic specificity quickly recede, however, when the candidates enter the castle to work together and reach their dreams, against the show's assertions of commonalities across regional differences and shared national heritage.

It would be unfair to imply, however, that *Star Academy* only constructs the local culture it is ostensibly representing through a nostalgic lens. As mentioned, newer arrivals on the French popular cultural scene are welcomed as representatives of a new generation of significant contributors to France's cultural identity. French rap and French rock are mixed in with the famous folk songs of singer-songwriters. Younger singers and newer genres are recognized as symbols of France's continuing engagement in popular cultural production. The show itself becomes such a symbol, as the winners from previous seasons, several of whom have gone on to successful careers, are invited to come back to the show as instructors or guests, and as their CD releases are heavily advertised during the show's commercial breaks. This bridging between young candidates and older professors, celebrated icons and newest fads serves to reassure viewers that a new cohort of cultural producers aware of the debt they owe earlier generations are being groomed to assure their masters' succession.

Perhaps more significantly, *Star Academy* also reconciles the audience with the changing nature of the French socio-cultural landscape. Candidates and professors on the show are clearly selected to represent the increasingly diverse racial, ethnic, and cultural make-up of the French population. Each season's cast of characters includes several black and/or North African aspiring artists.[27] The show's host, Nikos Aliagas, is of Greek origin. Kamel Ouali, the show's artistic director, is of Algerian descent. This mixing of races and ethnicities is typical of reality programs intent on creating drama by bringing together individuals of very different backgrounds.

The way *Star Academy* deals with race, however, significantly differs from the strategies used to address the issue in similar American texts. If instances of racial tension in the US versions of *Big Brother* or *The Real World* become occasions to suggest that friendship and discussion can alleviate racism – a neoliberal ideal that serves to conceal racism's *structural* nature – race is simply not addressed in *Star Academy*'s narrative beyond the obvious visual clues provided by the candidates' physical selves. If, in the United States, *The Real World* "constructs a reality that frees the audience of any implications in racism by blaming rural conservatives for the problem,"[28] *Star Academy* constructs a reality in which racism does not exist.

Mirroring the French government's official position of "color blindness," the show's narrative simply defines all candidates as (non-hyphenated) "French." One must search beyond the confines of the show's official texts – including its official website that provides biographical information on each participant – to find more detailed elaborations on the candidates' racial or ethnic identities.[29] It is difficult to assess whether racial tensions emerge among candidates in their daily life at the castle. If they do, the show fails (or refuses) to capitalize on them as dramatic elements of its narrative structure. Instead, everyone on the show, regardless of ethnic, cultural, or racial identity, is portrayed as equally sharing and enjoying the "French" cultural heritage described above, even if candidates are generally allowed to bring their own creative twist to these common cultural elements. Individuals whose "non-French" cultural origin is known due to their involvement in the broader French popular cultural scene, including Aliagas and Ouali, are portrayed as safely "integrated" into French culture.

Of course, this reality TV-style reality stands in sharp contrast to the intense racial tensions permeating the French socio-cultural landscape, as evidenced by the brutal riots that spread through the suburbs of France's major cities in the fall of 2005. Once again, however, the show's construction of a space in which urban and rural youths of varied ethnicities and races can not only adequately function as a group, but can do so while embracing the values of tradition, hard work, and trans-generational respect, reconciles white audiences with diversity, while reassuring minority audiences that they, too, can become celebrated contributors to the French popular cultural scene if they are willing to comply to the rules of French cultural integration.

Imagining the global

The process of localization – or, more precisely, of "nationalization" – described above, however, cannot be fully understood outside of the global context that defines reality TV formats. In a network society[30] where everyone is simultaneously engaged in the act of watching and aware of being watched, the show's claims about "the local" are developed with the global audience in mind. Thus, just as the candidates are (re)presenting themselves to the local audience that will ultimately have a chance to "vote them off the island" (or, in this case, the castle), the show (re)presents France for global consumption.

This sharp awareness of the global is particularly evident on the Friday night "primes," ostensibly marketed as transcending national borders. As one television magazine put it, "On the nights of the prime, *Star Academy* welcomes stars from around the world and becomes one of Europe's largest variety shows."[31] In this context, the show can be understood as not only serving to reconcile the French audience with elements of its contemporary socio-cultural "reality," but also as engaging in a process of promotion, commodification and, possibly, exoticizing of French culture, in all its regional diversity, on the global market.[32] More broadly, the primes serve to negotiate the candidates' (and, by extension, France's) position in the competitive environment of global cultural production.

On the most obvious level, "the global" is visually present on the set of *Star Academy*. The show's overall visual aesthetic – logo, graphics, color scheme – is modeled on a homogenized global format tightly controlled by Endemol. Thus, the French version of *Star Academy* is visually connected to its Lebanese, Brazilian, or Turkish versions. *Star Academy* also constantly makes references to "the global" in a postmodern pastiche of visual references to "Other" cultural environments – gangsters in US streets, samurai in full gear, Latin dancers. These visual clues are reinforced by the physical presence of a vast array of international stars on the set of the primes and, occasionally, in the castle. This serves to position

Star Academy's young candidates as highly engaged with the global through their familiarity with (and consumption of) hybrid popular cultural products originated in diverse cultural environments, and, consequently, as particularly well equipped to negotiate its demands. As the aspiring artists rap with 50 Cent, rock with Juanes, Kylie Minogue, and Johnny Hallyday, or sing romantic duets with Celine Dion, as they are seen writing their own songs in multiple languages and multiple genres or casually chatting with international stars, they emerge as both global citizens and global cultural producers.

More generally, France – or the version of France provided by producers – is itself positioned as a significant global player through the show's meta-narrative. The emphasis on the global nature of the primes in the larger cultural discourse surrounding *Star Academy*, as illustrated in the quote above, positions the show itself as a prized transnational cultural product. The frequently-mentioned fact that the show is able to attract celebrated international stars similarly highlights France's global cultural influence. If the likes of Madonna, Mariah Carey, Sting, or Ray Charles take time out of their busy schedules to perform in *Star Academy*, France must be on these artists' cultural radar. This suggestion is subtly reinforced through expressions of admiration for French culture on the part of international visitors – as when Colombian rock star Juanes engages in a short conversation in Spanish with Nikos Aliagas after performing with candidates to express his love for French culture and *Star Academy*, which the host translates as: "he says he loves France, can you blame him?"

The omission and/or representation of various elements of "the global" in the show's narrative serve to further (re)assert France's position on the international scene. For instance, the show tends to position France as the leader of an (imagined) global francophone community by defining this community almost exclusively in relationship to Quebec. On one hand, this exclusion of much of the actual worldwide French-speaking population conveniently allows producers to evade the uncomfortable matter of France's colonial past, the legacy of which is highlighted in the continuing influence of the French language in much of North and West Africa and parts of the Middle East. On the other hand, it (over)emphasizes France's influence in the francophone community by putting the focus on a relationship defined by a clear power differential, especially when considered in the context of the music industry where Quebecois artists are faced with the challenge of operating in a much smaller national market than their French counterparts.

Such a construction of the global francophone community is particularly interesting since the *Star Academy* format has been adapted with extreme success in the Arab world and Africa, often as a direct consequence of the success of the "original" French version. One might think that producers could find an economic advantage in linking the French show to these varied global incarnations, especially since a large segment of France's viewing audience has strong cultural ties to the areas of the world they represent. Their absence is not surprising, however, in light of the fact that areas of the world falling outside the confines of the traditional power blocks of North America, Europe, and Anglophone Australia (with the occasional Latin American thrown in for exotic flavor), are generally excluded from the show's upbeat postmodern global pastiche. So the performance of Tunisian Nader Quirat, winner of the 2008 edition of *Star Academy* in the Arab World, or that of Moroccan Hajar Hadnan who triumphed in *Star Academy* Maghreb in 2007, remain outside the frame of the French show's imagined reality.

Areas otherwise ignored in the show's narrative may, however, be reinserted into its negotiation of the global through other kinds of relationships. For instance, in 2007 the cast of *Star Academy* released a video titled Bangla Desh – a cover of the 1971 George Harrison song – to benefit disaster relief in the People's Republic of Bangladesh. By portraying the candidates, and, by extension, France, as benefactors of "less developed" nations while simultaneously ignoring these nations' cultural production, the show returns to a problematic vision of the world where some areas are positioned as significant cultural producers while others are portrayed as needing their paternalistic assistance to survive. To the critical viewer, the postmodern flavor of the show's free-flowing decontextualized references to various cultural environments does not fully conceal the neocolonial nature of this positioning.

Ultimately, just as the daily broadcasts serve to reconcile the audience with various contested arenas of France's contemporary socio-cultural landscape, the primes serve to reconcile the audience with the global. In a culture insecure about its position in the world where every hint of continuing transnational influence is noted and celebrated,[33] *Star Academy* (re)assures its viewers that France is still one of the "major players" of global cultural production. As the young French candidates – or, more precisely, the candidates positioned as French regardless of the actual complexity of their identity – are seen playing with the powerful on the set of the prime, the show suggests that the newer generations they represent are well equipped to negotiate the cultural, ethnic, and linguistic challenges of globalization. Their engagement in charity work benefiting "less developed" nations further suggests that they are not only powerful but also caring citizens of a global village constructed through an imagined reality that underscores France's contemporary influence all the while obscuring the historical legacy of its violent imperialist past.

Beyond the reality of reality TV

Jost argues that reality television claims to abolish the distinction between the "régions antérieures" – the "front stage" where social representation takes place – and the "régions postérieures" – the "back stage" where social actors are protected from judgment.[34] While, as Jost recognizes, this claim (on which rests reality TV's claims of authenticity) is dubious at best, the front stage/back stage distinction is useful in thinking about the local/global articulation in *Star Academy*. When inviting viewers into the back stage of popular music production in its daily broadcasts *Star Academy* also invites them into the back stage of French culture. Just as it constructs life at the academy as an "authentic" depiction of what goes on in show business and offers the candidates' everyday behavior as a reflection of their "authentic" selves – as opposed to the primes during which they are ostensibly asked to *perform* – *Star Academy* constructs these daily broadcasts as "authentic" representations of French culture. The "front stage" of the weekly primes transposes these representations onto the global stage where "French culture" performs through the candidates' interactions with the global and is ultimately offered for global consumption.

Considering such issues of representation and interpretation in reality television significantly informs our understanding of the multidimensional nature of the process through which licensed television formats are "adapted to local, national, and regional cultures but still bring complex transnational influences with them."[35] The case of *Star Academy* specifically highlights aspects of this complexity not adequately addressed by studies focusing either on global production or local reception. Particularly significant is the show's engagement with notions of national identity and national culture in relationship to the global. Indeed, while the show hints at France's regional, ethnic, racial, and generational diversity, it ultimately constructs – and offers its global audience – a vision of French culture as a national culture shared across these boundaries, supporting Straubhaar's suggestion that much television production and consumption still operates at the national level. This recognition is important since discussions of the relative decline of the nation-state have tended to deemphasize the continuing significance of national identity formation in "Western" nations. Indeed, if the role of media production and consumption in defining national identity has been usefully problematized in the case of post-colonial environments, the connection between media, national identity/culture, and globalization is more rarely considered in the "West." This oversight dangerously suggests that nationalism is the purview of "developing" nations enthralled in the process of negotiating modernity while their Western counterparts are comfortably installed in postmodernity.

Reality TV's multiple incarnations remind us that trans-local connections run in multiple and often unexpected directions, and that the common dichotomies that organize much of our academic thinking – between East/West, North/South, global/local – must be problematized. Like other localized and/or nationalized global genres, it forces us to recognize that the "localization of cultural forms can ... proceed simultaneously with an increasing global sharedness" and consider "the intersecting power lines that produce trans-national popular culture." It also simultaneously allows us to address "the mutual construction of what are often viewed as dichotomous analytical categories."[36] Finally, the case of *Star Academy* in France demonstrates how we must more assertively consider the politics of representation of the global both in local/national cultural texts *and* in our academic discourse about these texts and the processes of transnational influence shaping them.

Notes

1 Marwan M. Kraidy & Patrick Murphy, "Shifting Geertz: Toward a theory of trans-localism in global communication studies," *Communication Theory* 18, no. 3 (2008): 339.
2 Patrick Murphy & Marwan M. Kraidy, "International communication, ethnography, and the challenge of globalization," *Communication Theory* 13, no. 3 (2003): 310.
3 John Corner, "Politicality and the inter-generic settings of television: the indicative, the propositional and the symbolic," *Reel Politics: Reality Television as a Platform for Political Discourse* conference, Istanbul, Turkey, September 12, 2008.
4 Laurie Ouellette & Susan Murray, "Introduction," in *Reality TV: Remaking Television Culture*, eds S. Murray and L. Ouellette (New York: New York University Press, 2004), 2.
5 Damien Le Guay, *L'empire de la télé-réalité* (Paris: Presses de la Renaissance, 2005).
6 François Jost, *L'Empire du loft (la suite)* (Paris: La Dispute, 2002/2007), 24.
7 Richard Kilborn, *Staging the Real: Factual TV Programming in the Age of "Big Brother"* (Manchester, UK: Manchester University Press, 2003), 65.
8 Laurie Ouellette & Susan Murray, "Introduction," 2.
9 John Corner, "Performing the real," *Television and New Media* 3, no. 3 (2002): 255–70.
10 François Jost, *L'Empire du loft (la suite)*, 9.
11 Laurie Ouellette & Susan Murray, "Introduction," 6.
12 François Jost, *L'Empire du loft (la suite)*.
13 Richard Kilborn, *Staging the Real: Factual TV Programming in the Age of "Big Brother"* (Manchester, UK: Manchester University Press, 2003), 60.
14 Mark Andrejevic, *Reality TV: The Work of Being Watched* (Lanham, MD: Rowman and Littlefield, 2004).
15 Slavoj Žižek, *Interrogating the Real* (New York: Continuum, 2005), 14.
16 François Jost, *L'Empire du loft (la suite)*.
17 Richard Kilborn, *Staging the Real: Factual TV Programming in the Age of "Big Brother,"* 28.
18 Slavoj Žižek, *Interrogating the Real*.
19 Clifford Geertz, *The Interpretation of Cultures: Selected Essays* (New York: Basic Books, 1973).
20 Manuel Castells, *The Rise of the Network Society* (Malden, MA: Blackwell, 1996/2000).
21 Benedict Anderson, *Imagined Communities: Reflections on the Origin and Spread of Nationalism* (London: Verso, 1983).
22 See, for example, Damien Le Guay, *L'empire de la télé-réalité* (Paris: Presses de la Renaissance, 2005); Gareth Palmer, *Discipline and Liberty: Television and Governance* (New York: Manchester University Press, 2003); Lisbet Van Zoonen, *Entertaining the Citizen: When Politics and Popular Culture Converge* (Lanham, MD: Rowman and Littlefield, 2005).
23 A product of the European Broadcasting Union, which also produces the Eurovision Contest, *Jeux sans Frontières* was conceptualized by former French President Charles de Gaulle as a means for German and French youth to heal the wounds of WWII (European Broadcasting Union, n.d.).
24 The show was moved to a private hotel in downtown Paris in its latest season.
25 François Jost, *L'Empire du loft (la suite)*, 107.
26 The celebration of customs of religious (typically Catholic) origin on the part of non-practicing Christians (and, often, non-Christians) is not uncommon in France where the Catholic religion is perceived as one element of the country's cultural and historical fabric rather than as a personal lifestyle choice. Thus, viewers would be more likely to interpret *Star Academy*'s nod to Candlemas as pointing to a *cultural* tradition rather than to a religious practice.
27 Cyril was the first black candidate to win *Star Academy* in the show's sixth season (2006–7).
28 Jon Kraszewski, "Country Hicks and Urban Cliques: Mediating Race, Reality, and Liberalism on MTV's *The Real World*," in *Reality TV: Remaking Television Culture*, eds S. Murray & L. Ouellette (New York: New York University Press, 2004), 182.

29 The nature of the candidates' racial and ethnic identities is sometimes addressed, however, in blog discussions surrounding the show. So, for instance, the show's seventh season prompted an intense discussion about the possible Lebanese origin of one of the candidates. These rumors were neither denied nor confirmed by the show's producers or the candidates.

30 Manuel Castells, "The theory of the network society," in *The Network Society: A Cross-cultural Perspective*, ed. M. Castells (Northampton, MA: Edward Elgar, 2004).

31 Éva Roque, "Comment Star Ac' attire les stars," *Télé7Jours*, 15 December 2007, 19.

32 For discussions of this process see, Monica Heller, "Globalization, the new economy, and the commodification of language and identity," *Journal of Sociolinguistics* 7, no. 4 (2003): 473–92. Also useful is Joanne Sharp, "Writing over the map of Provence: the touristic therapy of *A Year in Provence*," in *Writes of Passage: Reading Travel Writing*, eds J. Duncan, & D. Gregory (New York: Routledge, 1999): 200–218.

33 Such as the recent award of the 2008 Nobel Prize for Literature to French writer Jean-Marie Gustave Le Clézio, which Prime Minister François Fillon claimed "blatantly refutes the theory of a so-called decline of French culture" (Lyall, October 9, 2008).

34 François Jost, *L'Empire du loft (la suite)*.

35 Joseph Straubhaar, *World Television: From Global to Local* (Thousand Oaks, CA: Sage, 2007), 5.

36 Ian Condry, *Hip-hop Japan: Rap and the Paths of Cultural Globalization* (Durham, NC: Duke University Press, 2006), 2.

Chapter 10

Reality television and the making of mobile publics

The case of Indian Idol

Aswin Punathambekar

In the summer of 2007, media coverage of *Indian Idol-3* focused attention on how people in the Northeast Indian state of Meghalaya cast aside decades-old separatist identities to mobilize support for Amit Paul, a finalist from the region. While some fans set up websites and blogs to generate interest and support from the rest of the country and abroad, others formed a fan club and facilitated efforts by a range of groups and organizations to sponsor and manage PCOs (public call offices) in different parts of Meghalaya, distribute pre-paid mobile phone cards, and set up landline voting booths. Recognizing the ways in which these activities were beginning to transcend long-standing ethnic, religious, linguistic, and spatial boundaries, state legislators and other politicians soon joined the effort to garner votes for Amit Paul, with the chief minister D. D. Lapang declaring Amit Paul to be Meghalaya's "brand Ambassador for peace, communal harmony and excellence."[1] It seemed that this three-month-long campaign around a reality television program could set the stage for a remarkable refashioning of the socio-cultural and political terrain in Meghalaya. As one commentator remarked:

> When Meghalaya's history is written, it could well be divided into two distinct phases – one before the third *Indian Idol* contest and one after it. A deep tribal–non-tribal divide, punctuated by killings, riots, and attempts at ethnic cleansing, would mark the first phase. A return to harmony and to the cosmopolitan ethos of the past would signify the second. The agent of change: Amit Paul, the finalist of the musical talent hunt on a TV channel.[2]

During this time, residents of Darjeeling and viewers in other cities and towns of West Bengal, Sikkim, and Nepal were rallying behind Prashant Tamang, the other finalist of *Indian Idol-3*. Tamang, who had taken time off from his job as a police officer in the city of Kolkata to participate in the contest, was able to capitalize on support from ethnic Nepalese across India, and even Nepalese working in countries like Hong Kong, UK, and UAE who financed a "Save Prashant" SMS voting fund. During the final stages of the contest, 600 people were reportedly hired to send SMSs round the clock to secure Tamang – dubbed the "pride of the hills" – a spot in the finals.[3] While Tamang's success soon attracted political attention, with politicians keen to leverage the occasion appearing at various public events to voice their support for the contestant, one prominent figure distanced himself.

Subhash Ghising, leader of the powerful Gorkha National Liberation Front (GNLF), refused to publicly back Tamang even when it was clear that Tamang's participation in *Indian Idol* had galvanized Gorkhas across the region. Spotting an opportunity, Bimal Gurung, an activist who claimed Ghising had betrayed the cause of Gorkhaland by reaching a compromise with the central government in New Delhi, launched a fund-raising effort to finance a mass SMS campaign for Tamang as a step towards renewing the struggle for Gorkhaland. Tamang's victory, furthermore, was marred by racist comments by a New Delhi-based radio jockey who called Tamang a *chowkidar* (guard/watchman), sparking riots in cities and towns in West Bengal. Capitalizing on these events and leveraging his position as chief advisor of the Prashant Tamang fan club, Gurung went on to form a new political party called the Gorkha Janmukti Morcha. Within days, Prashant Tamang fan clubs were transformed into Gorkha Janmukti Morcha offices and fans were drawn into Gurung's campaign for a separate state of Gorkhaland carved out of West Bengal.[4] Reality television, it seemed, had played a key role in altering the dynamics of Gorkha nationalism. And there was little doubt that this reality television phenomenon had drawn the attention of millions across India to the complex socio-cultural and political struggles in a region that continues to be neglected, and often misrepresented, by mainstream media institutions.

In this chapter, I focus on these events surrounding *Indian Idol-3* in order to assess the changing relationship between television, everyday life, and public political discourse in contemporary India. Situating this media phenomenon in relation to the changing landscape of Indian television and the socio-historical context of ethno-national politics in Northeast India, I argue that reality television and its plebiscitary logics have enabled new modes of cultural and political expression. I posit the notion of *mobile publics* to draw attention to the defining role of mobile media technologies and practices (public call offices, cell phones, texting) in the formation of publics, and to underscore the shifting and transient nature of such publics. To be sure, I am not suggesting a causal link between *Indian Idol-3* and the reconfiguration of political struggles in Northeast India. Rather, I seek to examine how convergence between television and various mobile media technologies is leading to the "mutual modification of politics and entertainment" in India and many other parts of the world.[5] I contend that *Indian Idol-3* is an exemplary media phenomenon that points to the importance of examining mobile publics as sites where politics, popular culture, and everyday life intersect in new and unpredictable ways. Mobile publics, I suggest, create possibilities for the renewal of everyday forms of interaction in public settings that may have been forgotten, subdued, or made impossible under certain political circumstances. As we will see in the case of *Indian Idol-3*, mobile publics that cohered around Amit Paul revealed the possibility, however fleeting, of everyday life in Meghalaya that transcended ethnic, linguistic, and spatial boundaries.[6]

Television and participatory culture: from *Antakshari* to *Indian Idol*

It would not be an exaggeration to state that television in India has undergone major changes over the past 10–12 years. As Shanti Kumar has documented, the establishment of influential transnational networks such as Star TV and translocal networks such as ZEE, Sun, and Eenadu during the 1990s "disrupted the hegemony of the state-sponsored network, Doordarshan," and transformed the ways in which television operated as a cultural institution.[7] What began with local cable operators stringing cables across rooftops to connect homes to the new and fascinating world of Star Plus, Star Sports, MTV, and BBC News had, by the mid-1990s, grown into a stable satellite and cable industry with rapidly expanding viewership. By the end of the 1990s, the number of cable and satellite television viewers was estimated at 110 million and current industry figures claim 425 million viewers across the country.[8]

In comparison to the pro-development and nationalist sitcoms, dramas, and documentaries that defined the Doordarshan era, these new television channels offered a wider range of programming, including American soaps, dramas, talk shows, music videos, and so on. While these programs initially attracted English-speaking urban elites, the launch of ZEE TV, which catered to Hindi-speaking viewers, and Sun TV and Eenadu targeting Tamil- and Telugu-speaking viewers in south India, forced Star TV to rethink its pan-Asian production strategies and begin formulating ways to "Indianize" its programming. The emphasis on "Hinglish"-language programming on channels like Star Plus and ZEE TV and the growing number of regional-language television channels thus led to several programming innovations. For the purposes of this essay, however, it would be useful to focus on film and film music-based programs that proved to be immensely popular across the country.

When state-regulated Doordarshan opened its doors to sponsored programming in 1983, signaling a departure from an earlier model of public service broadcasting with the express goal of utilizing television for "development" and "modernization," some of the earliest and most popular shows were film-based. The Saturday evening Hindi-language film, the film songs show *Chitrahaar*, and *Showtheme*, which used popular film songs and scenes to speak to a theme each week, always garnered high viewer ratings. By 1984, these shows had established an immensely lucrative "national audience" for Doordarshan.[9] During the 1990s, newly established television channels also discovered the appeal that film-based programming held with viewers, and thereby, the potential for advertising revenues. ZEE, Star Plus, and other channels introduced a number of innovative film music-based shows like *Antakshari, Sa Re Ga Ma*, and *Videocon Flashback*, and weekly countdown shows like *BPL Oye* and *Philips Top Ten*. Further, channels like MTV realized that they could not operate in India by offering Euro-American music-themed programming and turned instead to Hindi films and film music.

Indian Idol, I would suggest, could be traced back to these film-music-themed television programs and *Antakshari* and *Sa Re Ga Ma* in particular, shows which tapped into the enduring popularity of film songs and introduced an element of audience participation that further distinguished television channels like ZEE from Doordarshan. Popular across the country, *Antakshari* is a musical game played by two or more people in which participants have to sing a song that starts with the last consonant letter of the song sung by the previous participants. What had been a fun group activity that livened up journeys and family events took on another avatar when ZEE TV launched a television version of *Antakshari* in September 1993. While *Antakshari* was designed as an amateur singing contest, *Sa Re Ga Ma*, which premiered on ZEE TV in 1995, was framed as a serious competition that could launch contestants' careers in the world of playback singing in the Bombay film industry. These shows redefined film-based television programming in important ways and even anticipated some generic elements of what we today consider reality television. However, the show that marked the onset of a new televisual regime and set the stage for the formation of *mobile publics* around *Indian Idol* was *Kaun Banega Crorepati*, the Indian version of *Who Wants to Be a Millionaire*, which premiered on Star Plus in 2000.

At first glance, *Kaun Banega Crorepati* appears identical to any other international version of *Who Wants to Be a Millionaire*. As Kumar reminds us, "the producers of *Kaun Banega Crorepati* were contractually obligated to reproduce, down to the exact detail, the trademark title design, the show's sets, music, question format, and the qualification process, all of which are laid out in a 169-page document created by Celador Productions."[10] However, examining the ways in which the host of *Kaun Banega Crorepati*, the megastar Amitabh Bachchan, makes different elements of the show more relatable for Indian viewers points to the "interplay between generic innovation and imitation" in television programming.[11] While Kumar draws our attention to questions of genre, I would argue that *Kaun Banega Crorepati* also engendered important changes in television's relationship with new media technologies and how television industry professionals imagined and mobilized the "audience."

By all accounts, *Kaun Banega Crorepati* was a major gamble for the Star TV network and part of a strategy to re-brand Star Plus as a mainstream "general entertainment channel" that could cater to Hindi-speaking audiences just as well as ZEE, Sony, and other entrants like Sahara. With viewership and advertising at an all-time low, executives at Star approached the UK-based Celador Productions for the license to produce an Indian version of the *Millionaire* show and also managed to get Amitabh Bachchan, arguably the most popular film star in India, to host *Kaun Banega Crorepati*. Produced on lavish sets in Bombay's Film City and backed by one of the most expensive and aggressive marketing campaigns, *Kaun Banega Crorepati* attracted audiences immediately. By July 2000, over 200,000 people across India were calling each day for a chance to participate in the show and share a stage with Amitabh Bachchan, leading producers to recognize that the 570 telephone lines that had been installed in four major cities were grossly inadequate.[12] Further, *Kaun Banega Crorepati* represented a major departure in that it complicated industry professionals' understanding of the "audience" by bringing viewers in smaller cities and towns – ones that were never included in the audience measurement system of people meters – into the picture. "Middle India," as the English-language press dubbed this segment of viewers, had registered in metropolitan television executives' imaginations in an unprecedented manner. By 2005, when the second iteration of *Kaun Banega Crorepati* aired on Star Plus and *Indian Idol* premiered on Sony, phone usage had grown exponentially (256 million landline and mobile phone connections) and the practice of texting had become an unobtrusive and taken-for-granted feature of daily life.[13] It was clear that the television and marketing industries had to redraw the map of the "television audience" and grapple with the challenges of understanding novel and rapidly evolving patterns of new media usage surrounding television. There was, however, one element of certainty during this period of technological and cultural flux: television corporations, cell phone companies, and advertisers were quick to recognize the financial opportunities that this expanded and "interactive" viewership represented. In 2005, 55 million SMSs and phone calls for *Indian Idol* translated into interactive revenue of 150 million rupees and advertising sponsorship worth 450 million rupees for Sony.[14] It is in relation to these institutional and cultural transitions that we need to examine the events surrounding *Indian Idol-3* that I sketched earlier in this essay. But before that, a detour into the terrain of socio-political struggles in Northeast India would be in order. In the following section, I draw attention to the seemingly intractable nature of conflicts in the Northeast and the role of mainstream media institutions in contributing to the marginalization of this region in the Indian imagination.

The "northeast" in the Indian imagination

Northeast India, comprising the states of Assam, Arunachal Pradesh, Manipur, Meghalaya, Mizoram, Nagaland, Sikkim, and Tripura, is connected to the rest of the country by a narrow strip of land (20 kilometers wide at its narrowest point) commonly referred to as the "chicken's neck." Even as scholars recognize that the term "northeast" is a reductive construct for a "bustling terrain sprouting, proclaiming, underscoring a million heterogeneities," it remains unavoidable and widely used.[15] The region has been known as "Northeast India" since the 1960s, when the region's political map was redrawn by the Indian state in "an attempt to manage the independentist rebellions among the Nagas and the Mizos and to nip in the bud as well as pre-empt, radical political mobilization among other discontented ethnic groups."[16] Furthermore, even though states in this region share international borders with Bangladesh, China, and Myanmar, the complexities of India's relations with these nation-states have restricted cross-border flows and exacerbated this region's isolation. Over the past four decades, virtually every state in the northeast has witnessed the emergence of powerful militias that have contested the Indian state's narrative of socio-economic progress and of becoming a part of the "national mainstream." And as a number of academics and activists have pointed out, the Indian state's brutal repression of political struggles and implementation of draconian measures such as the Armed Forces Special Powers Act (1958), which gives security forces the authority to use lethal force and legal immunity from independent investigation of their actions, have done little to ameliorate the situation.

If, on the one hand, the Indian state is unwilling and unable to think outside the national development-nation building narrative and continues to maintain a colonial attitude towards managing difference, on the other hand, political movements in this region also seem unable to imagine a viable alternative to the logic of statehood. As Menon and Nigam point out, "in a context of extreme economic and cultural alienation of indigenous or local populations, the 'foreigner' issue is also on top of the agenda of many ethnic movements in the northeast."[17] For over a century now, the northeast region of India has attracted migration from different parts of the subcontinent and the resulting demographic shifts have been one of the major causes for ethnic violence and the implementation of a "protective discrimination regime" that seeks to safeguard the rights of historically disadvantaged "tribal" peoples to property, business, trade licenses, and so on.[18] However, this system has led to a "notion of exclusive homelands, where certain ethnically defined groups are privileged" and others are treated as outsiders.[19] And given the many other socio-cultural and economic changes in the region – transition to sedentary agriculture, redefinition of land and property rights, larger numbers of government jobs, new business opportunities, and reconfigurations of class and caste – there is now a marked disjuncture between the "idea of exclusive homelands … and actually existing political economy of the region."[20] Consider, if only briefly, Baruah's account of the tensions between Khasis, designated as one of the Scheduled Tribes of Meghalaya, and the "outsiders" (dkhars, in the Khasi language).

While tensions between Khasis and non-Khasis have shaped everyday life in Meghalaya for nearly three decades now, struggles over who could and who could not claim to be a Khasi became particularly fraught when the Khasi Hills Autonomous District Council passed the Khasi Social Custom Lineage Bill in 1997. While the district council introduced this measure as an attempt to codify the Khasi system of matrilineal kinship, other organizations such as the Khasi Students Union argued against the bill. Suggesting that it was more important to "modernize" the existing system, these groups "proposed a change that would have allowed only children of two Khasi parents to be regarded as a Khasi."[21] As Baruah explains, the question of who is and who is not a Khasi is of great importance given that their Schedule Tribe status entitles Khasis to "the lion's share of public employment, business, and trade licenses, and even the right to seek elected office," with 85 per cent of public employment and 55 out of 60 seats in the state legislative assembly being reserved for Khasis.[22] In recounting the controversy surrounding this bill, Baruah points out that "modernizing" the kinship system was a step backwards and led to rigid definitions of who could claim citizenship in Meghalaya; the existing system was far more progressive and would have been able to deal with demographic, cultural, and economic transitions in Meghalaya by keeping the "ethnic boundary of the Khasi highly porous."[23] However, the divisive language of insiders and outsiders continues to shape political struggles in the state and other parts of Northeast India and, as we will see, is central to understanding the region's mediascape and the significance of the *Indian Idol-3* phenomenon.

Given the Indian state's relationship with Northeast India, the intensity of ethnic strife in several states, and the strategic importance of the region, it does come as a surprise that neither All India Radio nor Doordarshan invested much effort in extending coverage and producing locally relevant programs. Even into the 1990s, All India Radio was broadcasting with low-power transmitters that could not compete with more powerful transmissions from border stations of neighboring countries including Bangladesh, Myanmar, China, and Philippines.[24] Besides, the lack of technical facilities and support for production staff meant that these All India Radio stations were, more often than not, unable to produce programs in local languages and tap into the history and cultural resources of the region. Hindi-language programming only served to alienate listeners further and reinforce perceptions of New Delhi's inability and unwillingness to understand the Northeast. The situation with television production was worse. For instance, the Doordarshan station in Meghalaya's capital city of Shillong was, as recently as 1995, operating with just two program executives who produced 75 minutes of daily programming. They did so, moreover, with no knowledge of the local language and without key production personnel such as editors and floor managers. And where news was concerned, New Delhi did not use dispatches from Northeast India, relying instead on correspondents who rarely ventured outside the confines of district headquarters in large cities like Guwahati in the state of Assam.[25]

This state of affairs did not change with the advent of cable and satellite television either. Not surprisingly, television networks like Star, ZEE, and Sony paid no attention to Northeast India simply because the region did not represent a commercially lucrative market. Compared to other parts of India, the number of cable and satellite homes in the northeast remains low, as does tele-density. In fact, Northeast India did not even figure in the 14-city auditions for *Indian Idol*; Prashant Tamang auditioned in Kolkata and Amit Paul was shortlisted in Mumbai. As Bhattacharjee notes in one recent commentary, "unfortunately, none of the [satellite television] channels are keen to treat the northeastern region as anything other than a repository of violence, cross-border drug trafficking, illegal immigration, and ethnic unrest."[26] Further, while one could point to numerous instances of stereotypical portrayals of people from the northeastern states of India across print, television, and film, a comment by Javed Akhtar, one of the judges on *Indian Idol-3* – that participants from the Northeast had "won the *dil ka daaman* and *ghar ka angan*" (heart and home) of viewers across India – speaks directly to the "othered" status of the Northeast in the Indian imagination and the racial fault line that marks relations between the Northeast and the rest of India.[27] This is the ethnoscape and mediascape in relation to which we need to situate the remarkable series of events that unfolded around *Indian Idol-3*.

Television, participation, and politics

Produced jointly by Sony Entertainment Television and two production companies, Optimystix Entertainment India and Miditech, *Indian Idol* emerged as one of the highest rated shows, attracting over 40 million viewers and 30 million SMSes during the first season in 2004–5.[28] With judges drawn from Bollywood, celebrities making guest appearances, and specially designed episodes in which contestants met *jawans* (soldiers) in New Delhi on Republic Day, attended workshops with Hollywood star Richard Gere, recorded songs to be used for tsunami relief fund-raising and so on, viewers' interest remained high. Further, public discussions of the show revolved, from the very beginning, around voting patterns and how "regionalism" ensured that participants from small towns and cities managed to stay on in the competition even if judges had given them poor evaluations. However, the first two seasons did not spark the kind of mobilization and intense debates around contestants that *Indian Idol-3* did.

The most striking aspect of the fan following that developed around Amit Paul was the sheer range and number of organizations and groups involved: the Shillong Arts and Music Lovers Forum, Civil Society Women's Organization, Society for Performing Arts Development, Bihari Youth Welfare Association, Frontier Chamber of Commerce, Marwari Ekta Manch (Marwari Unity Platform), and several smaller clubs in different localities of Shillong that drew in people from different ethnic, caste, linguistic, and religious backgrounds, with the Amit Paul fan club serving as an umbrella organization. In addition to organizing rallies through the city to raise awareness and drum up support for Amit Paul, these groups worked hard to ensure that their contestant received enough votes to stay in the competition. Working closely with local businessmen including influential figures like Dwarka Singhania, treasurer of the Meghalaya Chamber of Commerce and Industry, fans ensured that PCOs (public call offices) in residential areas and several prominent locations in Shillong remained open all night for people to come forward and cast their vote. And as Amit Paul progressed through the competition, attracting attention in Meghalaya and other northeastern states, fan activity intensified and funds were raised to create publicity materials (posters and banners placed throughout Shillong, for example) and even distribute pre-paid mobile phone cards for free. It is useful to note here that unlike *American Idol*, where viewers are allowed to vote for a period of two

Figure 10.1 A public rally in support of Amit Paul in Shillong, Meghalaya

hours after the show's broadcast, *Indian Idol* viewers are permitted 11 hours (from 9 p.m. until 8 a.m. next day). Viewers could cast their vote by sending an SMS via mobile phone or "televote" through a landline telephone, use an interactive voice service available for mobile phones and landline phones, or online through *www.indianidol.sify.com*. Further, voting for *Indian Idol* was open not only to viewers residing in India but also in the UK and the Middle East (UAE, Saudi Arabia, Kuwait, Qatar, Oman, and Bahrain).[29]

Over a period of 3 months, it became clear that the mobilization around Amit Paul had created a "neutral" space for a range of people to work together, and the many public activities had dramatically changed the way different groups inhabited the city of Shillong. In a city where areas are clearly demarcated along ethnic and linguistic lines – for instance, Bengali-speaking denizens tended not to wander into Mawlai, described as the "cradle of Khasi sub-nationalism" – the tumultuous reception that Amit Paul received when he visited Mawlai as part of his first visit to Shillong after competing in *Indian Idol* seemed remarkable even to the most jaded observers in Meghalaya.[30] While news organizations from New Delhi and Mumbai looked upon these events with incredulity, commentators in Shillong began debating how Amit Paul – a middle-class, Bengali, non-Khasi – had emerged as a catalyst for changing relations in Meghalaya. To begin with, the situation in Meghalaya had begun to change over the past 4–5 years, with tentative moves being made on the part of different groups to reach out and work towards peaceful resolutions of long-standing issues. Second, Amit Paul's background – a high-school dropout who had to struggle in a marginalized state and region of the country – resonated deeply with youth across the region, with questions of ethnicity receding into the background. As Manas Chaudhuri, editor of *Shillong Times*, remarked:

> In a place where there's nothing much to celebrate, Amit came as a god-send. He's talented, and has won all our hearts by singing Khasi, Nepali, Hindi and English songs on the show. It reminded people of the cosmopolitan culture that once prevailed in the state, and they have been overcome by the desire to restore the happy, multi-ethnic character of this state.[31]

Finally, Amit Paul's participation in a national contest like *Indian Idol* was seen as a unique opportunity for Meghalaya and other states in the Northeast to assert their presence in the nation and claim belonging in the "national family." Without a doubt, there were several schisms that threatened to disrupt the momentum generated by hundreds of fans across Northeast India, with groups like the Shillong Arts and Music Lovers Forum complaining that politicians were leveraging this moment for narrow reasons. And activist-writers like Patricia Mukhim did pose critical questions, asking readers why recognition from the rest of the country was so important and if it was because people in Meghalaya were unsure about their belonging in the nation.[32] For the most part, however, this reality television phenomenon was seen to have set the stage for a gradual reconfiguration of socio-cultural and political relationships in Meghalaya. The question then is, given the socio-historical context of Northeast India and the complex politics of ethnic strife, what happens when mobile publics that cohere around a reality television program dissipate? What are the cultural and political implications of mobile publics that last a few weeks or months at best?

Mobile publics: re-framing everyday life

> Viewers have seen what the shows do to people. They are a short-cut to fame, a bloodless revolution.
>
> Nikhil Alva, CEO Miditech

While we could certainly do without media executives' grand and irresponsible claims of reality television and "bloodless revolutions," what conceptual and theoretical frameworks might we draw on to understand this media phenomenon? To begin with, I would argue that it is problematic to regard such moments of participatory culture, enabled by mobile media technologies and practices, as nothing more than "free" fan labor harnessed by Sony Entertainment Television and cell phone companies.[33] Among other things, an in-depth account of this participatory culture would also need to trace and analyze the ways in which fan participation intersected with the interests and motivations of local businessmen, politicians, and varied civil society groups.

I would also argue against situating this phenomenon within the domain of a "cultural" public sphere and theorizing it as an interruption or intervention into the domain of "the" (political) public sphere. As Freitag, Chatterjee, and others have shown, the distinction between "public" and "private" and the notion of "the public" as "an intermediary realm that comes to be posed in opposition to the state itself" does not work in postcolonial contexts.[34] Building on these and other critiques of Habermas' theory of the public sphere, Arvind Rajagopal has argued for recognition of "split public(s)" that characterize and structure political discourse in countries like India.[35] The term "split public" draws attention to the "deep cultural fault line" between elite English-language publics and those that formed around the Hindi-language press, and more broadly, to "the relationship between the public's several parts."[36] However, it should be clear from the discussion thus far that the publics that formed around Amit Paul conform neither to the Habermasian ideal nor to Rajagopal's notion of split publics.

Therefore, I posit the term *mobile publics* as a way to draw attention to the centrality of mobile media technologies to the formation of publics, highlight the fluid and ephemeral nature of these publics, and suggest that the transient nature of mobile publics allows for the articulation of new cultural and political possibilities that might not be possible in more formal institutional settings. *Indian Idol-3* was a crucial media phenomenon precisely because the publics that cohered around Amit Paul created the possibility and the space for the renewal of everyday forms of interaction across ethnic, religious, spatial, and linguistic boundaries that had been subdued and rendered difficult, if not impossible, over the decades. In other words, *Indian Idol-3* created spaces in which people had to acknowledge their differences and set them aside, if only for a brief period of time. And in doing so, they were afforded a glimpse of the everyday that was not shot through with suspicion and the threat of violence.[37]

At one level, the term mobile publics relates to the emergence of a hybrid mediascape and the development of technological and cultural capacities to circulate and share ideas, images and information in ways that were not possible earlier. The question of *mobile technologies* – as Scannell puts it, how such technologies are in the world today – needs to be at the heart of any inquiry into the relationship between media and public political discourse in the world today.[38] At another level, it is important to recognize that mobile publics are more than just collectives that are informed and/or networked through new communication technologies. Mobile publics need to be understood more broadly as interventions – not stable formations – that evince, if only momentarily, new cultural and political possibilities within the realm of everyday life. As Veena Das, focusing on the violence of Partition in the Indian subcontinent in 1947 and the massacre of Sikhs in 1984, writes, "life was recovered not through some grand gestures in the realm of the transcendent but through a descent into the ordinary ... just as I think of the event as attached to the everyday, I think of the everyday itself as eventful."[39] Avoiding the theoretical impulse to explain moments of participatory culture solely in relation to the realm of "politics" is, I would argue, crucial if we are to understand why and how the everyday-ness of watching a reality TV show and sending a text message becomes deeply meaningful in places like Meghalaya. In a context where the idea of a coffee shop as a space for public deliberation has been unimaginable, the term mobile publics allows us to recognize how mobile media technologies are engendering new forms of sociality around television and, thereby, reshaping the terrain of everyday life.

Will such renewals of interaction and engagement sustain themselves over time? Can mobile publics strengthen other efforts to resolve long-standing tensions in Meghalaya? How might we trace and assess the impact of mobile publics? How do mobile publics intersect with and re-shape other spaces of conversation? These and other questions that emerge from this attempt to understand the relationship between television entertainment, public political discourse, and everyday life suggest not only the need for further critical examination, but also that the term mobile publics does not have to be limited to the socio-political context of Northeast India or reality television.

Acknowledgments

I would like to thank Marwan Kraidy and Katherine Sender for the opportunity to participate in the *Real Worlds* symposium. Marwan Kraidy, Amanda Lotz, Paddy Scannell, Henry Jenkins, and Jonathan Gray all provided valuable feedback. I am indebted to Rohit Chopra and Robin Coleman for their insightful comments and encouraging me to stick with "mobile publics" and consider its broader theoretical implications.

Notes

1 "MLAs' last ditch bid to garner votes for Amit Paul," *Shillong Times*, 20 September 2007.
2 Jaideep Mazumdar, "The hills are alive: a local lad on national TV unites a state," *Outlook*, 1 October 2007.
3 http://en.wikipedia.org/wiki/Prashant_Tamang.
4 Simon Denyer, "Gurkha secessionist fire stoked by *Indian Idol*," *International Herald Tribune*, 19 March 2008.
5 John Hartley, *Television Truths: Forms of Knowledge in Popular Culture* (Oxford, UK: Blackwell, 2008), 128. See Zala Volčič and Mark Andrejevic (this volume); Marwan Kraidy, *Reality Television and Arab Politics: Contention in Public Life* (New York: Cambridge University Press, 2010).
6 I have decided to focus on Amit Paul and the situation in Meghalaya partly because it would not be possible to also consider the case of Prashant Tamang and Gorkha nationalism within one essay. Second, Amit Paul's position as a Bengali-speaking non-Khasi, born and raised in Shillong, and able to speak and sing in Khasi, Bengali, Assamese, Hindi, and English, allows us to delve into the complexities of ethnic strife in Meghalaya. Finally, focusing on Tamang's case does not open up the

possibility to move past thinking about fan activity solely in relation to the sphere of politics.

7 Shanti Kumar, *Gandhi Meets Primetime: Globalization and Nationalism in Indian Television* (Urbana, IL: University of Illinois Press, 2005), 2.

8 Kaveree Bamzai, "Real Politics," *India Today*, 8 October 2007.

9 Shailaja Bajpai, "How Doordarshan Spends Rs. 133 Crores," *TV and Video World*, February 1985.

10 Shanti Kumar, "Innovation, Imitation, and Hybridity in Indian Television," in *Thinking Outside the Box: A Contemporary Television Genre Reader*, ed. Gary Edgerton and Brian Rose (Lexington, KY: University of Kentucky Press, 2005), 328.

11 Kumar, "Innovation, Imitation, and Hybridity in Indian Television," 333.

12 Shankar Aiyar and Anupama Chopra, "The Great Gamble," *India Today*, 17 July 2007.

13 Telecom Regulatory Authority of India, 2007.

14 Geetika Bhandari and Kaveree Bamzai, "The New TV Stars," *India Today*, 31 October 2005. These figures are comparable to the interest generated by *American Idol*, which attracted 41.5 million SMS votes in 2005. See Henry Jenkins, *Convergence Culture: Where Old and New Media Collide* (New York: NYU Press, 2006), 59.

15 Sanjoy Hazarika, quoted in Nivedita Menon and Aditya Nigam, *Power and Contestation: India since 1989* (New York: Zed Books, 2007), 138.

16 Sanjib Baruah, *Durable Disorder: Understanding the Politics of Northeast India* (New Delhi: Oxford University Press, 2005), 4.

17 Menon and Nigam, *Power and Contestation*, 139.

18 Baruah explains that as one of "South Asia's last land frontiers … these sparsely populated areas have attracted large-scale migration from the rest of the sub-continent" for much of the twentieth century, *Durable Disorder*, 185.

19 Ibid., 184.

20 Ibid., 184.

21 Ibid., 183–84.

22 Ibid., 184.

23 Tiplut Nongbri, 1998, quoted in Baruah, *Durable Disorder*, 207.

24 Amita Malik, "For AIR and DD, Northeast is far away," *TV and Video World*, 21 December 1995.

25 Ibid.

26 Kallol Bhattacharjee, "Northeastern India: Satellite TV's Forgotten Spectator," *Flow*. http://flowtv.org/?p=581.

27 Bamzai, "Real Politics."

28 Geetika Bhandari, "Making of an Indian Idol," *India Today*, 20 October 2004; Bryan Pearson, "Idol hands Sony auds in India," *Variety*, 14 March 2005.

29 For further details, see http://sify.com/indianidol/images/jun2007/voting_terms.html

30 Jaideep Mazumdar, "The hills are alive," *Outlook*, 1 October 2007.

31 Ibid.

32 Patricia Mukhim, "Trapped in the guile of reality television," *The Statesman*, 15 January 2008.

33 Terranova, "Free labor: producing culture for the global economy," *Social Text*, 18, no. 2 (2000): 33–57.

34 Sandra Freitag, "Introduction: the 'public' and its meanings in colonial South Asia," *South Asia* XIV, no. 1 (1991): 1–13. Partha Chatterjee, *The Politics of the Governed: Reflections on Popular Politics in Most of the World* (Delhi: Permanent Black, 2004).

35 Arvind Rajagopal, *Politics after Television* (Cambridge: Cambridge University Press, 2001), 25.

36 Ibid., 25.

37 Furthermore, as numerous news reports suggested, this renewal of everyday engagement between different people – at rallies and other public gatherings, fan club meetings, in queues at public call offices and so on – also evoked the cosmopolitan past of cities like Shillong and sparked discussions of how that cosmopolitanism could be a vital resource in struggles to overcome ethnic divisions. I use the term cosmopolitanism with the awareness that it has a very specific embodiment in a city like Shillong and is a matter for further inquiry.

38 Paddy Scannell, "The question of technology," in *Narrating Media History*, ed. Michael Bailey (New York: Routledge, 2008).

39 Veena Das, *Life and Words: Violence and the Descent into the Ordinary* (Berkeley: University of California Press, 2006), 7.

Part 4

Migrating economies

Introduction

Tara Liss-Mariño

To posit that the "reality" depicted on reality television is nothing more than a construct is cliché. We all know that producers privilege entertainment value over any promise of spontaneous representation. Yet, as the three essays in this section suggest, whether we believe reality television to be real is largely irrelevant. Instead what matters is that the genre's endemic deception points to a larger truth: the way that power is communicated and enacted. Thus the very same manipulations that incur such criticism can serve as windows onto the modalities of politico-economic power and social authority.

The following essays reject essentialist notions of power, in which authority is conceived of as a monolithic force. Instead they argue that any examination of reality television's claims of authority must be contextualized and the power behind these assertions understood as contingent and particular. Only then will we be able to tease out the ways in which authority is constructed and represented by this ever-growing genre – and, perhaps even more importantly, begin to come to grips with the implications of these portrayals. For as Nick Couldry points out, even if reality TV is taken to be trivial and contrived, the very real effect it can have on viewers' lives is incontrovertible. It is for this reason that an international frame is so important; by adopting a comparative approach we can most appreciate the various ways in which the genre makes power manifest. And though this section's authors move from the general to the specific, from the theoretical to the concrete, all three grapple with hegemonic dimensions of reality television and the methods by which it governs the popular.

Beginning this section, Yngvar Kjus demonstrates through his case study of Norway's tremendously popular talent contest, *Idols*, that the very nature of reality television can enable commercial television's central players to both preserve their economic power in an increasingly fragmented media landscape as well as reshape that landscape to suit their own interests. Kjus moves chronologically through the show's production process, identifying the myriad agents involved, as well as longitudinally, tracing the way that those agents evolve as a result of the show's growing popularity. In mapping this complex and dynamic genealogy, Kjus analyzes the various alliances that have been forged between internal agents – or those who are included under the official umbrella of TV2, *Idols'* broadcaster – and agents of those external media companies that are heavily invested in the show's success. But he also documents the way these relationships have shifted, as TV2 grew and acquired additional media outlets. Partnerships that were once mutually beneficial became hazards to TV2's subsidiaries, and the broadcaster has had to address the needs of the show (national coverage, often procured through external media) without cannibalizing its other holdings. Thus Kjus uses the Norwegian show to reveal the way that reality TV can serve as a locus of power exchange, a politico-economic site where access – and the financial gains that come with it – is continually negotiated amongst media old and new.

Kjus also broadens his scope, considering the relationship between the global and national forces behind *Idols'* production as well. The format of reality TV has proven highly useful for international multimedia corporations, as its tropes can easily be adapted to local customs and cultures without sacrificing its entertainment value. Moreover the genre's defining feature – its "eventfulness" or timeliness – has protected it from the threats posed by time-shifting technologies and digital piracy. And this, says Kjus, has allowed reality TV to become a "killer application," one whose impact is felt the world over. Of course, the continued viability of this application depends on agents' capacity to balance their immediate concerns with those of others, but the tremendous force of the genre cannot be denied.

Sean Jacobs also considers the global reach of the genre, tracing the profound impact that *Big Brother Africa* has had in Africa and the ways in which the show illustrates South Africa's increasingly hegemonic presence throughout the continent. Economic studies have generally forecast China as Africa's preeminent global player, but Jacobs argues that an examination of the circulation of popular culture – specifically via the medium of reality TV – complicates this picture. The third season of *Big Brother Africa* was an international tour de force, reaching audiences that spanned the continent. And while the show was trumpeted as an emblem of continental unity, it in fact served as an effective vehicle for the export of distinctly South African discourses of politics, sex, and class. The contestants were cosmopolitan, progressive in their sexuality, and challenged all sorts of gender and national stereotypes. As a result, viewers – typically cut off from such discussions – were exposed to questions of identity in a very real way.

Jacobs adds that, in this instance, the cultural is intimately bound with the politico-economic. Considered by many of its neighbors to be a "new imperial" power, South Africa has made significant inroads in areas like mining, retailing, and telecommunications. Despite this substantial presence, however, South Africa's hold on the continent has become increasingly threatened by China's growing influence. Jacobs sees *Big Brother Africa* as an attempt by M-Net, the South African television company responsible for the program, to reclaim some of this ground. In producing a continental version of the reality television show – one in which the countries represented mirror those in which M-Net is most invested financially – the company has effectively created a marketing platform that encourages viewers to both purchase television sets and become paying subscribers of its satellite service. Thus Jacobs's article makes clear the ways that reality television can serve political and economic ends that fall outside neoliberal accounts of the genre. In addition, Jacobs's analysis is an important addition to research on reality TV in the developing world, an area that has been gravely understudied.

If Kjus's and Jacobs's contributions stress the need for scholars to broaden their scope and consider the ways in which particular cultural contexts change the workings of the genre, then Nick Couldry's essay in the final chapter of this section offers an important platform from which to move in this direction. Couldry proposes a broad framework through which to conceptualize reality television, one that rejects all-encompassing views of the genre in favor of subtler – if harder to categorize – explanations of its underlying dynamics. While he acknowledges the relevance of neoliberal and biopolitical readings, or him neither adequately accounts for the form's enduring social effects. He sees reality TV as an instantiation of "the myth of the mediated center," or the idea that within society there exists a locus "that explains the social world's functioning and its sources of values". As such, reality TV serves specific political, social and economic functions that aren't accounted for in conventional interpretations. Moreover, for Couldry what is most important about reality TV's pedagogic content is not its neoliberal entreaty to improve one's self but rather its role as social arbiter. He believes reality TV is best understood as a site in which power is constructed, and the self-help message of these shows serves as a key conduit through which to communicate this authority.

Of course Couldry is quick to concede that these particular reference-frames, though much more nuanced than standard uni-dimensional explanations, are far from the only ways to approach the genre. In looking at reality TV on an international scale, he argues, we can see that there are still many more ways that these power struggles can play out. Couldry also underscores the need to move beyond reality TV's subject matter; for him an examination of how messages of social authority are embedded is just as important as the messages themselves. In creating a framework that looks at both the broad (the numerous dimensions responsible for reality television's persistent appeal) and the particular (how these messages become adopted in the day-to-day lives of viewers), Couldry offers us a solid foundation from which to launch the types of comparative analysis that he rightly argues are so needed.

Together, these essays complicate our understanding of reality television by demonstrating that its underlying power dynamics are dependent upon the cultural environment in which it is both created and viewed. Looking at the numerous ways that the genre manifests social authority – and the effects that these manifestations can have on its viewership – forces us to look beyond traditional accounts of the genre and instead open up the possibility for difference. The following chapters are important contributions to the questions of political economy and social authority that arise when reality TV is examined in a global context.

Chapter 11

New industry dynamics
Lessons from reality TV in Norway

Yngvar Kjus

Introduction

The rise of digital media has generally been accompanied by audience fragmentation. For instance, in 1995 225 shows reached audiences over 15 million in British television, but by 2005 none did.[1] However, the trend of reality TV has helped television enterprises around the world retain their audience's attention. One obvious reason for this is reality TV's increased social interaction with the audience. Also important, however, are the rapidly evolving interactions among media sectors, companies and departments on the production side of reality TV. This article studies these interactions, demonstrating that the reality TV phenomenon in fact does not promote the status quo in commercial television but gradually reinvents its value chains in digital environments. Spectacular events and live content are more essential than ever for extending audience reach and developing new revenues. *Big Brother* and *Idols* pioneered this development and were followed by numerous other reality gameshows, like *Dancing with the Stars* and *Got Talent*. The article relates their production to developments in television tabloidization and commoditization through a case analysis of *Idols'* production in Norway.

Studying evolving value chains

Although the cultural industries differ from other industries by producing experiences rather than utilitarian objects, they also standardize production chains and are affected by changing technological, economic and political conditions.[2] In Marxian terms, cultural production is also about the distribution of resources in society, and comprehensive investigations of cultural companies are particularly relevant today, as digitalization, deregulation and globalization tear down the walls between industries and enterprises.[3] As Castells has carefully revealed, new conditions especially affect businesses that trade in "information," whatever form it might take, as their transaction costs and barriers are ever more minimized.[4] By associating and interacting, these businesses have created new economies, and in his recent work Castells examines the networks of global multi-media conglomerates.[5] While acknowledging the importance of such structural analysis, Stalder hastens to add that important aspects of this new information-based capitalism are yet to be taken into account: "What is missing is the development of new information products, based on the creation of new forms of intellectual property, and a sustained analysis of the social dynamics created by these new property claims."[6] He thus encourages a more inclusive analysis of current media production processes.

Television studies is one of the academic fields that is rising to the new challenges – Caldwell and Deuze, for instance, have examined changes in the production chains of fiction TV-series.[7] The live-event shows of reality TV, however, activate production networks and circulate content in quite different ways. As pointed out by Schmitt et al., Moran & Malbon and Jensen, the format trade, and the engagement of national television companies at both regional and global levels, is increasingly centered on reality shows.[8] However, these studies seldom follow program formats throughout the production process and into their encounters with television companies, which are now turning into media houses while learning to cope with new media environment. To do so is to study value chains stretched to their full length, from design all the way to distribution and revenue streams.

In the past, relatively few companies comprised television's value chains beyond a broadcaster and a production company, and they generated relatively few products. However, in the present age of convergence, new forms of collaboration and specialization are surfacing, more agents are involved in the making of each product, and more products are connected to the same program. Each agent derives value from their contribution while taking revenue from other agents and/or selling various forms of access to the audience as well as advertising time to sponsors. However, this value chain of media production is not only measurable in monetary terms – it also has civic value and can contribute to democracy by sustaining a well-informed citizenry, for example.[9] Media industries are regulated and organized ideally to serve both forms of value production, although there is considerable variation among nations, sectors and companies.[10] It is therefore necessary to see their products in both lights and evaluate how audiences are addressed as citizens as well as consumers.

I will focus on three aspects of these emerging value chains. First, what networks of agents are involved in *Idols'* production, both within and between companies and on national and global levels? I am interested in the complementary links they establish with each other, and the gains and risks involved in doing so. Second, how are emerging multi-agent environments affecting *Idols'* production teams in a given national setting? I am particularly interested in the ways in which new agents apply digital technology and especially its unprecedented capacity for both live and delayed transmissions. Third, how do emerging networks and agents affect output? I will consider both qualitative and quantitative qualities of what the public is offered at this final stage of value production.

A multi-layered case study

The case-study approach is particularly relevant for exploring the relations between a phenomenon and its contexts, and the global success of *Idols* makes it a good candidate for analyzing reality TV. A key challenge is to identify and disentangle the media companies and production units involved in the show, a prerequisite for any contemporary study of the ever-increasing range of media phenomena. To do so I will work chronologically through the production process, beginning with the format trade and then moving on to the Norwegian broadcaster and its neighboring media.

This case study also has a longitudinal dimension, relating TV 2's transformation into a multi-media company with its annual production of *Idols* from 2003 to 2007. I combine three methodological tools: interviews, observation and output analysis. I conducted research interviews with key staff of TV 2 and *Idols* from 2005 to 2007, involving the project leader in TV 2's Program Department, the PR contact in TV 2's Information Department, the director and staff of TV 2's Interactive, the portal executive of TV2.no, and the producer, production leader and program hosts of the production company Monstermedia. I also interviewed a broader range of staff members more briefly while observing nine production days during the same period of time. I was generously given access to the making of the live television events, from rehearsals in the morning to the press frenzy as the given episode ended. Apart from *Idols'* official output, broadcast and online, I will also assess the program's coverage in various media, paying special attention to the special event aesthetics shared by numerous recent reality-formats.

International format trade and live event attractions

Over the last decades, a handful of multi-media corporations have come to dominate global media markets through acquisitions, mergers and partnerships. Big markets entail big actors, and the fourth biggest in this case is Bertelsmann, which owns the RTL Group, Europe's largest television production company, which in turn owns FremantleMedia, one of the world's largest program format agencies.[11] FremantleMedia was formed in 2000 through the acquisition of a number of established format companies, and it has since grown exponentially, along with the rest of the format industry.[12] Its dominant position made it a sought-after partner for *Idols'* creator, the entertainment brand corporation 19 Entertainment (bought by CKX in 2005), and FremantleMedia have so far managed the program format in more than forty territories around the world. Format enterprises have in fact been fuelled by reality TV, which for several reasons, discussed below, suits global television entrepreneurship extremely well.

Program formats are, in general terms, tools for reproducing content in the space and time of new national settings, and reality shows do this better than most. Significantly, reality formats generally feature ordinary people as participants, effectively incorporating local languages, cultures and temperaments. Moreover, reality concepts derive from universal conditions such as love, family life, careers and singing/dancing, which are likewise mobilized in traditional genres of public culture, including festive contests and various rituals.[13] They therefore accommodate local conditions while adapting to contemporary trends, like the singing contest *Idols* or the dancing contest *So You Think You Can Dance*. Programs adapted to local culture and language receive better ratings than those that are not; however, the significance of aligning programs to local time has been little considered.[14] Many reality formats are reproduced as live, continuous events that build to a climax at the end of the program season. This "eventfulness" lays claim to our attention and creates the water-cooler conversations, PR, and market visibility that are necessary to success in an overcrowded media landscape. Moreover, the full experience of a live-contest broadcast, whether a reality-TV episode or a football match, can only be had at the time and through the medium designated by the media company. The *immediacy* and *liveness* of the event protect it from time-shifting technologies such as the personal video recorders (PVR) and online file-sharing networks that increasingly threaten the advertising revenues of non-live (archived) television genres.[15] Live-event content like *Idols* thus not only protects television schedules but also accommodates developing online and mobile media services whose strategic importance and revenues are rapidly increasing.

All of this explains why television industries worldwide continue to embrace reality TV, and why format agents in turn try to claim intellectual property for their concepts. Courts generally deny copyright to formats, considering them to be general ideas rather than creative works, but there are lawsuits raising doubts about the issue.[16] Lobbying for copyrights is one of the reasons FRAPA (Format Registration And Protection Association) was founded in 2000. The big format players led the charge – FremantleMedia's entertainment president for North America, for example, headed the steering committee – because they are best served by a truly global control of the market. The ostensible motive was to fight "piracy" and unite all format actors behind the same rules, settling disputes and punishing transgression with banishment. Many television companies are in fact coming to depend upon global format agencies, both for purchasing other programs and for marketing their own. Successful formats offer commercial predictability, pre-existing production expertise and no development costs, whereas copycat accusations hurt business relations and can result in costly lawsuits.

The primetime schedules of Norwegian TV 2 have therefore become dominated by a handful of multiple-season reality shows, including *Idols*, *Dancing with the Stars*, *Got Talent* and *X-Factor* (which are all FremantleMedia's). Table 11.1 below presents the main weekend attractions on TV 2's spring and fall season during the last twelve years. The programs in grey cells are based on purchased format licenses.

Licensed reality formats have proven particularly successful in battling the traditionally dominant public service broadcaster in Norway (NRK). NRK has

Table 11.1 Primetime weekend programming on TV 2 from 1998 to 2009

	Spring season		Fall season	
	Friday	Saturday	Friday	Saturday
2009	Got Talent/Norske talenter	Det store korslaget	X Factor	Dancing with the Stars/Skal vi danse?
2008	Got Talent	The Farm/Farmen	Who Wants to be a Millionaire?/Vil du bli millioner?	Dancing with the Stars
2007	Deal or No Deal	The Farm	Idols	Dancing with the Stars
2006	Idols	Alle mot en	Dancing with the Stars	Deal or No Deal
2005	Idols	Hilde og Brede	Filmstjerne	Klisterhjerne
2004	Idols	God morgen Norge	Farmen	God morgen Norge
2003	Idols	De syv søstre	Tommys popshow	Klisterhjerne
2002	Who Wants to be a Mill.?	Oles Ark	Who Wants to be a Mill.?	Mot i brøstet
2001	Who Wants to be a Mill.?	Who Wants to be a Mill.?	Who Wants to be a Mill.?	Nimme og Gundersen
2000	Who Wants to be a Mill.?	De syv søstre	Who Wants to be a Mill.?	Gladiatorene
1999	Rebusløpet	De syv søstre	TV 2000	Film (Olsenbanden)
1998	Stol aldri på en kjendis	De syv søstre	European soundmix show/Stjerner i sikte	De syv søstre

long enjoyed an exceptionally strong position in comparison to most other license-funded broadcasters in Western Europe, but from 2005 to 2008 the total market share of its TV-channels dropped from 43.9 per cent to 37.7 per cent. TV 2's total share grew in the same period, from 29.4 per cent to 30.4 per cent, along with the strategic importance of the main channel's weekend attractions. Using well-tested formats TV 2 first got a firm grip on Friday nights, and then moved on to Saturday nights. During the same period, the pace of the format trade has picked up considerably, and to obtain the most attractive formats, broadcasters must be both fast and well connected. TV 2 executives in Norway have therefore allied with executives of TV 4 in Sweden and TV 2 in Denmark – representing the largest commercial broadcasters in Scandinavia, this group is a favored partner for global format holders. In the last four or five years, the ability of formats to generate new media revenues has become the reason this group chooses formats. Format agencies, on their side, are no longer concerned about the ability of television companies to generate ratings alone but also new media profits, for which license deals often set a fifty-fifty split.[17] Due to their remit and regulation, public service broadcasters may therefore be less attractive as partners for format agencies, which explains why reality TV has been a predominantly commercial phenomenon.

Reality formats are also uniquely effective at linking to various industries in ways that are thematically engrained in their very concepts, be it the music industry (*Idols*), fashion (*Top Model*), tourism (*The Amazing Race*), or business (*The Apprentice*). The participants are typically offered whatever might be most desirable within the given industry. In *Idols* the winner is awarded a record contract with Sony BMG, and in fact these winners and runner-ups often sell very well – Chris Daughtry, the fourth-place *American Idol* finisher in 2006, sold 4,330,000 copies of his first album. All *Idols* contestants are contract-bound to Sony BMG, which is a fifty-fifty joint venture between Bertelsmann Music Group and Sony Music Entertainment, so yet another link in this value chain is kept by Bertelsmann. The owner of *Idols'* brand, 19 Entertainment, in turn demands 20 per cent of the music revenue. For Sony BMG, of course, the "eventfulness" of the big television show boosts record sales at a time when online piracy is threatening the entire music industry. But *Idols'* intense attraction is relatively short lived, and commercial aims (to get albums out on the market as fast as possible) tend to overpower quality concerns (according to most music critics).

By staging a national talent contest with auditions all over the country, *Idols* functions as an extensive popularity campaign for the winner. The program emphasizes the universal: everyone is invited to audition, and everyone watching is invited to vote via telephone. The contestants must, however, be within the age limits that best answer to the show's marketing aims (usually sixteen to thirty or thirty-five). The format forcefully enacts a dream held by many young people, to become a pop star, and further holds the attraction of seeing an ordinary Joe trying to be someone extraordinary. The program follows the drama of the competition closely and always addresses the audience in the present, orienting them toward the next turn of events. This intense prospective quality is shared by many reality shows and is borrowed from sports and football leagues; *Idols* is even structured as auditions, semi-finals and finals.[18] It exerts an attraction that has set records for media companies around the world, in terms of television ratings as well as online and telephone services (for the American version, see Jenkins).[19] This is certainly the case in Norway, where the show has run for five seasons following TV 2's purchase of the format license in 2002. *Idols* is closely connected to TV 2's expansion since the turn of the century, a process that is examined in following sections.

A television company in transition

TV 2 was established in 1992 by three Nordic media conglomerates – A-Press, Schibsted and Egmont – and it started up as a television enterprise only. It was the first commercial channel allowed access to the state-owned terrestrial broadcasting system, the analogue signals of which had national reach but limited channel capacity. TV 2 therefore had to accept some public service requirements, including universal availability (free of charge) and minority programming. These limitations and regulations did, however, not apply to online and mobile media, and the subsidiary company TV 2 Interactive was founded in 2000 to develop new media revenues, partly by commoditizing existing services (including online TV-subscriptions). However, newspaper agencies were the first group to really profit online, and in order to truly enhance its web presence, then, TV 2 Interactive bought the largest independent Norwegian online newspaper, *Nettavisen*, in 2002. This same cross-sector, empire-building strategy then led to the purchase of the radio station Channel 24 in 2004 and the founding of the online celebrity magazine *Side2* in 2005. Along the way, TV 2 established a series of theme channels (news, sports, entertainment and film) while expanding onto the new national digital broadcasting system, one third of which it owns as well. This new distribution capacity reduces the legitimacy of public broadcasting regulations, and TV 2 might become a subscription-based and entirely commercial enterprise when its current state contract expires in 2010.[20]

In this way TV 2 has speedily acquired several media outlets and channels to serve its commercial aims, and reality shows and major league football, both growing markedly in popularity, represent two key components of this. Their "eventfulness" and immediacy pull audiences most successfully to online and mobile media, and new media revenues rose by 30 per cent from 2005 to 2007, ultimately amounting to 13 per cent of total TV 2 profits (Stavrum 2007). However, in 2009, TV 2 lost football distribution rights to the energy and broadband company Lyse (which startled TV 2 by outbidding it), making reality shows all the more important now. Taking TV 2 and the Norwegian public by storm, *Idols* has since been followed by a series of similar formats, like *Dancing with the Stars* and *Got Talent*, and in 2003 it was already a reference point for corporate strategists:

We can't afford to produce many big program concepts; we'll have to make the most of those we have. I think, for example, that *Idols* 2007 will be huge on web, radio and television for TV 2, as opposed to this year where *VG* and *Dagbladet* [newspapers] profited from all the aspects and issues we did not utilize.[21]

Corporate management continuously seeks profitable synergies, but this is difficult because decisions must be based partly on future cooperative scenarios that might not work out and partly on the current (but by no means guaranteed) profitability of subsidiaries. The radio channel, for instance, was never integrated in cross-production; after several years of draining the company balance, it was sold in 2007. The same year, Schibsted sold its TV 2 stocks as TV 2 hired a new director with a long history from A-Press. The new management team then dissolved TV 2 Interactive and established Nettavisen (with Side2) as an independent online media house in the hope of developing synergies with A-Press and its fifty local newspapers. All of the departments in TV 2 Interactive with a close connection to the channel brand were integrated into TV 2, including TV2.no, which was given a high priority. Although TV2.no was to represent a more direct online continuation of TV 2 programs, TV 2 management continues to experiment with synergies and cross-linkages to its subsidiaries. The ultimate outcomes of this are uncertain, and several studies have in fact found that agents within conglomerates tend to only care for their own bottom line.[22] The next section examines how these new circumstances affect *Idols'* production team and its relationship to other TV 2 actors and interested parties.

Idols' production team

A production team consists of actors working together to maximize the value of a program, and who share an understanding of the means for achieving it. When TV 2 was established in 1992, its production teams consisted primarily of personnel from TV 2's Program Department and an external production company, but also included press contacts from TV 2's Information Department. These press contacts would work closely with the other team members to generate suitable media coverage/PR, which is important for interesting people in the programs and thereby completing the value production. The turn of the century marked a very basic shift, however, as TV 2 Interactive arose and then began allocating personnel to program productions specifically to exploit their commercial potential in terms of new media. At the same time, international format agents increasingly intervened and profited from TV 2's television, online and mobile media production.

This growing body of agents has generally integrated itself well, and in the case of *Idols*, in fact, they all seem to profit too. FremantleMedia's format represented one of the major triumphs of TV 2's Program Department, and several other successful purchases followed. To produce *Idols*, TV 2 engaged the small Norwegian production company Monstermedia, which had been formed only a year before. The deal gave Monstermedia almost no monetary gains, but the prestige of producing *Idols* made it a big player, and it subsequently produced other reality shows for TV 2, including *Dancing with the Stars, Got Talent* and *X-Factor*. *Idols* also made TV 2's Information Department busier than ever before, not least in handling specifically online PR. The department had for some time produced the official program websites, but *Idols'* website generated far more traffic than any other TV 2 program and was the first, according to the chief press contact, to really further a format's PR. The web traffic was immense, particularly immediately following each broadcast, and when *Idols* was not being produced, overall traffic on TV2.no decreased dramatically.

Idols was also a turning point for TV 2 Interactive. First of all, its Tele Department was in charge of the telephone voting system, which drew upon the expertise of telephone operators and computer companies as well. Each vote cost about 0.65 Euro, and although the returns were split among TV 2, Fremantle-Media and the telephone operators, they comprised a substantial bonus. *Idols* often garnered more than six million votes in a season, more than the Norwegian population, which earned the program a reputation as the mother of all voting programs (many of which soon followed). Second, because of *Idols'* popularity, TV 2 Interactive could develop various profitable payment services, including extra show-related material online, song downloads and mobile phone club memberships. Its staff did not create new content but used existing and surplus content to expand the *Idols* universe and gratify fans. This dovetailed well with the interests of TV 2's Program Department, and in order to develop the best possible services, key staff from the Tele Department soon moved physically into the Program Department offices. When TV 2 Interactive was dissolved in 2007, these people continued their work, and the Tele Department was incorporated into TV 2.

Over the last decade, then, program production teams have been comprised of more parties interacting in more complex ways. *Idols*, however, exemplifies how these parties can successfully co-operate in projects as each develops a sense of being part of a team sharing a common understanding of aims and means.[23] Although the staff from TV 2 Interactive, for instance, focused on developing payment services for new media, their constant contact with the rest of the production team served to remind them that their individual success depended on the popularity of *Idols'* broadcasts. This contact also cultivated a joint understanding of program concepts necessary for extending them to new media. A fundamentally different dynamic, however, developed with the other TV 2 media.

Idols in other TV 2 media

The expanding range of parties related to TV 2 media soon attempted to benefit from the immense popularity of *Idols*, first by covering it through interviews with participants and so forth. However, *Idols'* press contacts in the Information

Department insisted on treating internal media just like external media, offering access only when it strengthened the attraction and reputation of the program. In terms of other TV 2 programs, those preceding and following each live *Idols* episode have been routinely allowed to feature participants, building expectations beforehand and creating a sense of release afterward (in light talkshows such as *Friday* and *Late-Night*).

TV 2 Interactive's online media were also keen on the program, particularly the celebrity magazine *Side2*, which soon discovered that it could attract twice as much traffic for its *Idols* coverage as the official program website did. Importantly, its journalists had no obligations regarding the contestants or the long-term success of the show and could be far more "juicy," speculative and sensationalist.

Both *Side2* and *Nettavisen* are routinely used by *Idols'* press contacts for PR purposes. However, the biggest national newspapers, including *VG* and *Dagbladet*, have ten times the reach and visibility. At important points in the program – for instance, the premiere, or transitions from one contest stage to another – the big newspapers are therefore regularly offered exclusive access. In the words of *Idols'* chief press contact, "We need to reach outside the TV 2 island to recruit new audiences." For TV 2's online ventures, however, this practice often appears irrational, even disloyal, in terms of developing TV 2 through new media. This debate receded with the disbandment of TV 2 Interactive and installation of *Nettavisen* (with *Side2*) as an independent company. But it soon remerged as TV2.no was staffed up and re-launched with the aim of profiting more from TV 2 programs. These struggles continue and point to the general challenges of expanding value chains: how is it possible to introduce new value links without damaging existing ones, and to survive with the advent of new agents? The latter challenge, in particular, increasingly entails warding off the external media.

Idols in the external media

Media agents outside TV 2 also try to benefit from the popularity of TV 2 programs, particularly the big newspaper tabloids, and *Idols* became the most written-about television show of the new millennium. Key explanations are related to increased competition, cuts in staff/budgets, and the growth of new media journalism outlets, for which *Idols* provides cheap, accessible and popular content through its hoards of wannabe pop stars.[24] For *Idols'* chief press contact, the immense media interest was both a blessing and a curse:

> In season one, in 2003, my job was to approach the press as much as I could and offer interesting stories and news angles. However, as *Idols* became a major hit, my job reversed, and was increasingly about protecting the program and preventing too much information from leaking out. We deeply appreciate press coverage, but at the same time we do not want to bore the audience and we want to retain *Idols* as an exclusive TV 2 event.[25]

The quote reflects the increasing challenge of portioning out content in program production, and the press contact affirms that about 90 per cent of all approaches are rejected to stay on the safe side. Ultimately, the aim is not to deny access entirely but to make it serve the show's dramatic ends. For example, the press are eagerly welcomed at the studios on the nights of the live-to-air contest episodes and are thus encouraged to focus on the festivity and drama of the contest. The biggest online newspapers in turn continuously feature *Idols* on their front pages, pointing to TV 2's broadcast. To accommodate this, TV 2 provides the press with high-speed Internet facilities, which also help the newspapers make the deadline for the paper issue the following morning.

To maintain interest between broadcasts, *Idols'* press contacts often sought the front page of the largest tabloids, and recent newspaper industry transformations support this strategic PR-work. Digitalization has reduced the release of unforeseen events in the established newspapers, particularly their paper issue because numerous online media generally get to them first.[26] However, in the case of planned events like *Idols*, program producers can contain their stories and offer exclusive access – for instance, to the new board of musical judges for the upcoming season, or to the finalists before the ultimate showdown. The big news tabloids generally swallow the bait, and in spring 2005 *Dagbladet* featured *Idols* a staggering thirty-eight times on its front page (paper issue). Journalists even began to pejoratively call *Dagbladet*'s light culture section "the *Idols* department." The collaboration has become relatively standardized over the years, and before the 2007 season journalists from the other biggest tabloid, *VG*, also approached *Idols'* press contacts to arrange a meeting about the attractions of the upcoming season. It is difficult to measure accurately the effect of press coverage on television market shares, but a yearly word count for "Idol" in the twenty-nine largest Norwegian newspapers (paper issue) demonstrates that they generally coincide (see Table 11.2).

The increase in coverage was ironically a growing concern for *Idols'* press contacts, who view over-exposure as a key explanation for the drop in ratings in 2006. For the 2007 season, access was more severely restricted, which might have resulted in a corresponding rise in market shares.

The PR challenge has paralleled the rise of new media for recording and distribution, the impact of which was particularly blatant in 2007. By then all of the major Norwegian newspapers had invested heavily in web-TV, and the

Table 11.2 The yearly press coverage of *Idols* and television market shares

	2002	2003	2004	2005	2006	2007
Word count for "Idol" in Norwegian newspapers. Source: Retriever Norway.	263	1870	3247	3738	2772	2592
Market shares for *Idols*. Source: TV 2.			35.4%	47.5%	48.0%	40.4%	43.3%

journalists who showed up to cover *Idols'* auditions wanted to tape contestants and their nervous journeys through long queues stretching from the streets into the studio. They would no longer stick to print and picture, instead threatening to leak the audiovisual stories that were once held as exclusive to the TV 2 program and were now necessarily stopped at the studio doors. Online video sites of different kinds can, of course, also be effective PR vehicles or new revenue sources. The performances of the amateur opera singer Paul Potts and Susan Boyle in *Britain's Got Talent*, for instance, reached audiences worldwide via YouTube in 2007 and 2009. Television companies are increasingly controlling uploads and exerting copyright claims on such sites. A more problematic form of content raiding was initiated by the user-generated content site www.Snutter.no, which *VG*, the biggest national tabloid, started in 2007 with inspiration from YouTube. As *Idols* began on TV 2, Snutter launched its own amateur song contest, called *Become an Idol on Snutter*, and in 2008, as *Got Talent* began on TV 2, Snutter launched *Young Talents*, which attracted substantial traffic. TV 2 wanted to stop this activity by legal means, but its lawyers found that copyright law did not apply.

These examples indicate the unanticipated complexities of protecting and managing content across media outlets, which is increasingly important to the success of programs and particularly live-event reality shows. Digitalization creates a proximity that facilitates collaboration as well as exploitation. Whereas new media agents try to take over parts of *Idols'* value production, *Idols'* production team in turn tries to regulate the new activity to serve their own ends.

Disentangling new value chains

Idols exemplifies how reality TV is in the vanguard of program production in new media environments with a new range of agents. In order to disentangle its value chains, I have found it useful to distinguish between global and national players, between agents engaged in official versus unofficial *Idols* output, and between agents with proprietary affiliations and those without. Figure 11.1 surveys the most important agents in these terms, locating the global players at the top and the national at the bottom.

The global and the national level is connected through FremantleMedia's licensing contract with TV 2, and the thick line trails the agents involved in *Idols'* official output, from the owner of the format brand to the local production company. The global actors provide high-end content formulas and safety behind the investments, while the national actors adapt programs and realize consumption. The thin lines indicate proprietary connections between agents that in various ways engage in *Idols'* value chain. On the global level, Bertelsmann benefits from owning both FremantleMedia and half of Sony BMG; on the national level, TV 2 benefits from owning *Nettavisen* and *Side2*. The agents on the right side, YouTube, VG and *Dagbladet*, represent agents without a

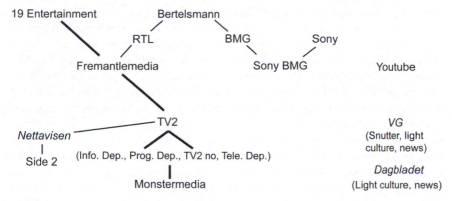

Figure 11.1 Key media agents involved in *Idols*

proprietary connection that still are increasingly involved in *Idols'* production and profitability.

All of these agents are working more closely together and increasingly forming network structures where each agent, or node, depends upon the others. The main nodes are companies, which consist of a central management, various departments, and, increasingly, subsidiaries. I have examined some patterns in how managements try to facilitate productivity in the ways they organize departments, incorporate subsidiaries and set up production teams. Those departments, subsidiaries and production teams in turn attempt to be as valuable as possible to their managements. These forces, top-down and bottom-up, together shape the networks. The motivation of the agents (in this case study) is commercial, and their association is, in general terms, either formal, entailing contracts and money transactions, or informal, with more loosely connected agents exchanging content and publicity. The main commodity of these associations is live-event content. The central agents increasingly try to wield legal authority over this content, and to follow their struggles at close range provides an access point to the ongoing negotiations between old and new media, and the effect of this on the value produced.

Conclusion: the rise and fall of a killer application?

The spectacular events of reality TV have over the last decade been a "killer application" through which the big players of the commercial television industry retain market domination in new media environments. Importantly, event formats help global agents reach national markets in full force, and they help national television companies attract audiences' attention in a time of increasing competition. Live events offer close connections to sponsors and audiences, massive publicity, and an abundance of popular material to apply across outlets and services. Their "eventfulness" can even be applied as intense marketing for other industries, such as the music industry. A key characteristic of live events is that they only exert their full attraction for a limited time, which presents certain opportunities for controlling content and audience attention at a time when digital media (legally and illegally) are bypassing established systems for containing, marketing and profiting from archived content, including broadcasting, cinema, books and CDs. With enough control over it, this live content is highly suited to the development of payment services. Live events thus assist commercial media both in reaching out – their centrifugal force – and in retaining control over content and consumption – their centripetal force. As we have seen, television agents are now finding ways to exert these double forces continuously and across media, which include circumventing old media regulations and lobbying for new copyright laws, and the outcome is important to the values generated.

The centrifugal and centripetal forces of reality TV emphasize key dimensions in its value production, in terms of commercial as well as public values. For one thing, a broad reach not only suits commercialism but also public service endeavors, and several reality shows superiorly summon national audiences to the same events. Simultaneously, however, parts of the events are increasingly walled off and charged for – in this way, reality TV in the 2000s can be seen as building upon the commoditization of major league football in the 1990s.[27] Reality TV thereby has ambiguous public value effects. On the one hand, it creates huge events that can promote social integration in a time otherwise characterized by fragmentation. On the other hand, it threatens to turn ever greater areas of the cultural domain into commodities.

These forces made reality TV the "killer application" of commercial television, but over time they can also harm both commercial and public value production. For one thing, a strong centrifugal drive threatens to overwhelm the media and the public eye with reality TV sensationalism and celebrity news in a way that does not best serve citizen interests.[28] Reduced social relevance and tabloidization may in turn reduce the attractiveness of content, and the willingness of people to pay for it, particularly when many agents go down the same road at the same time. Many reality shows flop or decline after their initial successes, including even *Idols*' ratings and CD sales, and in Norway too much coverage of celebrities and reality TV is viewed as one reason why the big tabloids have lost ground over the last few years.[29] Smaller and more serious news agents, on the other hand, are growing considerably. If this trend escalates, the big commercial players for whom reality TV has been such an important strategy in the 2000s may see a diminished return.

Notes

1 Amelia H. Arsenault & Manuel Castells, "The Structure and Dynamics of Global Multi-Media Business Networks," *International Journal of Communication* 2008: 707–48.
2 David Hesmondhalgh, *The Cultural Industries*, 2nd edn (Los Angeles: Sage, 2007).

3 Simon Cottle, "Media Organization and Production: Mapping the Field," *Media Organization and Production*, ed. Simon Cottle (London: Sage, 2003), 3–24.

4 Manuel Castells, *The Rise of the Network Society* (Cambridge and Oxford: Blackwell, 1996).

5 Arsenault & Castells, "The Structure and Dynamics of Global Multi-Media Business Networks," 707–48.

6 Felix Stalder, *Manuel Castells. The Theory of the Network Society* (Cambridge: Polity, 2006).

7 See John T. Caldwell, *Production Culture: Industrial Reflexivity and Critical Practice in Film and Television* (Durham, NC: Duke University Press, 2008) and Mark Deuze, *Media Work* (Cambridge: Polity, 2007).

8 See Daniel Schmitt, Cristoph Fey & Guy Bisson, *The Global Trade in Television Formats* (London: Screen Digest, 2005); Albert Moran & Justin Malbon, *Understanding the Global TV Format* (Bristol and Portland: Intellect, 2006); Pia Majbritt Jensen, *Television Format Adaptation in a Trans-National Perspective: An Australian and Danish Case Study*, Ph.D. dissertation (Aarhus University, 2007).

9 Graham Murdock, "Building the Digital Commons: Public Broadcasting in the Age of the Internet," in *Cultural Dilemmas in Public Service Broadcasting. RIPE@2005*, ed. Gregory F. Lowe & Per Jauert (Gothenburg: Nordicom, 2005), 213–330.

10 Hesmondhalgh, *The Cultural Industries*.

11 Arsenault & Castells, "The Structure and Dynamics of Global Multi-Media Business Networks," 9.

12 Schmitt et al., *The Global Trade in Television Formats*.

13 Stijn L. Reijnders, Gerard Rooijakkers & Liesbet Van Zoonen, "Community Spirit and Competition in *Idols*: Ritual Meanings of a TV Talent Quest," *European Journal of Communication* 22, no. 3 (2007): 275–92.

14 Silvio Waisbord, "McTV: Understanding the Global Popularity of Television Formats," *Television and New Media* 5, no. 4 (2004): 359–83.

15 Arsenault & Castells, "The Structure and Dynamics of Global Multi-Media Business Networks," 11.

16 Albert Moran & Justin Malbon, *Understanding the Global TV Format* (Bristol and Portland: Intellect, 2006), 127.

17 Moran & Malbon, *Understanding the Global TV Format*, 67.

18 See Paddy Scannell, "*Big Brother* as a Television Event," *Television and New Media* 3, no. 3 (2004): 271–82.

19 Henry Jenkins, *Convergence Culture: Where Old and New Media Collide* (New York: New York University Press, 2006), 59.

20 Tanja Storsul, "Bakkenettet og allmennkringkastinga," *Norsk Medietidsskrift* 15, no. 1 (2008): 38–56.

21 Gunnar Stavrum, Director of TV 2 Interactive, interviewed 4 December 2003 by master's student Hans-Martin Cramer; see http://www3.hf.uio.no/imk/wp-pap/?page_id=28 (accessed 10 October 2009). All Norwegian quotes in the article are translated into English by the author.

22 See Stalder, *Manuel Castells. The Theory of the Network Society*, 57; Deuze, *Media Work*, 177; Caldwell, *Production Culture: Industrial Reflexivity and Critical Practice in Film and Television*, 272.

23 Stephen Jeffrey-Poulter, "Creating and Producing Digital Content across Platforms," *Journal of Media Practice* 3, no. 3 (2003): 155–64.

24 See Deuze, *Media Work*, 141, on developments in journalism.

25 Bjarne Laastad, press contact in TV 2's Information Department, interviewed 9 April 2007.

26 For an overview of this development in American media, see http://www.stateofthe newsmedia.com

27 Raymond Boyle & Richard Haynes, *Football in the New Media Age* (London: Routledge, 2004).
28 Colin Sparks & John Tulloch, eds, *Tabloid Tales: Global Debates over Media Standards* (Lanham, MD: Rowman and Littlefield, 2000).
29 Sigurd Høst, *Avisåret 2006. Salget av Orkla media* (Fredrikstad: The Norwegian Institute of Journalism, 2007).

Chapter 12

Continental reality television and the expansion of South African capital

Sean Jacobs

Introduction

This chapter wants to argue two things: the first part suggests that reality television in Africa – specifically the series *Big Brother Africa*, which completed its third season in November 2008 – has had profound impacts for identity politics, gender politics, and the politics of class on the continent. In fact, these are the issues most commonly illuminated by reality television and I wrote about these in a previously published article.[1] The second part of the chapter moves into less explored territory. In that previous article, I briefly discussed how specifically *Big Brother Africa* can illuminate the workings of globalization in Africa and, in particular, South Africa's hegemonic role in that process. Here, I expand on my earlier argument by exploring that hegemony in the context of the growing Chinese presence in Africa. All economic and political indicators suggest that China's growing investment in mining and infrastructure and its political clout relative to South Africa mean that it is destined to assume a place of prominence on the continent. But here I want to argue that if we want to understand how globalization plays out in Africa, we need to look beyond China's military and economic expansion. For me, *Big Brother Africa* can help us make sense of these dynamic processes.

South Africa has consistently remained the highest-ranking country in Africa in terms of its "global competitiveness" as measured by the World Economic Forum.[2] South Africa dominates regional markets in Southern Africa as well as remaining competitive in the rest of the continent against business rivals from United States and Europe. As it was under Apartheid, there is a close symbiosis between the continental aspirations and interests of the postapartheid state and that of South African business. The advent of democracy in 1994 has opened up African markets for South African business on an unprecedented scale. The South African state is very active on the African continent and keen to develop a leading role for itself. In fact, successive United States governments have viewed South Africa as a continental leader.[3] For example, former President George W. Bush referred to former South African President Thabo Mbeki as his "point man in Africa."[4] The South African government underwrites and actively promotes South

African business's continental schemes through its "Proudly South African" campaign coordinated through an International Marketing Council situated in the Office of (the country's) President since 2002, which links state nationalism with consumption. Separately a statutory Industrial Development Corporation (established in 1940) underwrites the business expansion of South African capital.[5]

More recently South African businesses have been challenged – some would say supplanted – by Chinese state-led investment on the African continent. Chinese investors and developers have carved out a clear advantage in mining and infrastructure investment. But merely looking at China's "hard" economic power does not tell the full story of globalization in Africa. For that we have to look at the production of popular culture which points to a more complicated tale. The story I tell here is that entertainment media, including reality television, have not just given South Africa's business and entertainment industry the opportunity to export the country's cultural products to the rest of the continent, but it also becomes the conduit for exporting discourses of aspiration, continental union and progressive sexual politics. As a result, South Africa (especially South African capital) remains competitive in the scramble for resources and new markets in the rest of the continent.

South Africa as "territorial figure"

The South African-based cultural theorist Achille Mbembe makes a strong case that the old schemas by which we represent and understand political and cultural change in Africa, and by which Africa is presented as being on the margins of the world, cannot capture the continent's complexity and development. Here Mbembe is referring to colonial boundaries (French, British and Portuguese among others) and regional demarcations (e.g. North and Sub-Saharan Africa). Mbembe points to the emergence of "new forms of territoriality and unexpected forms of locality" where "new internal and external actors, organized into networks and nuclei, claim rights over these territories." Two of Mbembe's assertions are important here: the emergence of what he terms "cultural and symbolic territorialities" and, second, South Africa surfacing as a major "territorial figure."[6]

Mbembe singles out a select group of the continent's capital cities and major commercial hubs as cultural centers where "… a new African urban civilization is emerging." For Mbembe their residents represent a "new [African] urbanity." The cities included in this category are Cairo, Kinshasa, Cassablanca, Nairobi, Lagos, Douala, Dakar, Abidjan, and, crucially (for this chapter), Johannesburg:

> This new urbanity, creole and cosmopolitan, is characterized by combination and mixture in clothing, music, and advertising as well as in practices of consumption in general.[7]

New notions and practices of gender and sexuality also take shape in these new spaces. For Mbembe,

> ... the dimension of individual behavior, the universe of norms, and the forms of morality that are supposed to govern private practices [in these   cities] have undergone deep transformations. The last twenty years have witnessed, in fact, a generalized loss of control over sexuality by families, churches, and the state. A new moral economy of individual pleasures has developed in the shadow of economic decadence.[8]

To underscore the relative importance of Johannesburg in relation to these other cities, Mbembe (along with Sarah Nuttall) later edited a special issue of the journal *Public Culture* (October 2004) to investigate Johannesburg's status as an "African Metropolis."[9] The aim with the *Public Culture* special issue was also to "de-familiarize" the way that Africa, and Johannesburg as an African city, is understood.[10] As opposed to an Africa usually treated as uncharacteristic from the rest of the world, Mbembe and Nuttall wanted to emphasize the dimensions of what they call the "worldliness," the "being-in-the-world" of Africa or the "sameness-as-worldliness."[11]

South Africa's economy is fully integrated into the world economy, especially with European markets, North America and, increasingly, Asia, in contrast to other African states and territories. Only some North African states (Tunisia, Morocco) can claim a similar relation. South Africa vies with North African states as well as other non-African actors for control over resources in a number of weaker states and territories (e.g. the Democratic Republic of Congo, Sierra Leone, countries in the Sahel, etc.). In addition, South African business dominates economic relations with its Southern African neighbors (like Zimbabwe, Namibia, Botswana and Mozambique, to name a few) to the extent that these countries "are well on their way to becoming South African provinces," if they already are not. Further north, South African capital (with the symbolic support of the South African state) dominates national markets in tourism, mining, transportation, electricity and banks in a number of African states. Mbembe concedes that South Africa's growing influence is subject to global financial fluctuations and that its "position on the continent is still highly ambiguous, and [that] the terms on which it can be reintegrated into the continent remain unclear." However, Mbembe emphasizes that "... *South Africa's political, diplomatic, and cultural influence is far greater than economic power, which itself remains very relative*" [my emphasis].[12]

Mbembe was not the first to point to the growing cultural, political and economic importance of Johannesburg and South Africa in Africa. The South African central state actively promotes such a vision, and so does the city of Johannesburg, the city's intellectual and cultural elites, and multinational corporations. In fact, in the aftermath of Apartheid, Johannesburg fast eclipsed previously regional hubs such as Nairobi and Harare as the base for multinational media or other private business corporations.

Identity, gender and class

Big Brother Africa was first aired in the summer of 2003. It was the third season produced by M-Net, a South African television company based in the suburbs of Johannesburg and trading in the rest of the continent as MultiChoice Africa.

The South Africa-specific edition of the Big Brother franchise was defined by the fact that the balance of the contestants on the first two seasons was white. In both editions of the South African iteration of the reality series, six of the twelve contestants were white and in each case the winner was a white male. (Similarly, the inaugural winner of the *Pop Idols* program, another much-watched TV show, was also a white male.) M-Net came in for heavy criticism as a result, from some commentators in the South African media and cultural critics alike. The producers of *Big Brother South Africa* insisted this was unfair criticism. They countered that *only half* of the contestants were white. This, they maintained, represented significant progress, a rather extraordinary statement given that whites make up only 10 percent of the South African population. What they did not want to say publicly, however, was that the rationale behind the skewed demographics of the first two series of *Big Brother* in South Africa was, of course, the fact that whites constitute an economic elite in South Africa and, for this reason, are more attractive to advertisers.

The decision therefore to mount a continental production was on M-Net's part definitely an attempt to keep interest in the *Big Brother South Africa* franchise alive – and profitable. However, it does not tell the full story of how *Big Brother Africa* is bound up with and reflects the politics of South Africa's place in relation to the rest of the continent.

In January 2003, M-Net announced that it would host a "continental" series. Following auditions, twelve contestants – one each from Ghana, Kenya, Uganda, Tanzania, Malawi, Zambia, Angola, Namibia, Botswana, Zimbabwe, Nigeria and South Africa – were chosen. They entered a specially equipped house in suburban Johannesburg on 26 May 2003. The house was also equipped with 27 cameras and 56 microphones (concealed behind mirrors or mounted in walls) running continuously to catch every moment of the housemates' activities. The footage was broadcast non-stop on a satellite television channel created specifically for this purpose by MultiChoice Africa. Highlights were also streamed via the Internet.[13] A daily 30-minute highlight program and a Sunday night 60-minute "eviction" program were broadcast on M-Net's regular channels in forty-seven countries. These also appeared on free-to-air services through an agreement with terrestrial broadcasters in a number of African nations. The series managed to attract huge audiences, averaging thirty million people tuned in nightly throughout its inaugural 2003 run: a feat for the African continent. This was all the more remarkable as M-Net had only 1.3 million subscribers, 80 per cent of whom lived in South Africa in 2003.

The producers repeated this formula in subsequent seasons of *Big Brother Africa* in the summers of 2007 and 2008.

Thanks to national broadcasters throughout Southern Africa and beyond who signed up to carry the daily updates, the show's viewership grew exponentially, beating all previous records. *Big Brother Africa 2* received one million SMS or text messages. At least 14 million registered page impressions were registered on the show's website and more than 4 million people viewed video clips online.[14]

For the show's full run – 106 days, beginning in late May 2003 – the house-mates were isolated from the rest of the world. They could not leave their "home" and were banned access to television, radio, telephone or other communications media. Each was required to carry out special "tasks" set by the producers. How these tasks were performed was meant to reveal how "creative and original" individual housemates were and served to determine their popularity both among their fellow contestants and with the public.

Each week, viewers voted their least favorite candidate out of the house and off the program. The final contestant remaining walked away with US $100,000. As in similar shows elsewhere (*Big Brother* in its US and British iterations, *Loft Story* in France), contestants spent most of their time doing rather ordinary things – eating, arguing, playing in a strategically-positioned hot tub and hamming it up for the camera.[15]

Big Brother Africa shares characteristics of the reality program genre that have been well documented and critiqued in the academic literature and popular media alike. By way of carefully chosen camera angles and editing, the producers determined what viewers saw, belying the series' much-touted claims to unscripted "reality." Activities on the set were driven by daily and weekly "storylines," with contestants coming to represent stock characters and stereotypes. Audience reception was actively shaped by these views and plots imposed from above. The producers' continual emphasis on certain, very particular types of "creativity" and "originality" and on what they termed "a willingness to play the game" determined who stayed in the house and who got evicted, belying still another of the show's claims – that the winner would be chosen by the audience and audience alone.

However, since it first broadcast *Big Brother Africa* has been more than just a reality show and has reflected, and managed to insert itself, into larger debates about cultural politics and economic globalization, both in South Africa and elsewhere on the continent.

The show was hailed – both by its boosters (including ordinary viewers) and critics – as an avatar of continental unity, contrasting the relative goodwill among its contestants with the fragmentation that many in the "North" see as Africa's downfall. "Three decades after the concept of Pan-Africanism fizzled out," *Time* magazine reported, "satellite television is working where liberation philosophy did not: connecting and modernizing the world's poorest continent."[16] And the influential South African *Sunday Times* newspaper editorialized:

> *Big Brother Africa* has succeeded where the Organization of African Unity failed, by unifying the ordinary people of Africa.[17]

The Johannesburg correspondent of the (US) *Christian Science Monitor* praised the series echoing common sentiments: "[*Big Brother Africa* is] ... an unlikely catalyst for cultural understanding on a continent often divided by ethnic conflict, nationalism, and xenophobia."[18]

By and large, people seemed to share the view expressed by Sammi Bampoe, a Ghanaian contestant participating in the first season of the reality show: Bampoe told his country's national media after being evicted from the house, that it had had no negative impact on his opinion of other African countries or their nationals. In any event, he had found that the housemates had a lot in common. The only difference, according to Bampoe, "was in terms of food and music. Apart from that *we were all the same*."[19]

Big Brother Africa's producers encouraged such views. Carl Fischer, a veteran producer of TV shows for M-Net's South African market and a key player in producing the earlier, all-South African iterations of *Big Brother*, made this claim about the continental version: "For the first time [African viewers] are getting just African images, African people, African heroes, African music."[20] For Marie Rosholt, the series' executive producer, *Big Brother Africa* was properly ground-breaking: "It's serving to break down misconceptions. There's a perception in the rest of Africa that Nigerians are less than honest, that South Africans are arrogant. I think our show challenges those views."[21] Fischer also insisted that *Big Brother Africa* represented a significant rebuke to generally dour views of the continent: "We are educated, can engage one another and don't always have wars."[22]

The series continues to challenge long-held gender stereotypes, sexual identities, and sexual anxieties. Unmarried and single young men and women lived in the same house. Nudity is on full display (during the "shower hour" – the segment which records the highest average daily viewership). There have been sexual relationships between contestants. In other instances a bisexual contestant was outed (*Big Brother Africa 3*) and the men were challenged for their treatment of women (*Big Brother Africa 2* and *3*).[23] Many of these issues are treated matter-of-factly among the housemates. For example, the Tanzanian contestant, Munya (one of the three finalists in *Big Brother Africa 3*'s last round), was involved in a "love triangle" with one of the female contestants and the eventual (male) winner. Post-show he was later forced to apologize for his treatment of that female contestant.

Outside the house the behavior of housemates has often resulted in passionate debate.[24] Some contestants – particularly female contestants – have been derided for "loose morals," they have also publicly defended their behavior. During the third season Tawana Lebale, a 31-year-old contestant from Botswana, was criticized in media reports, chat rooms, and via SMS for her multiple sexual relationships in the house. At one point, she was attached to two of the male contestants at the same time. Lebale was very frank about her sexuality in a way that was unusual for women in Southern Africa at least:

> Nothing happens by coincidence! I felt comfortable sleeping with both Ricco and Munya [two male contestants] and if they feel they'd played me, I had the most fun. I was spoilt for choice. When I wanted it rough I went with Munya and when I wanted it gentle I did Ricco. I can't speak for them and what they did behind my back. All I know is that there are times when a woman wants to be treated like a slut. And if you think I chased Munya you are wrong. I never went to his bed. He always came to mine. I slept with Ricco because he was open to suggestions. I know morally upright people saw me in bad light but I'm comfortable with what I did. I have no regrets.[25]

Critics of *Big Brother Africa* – in governments and churches and defenders of "high culture" – invoked "invented traditions" to damn the show as somehow "un-African" or "immoral."[26] Essentialized conceptions of African kinship and patriarchal values fast on the wane found common cause with the moralism of missionary Christianity; the series' voyeurism was condemned and, in the process, notions of "privacy" – commonly (if erroneously) associated with Western individualism – to "protect the honor of women," were conflated with ideals of African "cultural heritage." The writer Wole Soyinka was particularly brutal in his dismissal of the series: "All we need is just get some prostitutes on the streets and lunatics. They will go naked for nothing."[27] However, attempts to block transmission of the series on national broadcasters – in Nigeria, Malawi, Zimbabwe, and Namibia – were met with widespread opposition.[28]

Or as Tashi Tagg, a well-known South African television blogger wrote on the eve of the *Big Brother Africa 3* finale, about Tawana Lepale's actions:

> The truth of the matter is I don't have any problems with Tawana's sex[ual] [ex]ploits – I fully believe women should be allowed to enjoy and say they like sex in the same way men do and go as wild as they please. To top it all off I'm annoyed by society in general and feeling trapped by global sexism.[29]

Similarly, a columnist in *The Namibian* opined:

> [S]he's [Tawana Lepale has] never been one of my favorite housemates. But I hate the hypocrisy teeming across the BBA3 [*Big Brother Africa 3*] TV text strip like maggots swarming over a dead corpse. Munya and Ricco are men and have needs, but Tawana, who quite obviously also has needs, is

every unthinkable name under the sun. Some of the messages are downright cruel. Guys do "it" – as often and as much as they want – and it's all about bragging rights; a woman does "it" and boy, oh boy, they're all but burnt at the stake. Look it's not my scene, but let's be fair. Tawana should not be made a scapegoat.[30]

The promise of new identities – both "national" and sexual – was therefore certainly attractive.

Official responses were not always dismissive or negative towards the show. Instead they often marshaled the show's discourses for their own political ends. The government of Botswana actively promotes its contestants. Nelson Mandela, the former President of South Africa, referred to the winner of the first season, Cherise Makubale (of Zambia), as "an example to African youth."[31] When Cherise Makubale, the winner of the inaugural season of *Big Brother Africa*, returned to Lusaka, Zambia's then-President Levy Mwanawasa announced that Makubale would become an "ambassador of goodwill." She would represent Zambia and be granted diplomatic privileges when traveling. President Mwanawasa also publicly praised Makubale for exhibiting positive national traits that simultaneously conflated a particular set of gender relations – economic, cultural ("national") and familial: " … A Zambian woman must sweep and cook and you did exactly that. I am not surprised that you have received so many marriage proposals."[32] Later, Mwanawasa's spokesperson praised Makubale for exhibiting "high moral standards in the house."[33]

Yet over time that view of women changed on *Big Brother Africa*. In fact, though a Malawian contestant who resembled Makubale (she cooked and cleaned for the rest of the group) made it to the final round of *Big Brother Africa 3* she lost out to a male Angolan contestant as viewers and media critics criticized her attempting to secure the "kitchen vote."[34]

However, more is going on than just nationalism and a reworking of gender roles. A close look at the social backgrounds and economic status of the contestants throughout the three seasons gives a clear sense of the class politics at work. Most, if not all, the housemates had finished college, were fluent in English, lived in the major African cities (and not their slums), had some exposure to the entertainment industry or had worked in it (in television and modeling among others), and had either traveled or lived outside the continent at some time or other. As one journalist noted: "They are drawn from their respective countries' cultural elite and are in no way representative of Africa's impoverished and downtrodden millions."[35]

A leading Ugandan journalist – also an emphatic supporter of *Big Brother Africa* – told a US public radio station:

There's been criticism that the bulk of the contestants didn't really grow up [here] – like Gaetano [Kagwa, the Ugandan contestant in *Big Brother Africa 1*] – he didn't do most of his schooling here. Some of … the contestants have been criticized for not having been through or probably lived through Africa enough. But you must look at some of the requirements that the show organizers wanted. They wanted people who were fluent in English. They really wanted people who had had some form of exposure – *not people who were really raw* [my emphasis].[36]

According to Neil McCarthy, a South African who was series editor on the first *Big Brother* program, in dramas and reality TV shows South African broadcasters actively promote what they refer to as the "aspirational":

[It] translates to mean that the lives we see on TV should be ones that give ordinary people something to aspire to, not ones that mirror their fears. It seems to be based on a view that popular culture in South Africa has an ethical obligation to be encouraging. That social ills such as crime, poverty and corruption and illiteracy should be handled with extreme caution. [As a result] ... we get [shows] that reflect a slightly idealized, middle-class world where the problems are small ones and the delights are many.[37]

The struggle for hegemony

In a study of economic relations in Southern Africa, sociologist Bill Martin has argued that " ... South Africa has long dominated its neighbors." The advent of the post-apartheid epoch " ... has certainly not brought about the withering away of the power of South African firms or the South African state."[38] In fact, since 1994 South African firms have expanded across the Southern African region and the continent. The privatization of state enterprises and relaxation of controls on foreign investment in other African countries since the late 1990s have proved very timely for South African expansionism.[39]

The South Africans are not always welcomed. In a number of countries, South African corporations are considered "new imperialists," "subimperial" or derided as "semi-peripheral." In March 2004, a member of the South African Cabinet, Jeff Radebe, admitted as much when he told journalists:

There are strong perceptions that many South African companies working elsewhere in Africa come across as arrogant, disrespectful, aloof and careless in their attitude towards local business communities, work seekers and even governments.[40]

There are, of course, many reasons for this. Among them are accusations of disregard for local production and workforces and allegations of corruption. For example, South African retailers who have opened shopping malls in countries to the north are often criticized for contributing to deindustrialization there, and to undercutting the value of local products, by sourcing cheaper goods from

South Africa. More controversial still, South African mining interests there have become embroiled in allegations of looting mineral assets abroad, notably in the Democratic Republic of Congo.

In Tanzania, where more than 150 South African firms have entered the country since 1994, and "with virtually every major South African firm active in the region now operating in Tanzania,"[41] the presence of South Africans remains a contentious issue. Objections to the South African presence include their role in the rapid privatization of nearly 400 state-run institutions (e.g. the largest banking chain, national airline and national brewery), control of new industries (cell phones service providers, private television stations), the dumping of cheap South African goods on Tanzanian markets by Shoprite, a supermarket chain now present in a number of SADC countries, as well as the domination of extractive industries (gold, gemstones) by South Africans on very favorable concessionary terms.

According to Richard Schroeder, a geographer who has studied South African investment in Tanzania, what irks ordinary Tanzanians more is the role and behavior of white South African representatives of these firms. The South Africans, mostly white expatriates, are often accused of importing racism from home. This includes establishing exclusive schools, social clubs and the use of violence against Tanzanians. Schroeder describes their behavior in the gemstone sector, for example:

> In the gemstone sector, hundreds of small-scale miners were forcibly removed from the core of a lucrative tanzanite mining site in the mid-1990s, clearing the way for acquisition by a South African mining firm. In the ensuing decade, South African security personnel at the mine were impli-cated in numerous shooting incidents, which resulted in several fatalities and the wounding of dozens of small scale miner "trespassers." The corporate miners later established an exclusive tanzanite brand, which was then used to discredit unbranded gems (like those produced by the small scale sector) as potentially illegal and unreliable.[42]

As a result the South Africans have a perception problem. Schroeder quotes a rural activist: "We now live in the United States of Africa."[43]

To compound matters, the South Africans do not have free rein. More recently, the hegemony of the "old World" (including the Middle East) and North American governments and firms have been challenged by the increasing presence of China on the continent and African countries' growing relationships with Asian countries in general. As the World Bank summarized China's growing influence in 2007:

> Since 2000 there has been a massive increase in trade and investment flows between [sub-Saharan] Africa and Asia. Today, Asia receives about 27 percent of Africa's exports, in contrast to only about 14 percent in 2000.

This volume of trade is now almost on par with Africa's exports to the United States and the European Union (EU) – Africa's traditional trading partners; in fact, the EU's share of African exports has halved over the period 2000–2005.[44]

That also has consequences for South African capital's – both public and private, including media companies – continental ambitions. China's growing influence is negatively impacting South Africa's "pivotal position" on the African continent.

[South African] exports to Africa as a percentage of total exports have barely changed since 1998 (at around 13–14%). Exports to SADC [Southern African] states have actually declined to around 10% of South Africa's total exports. As these figures suggest, industrialized South Africa faces potential competitive pressures from the industrialized East that are unlike those of Africa's primary producers.[45]

At first these figures may appear insignificant, but as Martin argues they " … hide the fact that African markets have long represented a significant market for South Africa's more advanced industrial, financial, commercial and mining firms."[46]

In October 2007 the Industrial and Commercial Bank of China (one of the "Big Four" state-owned banks), in what was its largest foreign investment ever, committed US$5.45 billion to purchase a stake in the South African Standard Bank, the largest commercial bank in the continent.[47]

As Europe and the United States de-industrialized, Asia and particularly China have become, like South Africa, exporters of both low- and middle-range industrial goods. Chinese manufacturers produce these goods with much larger and lower-cost labor reserves. Increasingly South African firms – while relatively competitive in the mining sector – are facing strong competition from the Chinese in retail trade and financial and banking investment.

Growing African ties with the East are likely to bypass or be at the expense of South African capital. Second, these shifts can displace, as can already be seen in the commercial, mining, and financial sectors, South Africa's historically privileged, and underdeveloping, ties with the region. It is thus not simply that the hold of the North is declining as the East rises: it is clearly the case that the region as an integrated social and economic formation may well break apart – at South Africa's expense.[48]

Martin suggests the South African state and South African capital are oblivious to the depth and implications of this transformation as they are either confident of their sub-imperial role or "focused on short-term calculations and policies."[49]

I want to complicate the picture and suggest that South African capital is acutely aware of its limitations. In fact, the South Africans are banking on cultural productions to compete for capturing these markets and remain competitive with the Chinese. As I have pointed out earlier South Africa's cultural production is spreading across the continent, creating opportunities for South African capital and exposing millions to its political and social discourses and these dynamics are visible in the case of reality television.

Big Brother Africa and the other host of continental reality TV shows that followed in its wake are therefore an attempt by M-Net/Multichoice to secure a greater share of the television market in Africa and to expand its existing footprint. The shows developed in *Big Brother Africa*'s wake include ones with continental reach (*Project Fame, Face of Africa, The Apprentice Africa*, etc.) as well as regional or national versions (*Idols West Africa, Idols East Africa, Big Brother Nigeria*). As an M-Net producer told journalists, MultiChoice Africa aggressively pushed a continental *Big Brother Africa* in an attempt to encourage middle-class people outside South Africa to buy their own television sets, and eventually to subscribe to satellite television services:

> The decision to expand *Big Brother* across Africa was taken for purely business reasons. M-Net is growing faster in other African countries than in South Africa.[50]

Such considerations were clearly behind the choice of contestants for the inaugural *Big Brother Africa* show. Of the twelve contestants in the first series, eleven came from countries where English was the lingua franca among elites, while one contestant was from a Portuguese-speaking country (Angola). The overwhelming presence of contestants from Southern Africa reflected the region's status as M-Net's number one decoder and satellite television services market. Market considerations dictated the inclusion of Ghana and Nigeria too and the choice of Angola – M-Net's fastest-growing client base outside South Africa – as well. That formula has held in subsequent editions of the show.

The maturation of the local pay-TV market in South Africa means M-Net has to expand beyond the country's borders. As a result it has developed specialized "bouquets" of channels specifically targeted at niche markets within the continent. These include series of channels aimed at Francophone and Anglophone Africans respectively, the Portuguese-speaking countries, and a large Asian audience in East Africa.[51] *Big Brother Africa* helped to increase this market considerably. One report pointed to the show's effect in this regard:

> From a business perspective, *Big Brother* [*Africa*] has been a runaway success for M-Net and MultiChoice … Satellite dishes and cable subscriptions are up since the show began in late May, and cell phone usage is booming as well with text messages voting out contestants every week.[52]

Second, a number of South African corporations investing heavily in the rest of the continent underwrote the program. They included M-Net/MultiChoice Africa itself and the main South African cell phone providers, Vodacom and MTN. All three companies aggressively market their products on the continent, primarily (though not exclusively) to middle-class audiences.

M-Net is keenly aware of the potential that the wider African market represents and, in response, has launched a variety of programs aimed at audiences across the continent. Among these is an African version of the US music television channel MTV, called MTV Base and sited in Johannesburg, as well as continental versions of the reality talent contest *Project Fame* (where contestants compete for a recording contract). It has also débuted *Face of Africa*, a program in which competitors vie for the prize of a modeling contract in North America or Western Europe.[53]

Does China's presence seriously challenge South Africa's strategy to combine capitalist and cultural expansion? The Chinese investment does not prevent any threat to the South African media and cultural domination.

There are a number of reasons why this won't happen soon. First the Chinese investment is very focused: in construction, exporting cheap commodities (second, clothing, which is hardly associated with upward mobility), and resource extraction (through mining). Cultural relations hardly forms part of this investment strategy. One criticism of the Chinese workers and investors in Africa is that they keep to themselves in compounds. The South African behavior in Tanzania is an exception. Second, as far as media is concerned, Chinese television does not need or see African TV markets as desirable. Chinese TV is very inward looking. While the Chinese state okayed the financing of an international news channel (with some cultural programming) to promote China overseas, that channel does not have a strategy for Africa. (In contrast, CCTV launched an Arabic language channel in mid-2009.[54]) Instead CCTV 9 (the international news channel) is aimed at Chinese expatriates (it reaches 30 million Chinese living overseas via satellite and broadcasts in English, Spanish and French) and the presentation of program content is very formal (it copies the news studio format of most major American and European broadcasts).

The audience numbers for the state-run CCTV, whose multi-channel package dominates television in China (and which also hosts the international news channel), are astronomical. It has a TV audience " ... vastly larger than every major television in the United States and Europe combined." For example, " ... while NBC [which had a monopoly on coverage of the Beijing Olympics, celebrated] average prime-time audiences of 29 million viewers in the United States," CCTV recorded an average audience of half a billion people for the opening ceremony of the Olympics, with 842 million people watching at least a minute of the opening ceremony.[55]

CCTV's status as an instrument of the state and its ties to the ruling party's views of China, means – in contrast to the South African M-Net – that its news and programming is heavily censored " ... and packaged largely to show the country's happy, harmonious moments, to inspire pride in the people, and, if necessary, unify them against a common enemy."[56] Chinese investors work closely with African governments – many who are repressive, socially conservative and do not take easily to criticism. The kind of politics that M-Net's *Big Brother Africa* encourages – conflict, questioning of authority, sexual freedom, etc. – is hardly in sync with CCTV's values. CCTV also bans "Western programming" during prime time.[57]

More significant factors, however, are what are often referred to in shorthand as "cultural differences," but which can be more accurately described as a mix of low levels of immigration to and emigration from Africa as well as little knowledge of the African continent or Africans. Some scholars have suggested that immigration, especially African immigration, is an "unfamiliar issue" among Chinese.[58] Chinese anti-black racism also plays a major role.

Conclusion

Reality TV certainly – and predictably – taps into and engages with existing discourses about national (and, in the case of *Big Brother Africa*, continental) identities, gender as well as class politics. But as I argue here, it also cements South Africa's place as a globalizing force, separate and independent from those countries and corporations academics and researchers usually associate with globalization.

South African-produced reality television exposes millions of Africans to that country's political and social discourses. South Africa is the only country on the continent that constitutionally protects its subjects' sexual orientation. It also has the most developed television industry on the continent, both in terms of its reach, its resources, but also the diversity of its content. Through reality television, continental audiences – often shielded from such open and robust debate in their countries – are exposed to questions of identity, class and gender, in a very matter-of-fact way. It is also not surprising that when the season wraps up, the winners or at least the balance of the contestants usually declare that they will stay in South Africa "forever." Reports quote contestants saying "the best opportunities are here," and that South Africa "is rich in opportunities."

The expansion of South African reality television products increasingly takes on a continental flavor and South African producers retain either primary or considerable co-production credits for these new reality shows.

Studying reality television in South Africa broadens the manner in which scholars approach cultural, especially media, phenomena. Despite increasing attention to reality television and its wider impact, there is still very little scholarly research on the genre in the developing world. The research and commentary that exist deal largely with the North American and Western European contexts and focus very much on "the implications of questionable production techniques, ethics, and the effects of globalization for television culture and production."[59] Africa is missing in these analyses, and when developments on the continent are addressed there is a tendency to transfer insights and conclusions from the rest of the world uncritically to its shores. While some of the characteristics of reality television encountered elsewhere are also present in Africa, it seems clear that generalizations are of little use in analyzing the phenomenon as it presents itself on the continent.[60] An African, and here specifically South African, focus does a lot to alter this scholarly reality.

Notes

1 The arguments in the first section of this chapter are discussed at length in my article, "Big Brother, Africa is Watching," *Media, Culture and Society*, 29 (6), 2007: 851–68.

2 "How the world rates South Africa," http://www.southafrica.info/business/economy/globalsurveys.htm (October 2008).

3 See Robert Kinloch Massie, *Loosening the Bonds: The United States and South Africa in the Apartheid Years* (New. York: Nan A. Talese, 1997); James Sanders, *South Africa and the International Media, 1972–1979: A Struggle for Representation* (London: Routledge, 2000); Mahmood Mamdani, *Good Muslim, Bad Muslim: America, The Cold War and the Roots of Terror* (Pretoria: Jacana, 2005).

4 Sean Jacobs, "The Exit of George Bush's Point Man in Africa," Huffingtonpost.com, September 26, 2008; Sean Jacobs, "Could Africa be the Real Legacy of George Bush," *The National*, October 23, 2008, http://www.thenational.ae/article/20081022/OPINION/193766832/1006/FOREIGN

5 For more on the *Proudly South African* Campaign see http://www.proudlysa.co.za; for the International Marketing Council see http://www.brandsouthafrica.com/; and the Industrial Development Corporation see http://www.idc.co.za/Overview%20of%20the%20IDC.asp

6 Mbembe, "At the Edge of the World: Boundaries, Territoriality and Sovereignty in Africa," published in *Public Culture*, 12 (1), 2000: 260–61. See also Philip Rekacewicz (Translated by Anne-Maria Boitumelo Makhulu), "Mapping Concepts (Cartographier la pensée)," *Public Culture*, 12(3), 2000: 703–6.

7 Mbembe, "At the Edge of the World: Boundaries, Territoriality and Sovereignty in Africa," published in *Public Culture*, 12 (1), 2000: 268.

8 Mbembe 2000, p269.

9 *Public Culture*, vol. 16, no. 3 (2004): 347–72.

10 Achille Mbembe and Sarah Nuttall, "Writing the World from an African Metropolis," *Public Culture* 16 (3), 2004, p352.

11 Mbembe and Nuttall, p351, 357.

12 Mbembe, 2000, p276.

13 http://www.mnetafrica.com/bigbrother/Default.aspx [Accessed on November 26, 2008].

14 See http://www.dstvafrica.com; http://www.bigbrotherafrica.com/

15 See "An African Big Brother Unites and Delights," *Washington Post*, July 14, 2003: A1; "Africa's Sexy Big Brother Cuts Across Great Divide," *The Times* (London), July 16, 2003; "Africa's Satellite Effect: They Are Creating the First Pan-African TV Networks – and Hits," *Newsweek* (International Edition), August 18, 2003: 19; "Reality TV, African Style," *Time* (European Edition), June 23, 2003; "Reality TV Houses Africa Under One Roof," *International Herald Tribune*, September 10, 2003.

16 *Time* (European Edition), June 23, 2003.

17 "A Chance to 'Visit' the Birthplace of our BBA Housemates," *Sunday Times* (South Africa), August 24, 2003.

18 "Reality TV Hit Unites Africa in 'Brother'-Hood," *Christian Science Monitor*, July 8, 2003: 1. See also: "Zambian churches Demand End to 'Immoral' Big Brother," *Mail*

& Guardian, July 4, 2003; "Sexy Reality TV Show Angers Church Leaders," *InterPress Service/Global Information Network*, July 23, 2003; "Now KK joins BBA winner Cherise frenzy," *Times of Zambia*, September 12, 2003; *Daily Independent* (Nigeria), July 21, 2003.
19 *Accra Daily Mail* (Ghana), August 11, 2003.
20 *Time*, June 23, 2003.
21 Ibid.
22 *Times of Zambia*, September 12, 2003.
23 "So, why watch *Big Brother?*" *The East African*, September 27, 2008.
24 Natasha Uys, "*Big Brother Africa 3*. Munya, the Bridesmaid," *The Namibian*, November 27, 2008.
25 " 'I love Men': Tawana," *Sowetan*, November 18, 2008. Online at http://www.sowetan.co.za/News/Default.aspx?id=127724
26 "*Big Brother Africa*: What is the Point?" *Accra Mail*, November 25, 2008.
27 "Reality TV Houses Africa Under One Roof," *International Herald Tribune*, September 10, 2003.
28 "*Big Brother Africa 3* – Is Malawi Going to Clean Up," *The Namibian*, November 19, 2008.
29 *The Namibian*, November 12, 2008.
30 *Mail & Guardian Online*, September 9, 2003; "The Lady Who Charmed Africa," *Saturday Nation* (Zambia), September 13, 2003.
31 "Controversial Big Brother Winner Becomes Zambia's Ambassador," *Xinhua News Agency-CEIS*, September 10, 2003.
32 *Times of Zambia*, September 12, 2003. It is telling that, in September 2004, another Zambian winner of a continental reality television series – Lindiwe Alamu, winner of *Project Fame*, the next big continental reality show after *Big Brother Africa* – was also granted a diplomatic passport by the Zambian government. She was only the third person to have been so rewarded. The other was the former captain of the national football team, Kalusha Bwalya.
33 "*Big Brother Africa 3*: Coming oh so close!" *The Namibian*, November 27, 2008; Maureen Odubeng, "BB3 was quite an experience – Hazel," *Mmegi*, November 26, 2008.
34 See biographies of contestants on the official website: http://www.bigbrotherafrica.com/
35 *The Times* (London), July 16, 2003.
36 "On the Media," WNYC Radio, New York City, August 8, 2003. Transcript of Broadcast.
37 Neil McCarthy, "The New Aspirational," *The Media* (supplement to the *Mail & Guardian*), March 1, 2005.
38 Bill Martin, "South Africa's Subimperial Futures: Washington Consensus, Bandung Consensus or a People's Consensus," *Afriples*, 6 (October 2008), p2.
39 Martin, p7.
40 Quoted in Patrick Bond, "African Development/Governance, South African Subimperialism and Nepad," CODESRIA Conference on "The Agrarian Constraint and Poverty Reduction" (Addis Ababa, Ethiopia), December 17–19, 2004, p38.
41 Richard Schroeder, "South African Capital in the Land of Ujamaa: Contested Terrain in Tanzania," *Afrifiles*, 5 (September), 12, 2008.
42 Schroeder, p19.
43 Schroeder, p14.
44 Quoted in Martin, p4.
45 Martin, p5.
46 Ibid.
47 *Far Eastern Economic Review*, October 2008, p64.
48 Martin, p6.
49 Ibid., p2.

50 *"Big Brother Africa* Sparks Controversy," *Times of Zambia,* July 5, 2003.
51 "Endemol Appoints Joint MDs in South Africa," Press Release, 10 November 2008.
52 *International Herald Tribune,* September 10, 2003.
53 *"Project Fame* to Replace *Big Brother Africa," Accra Daily Mail* (Ghana), April 13, 2004.
54 "CCTV launches Arabic international channel," CCTV.com, July 24, 2009.
55 David Barboza, "Olympics Are Ratings Bonanza for Chinese TV," *New York Times,* August 22, 2008; CCTV.com ("About Us"); see also CSM Media Research, online at: http://www.csm.com.cn/en/business/b4.html
56 Barboza, 2008, Ibid. See also Shirong Chen, "China TV faces propaganda charge," BBC News, January 12, 2009.
57 Noreen O'Leary, "CCTV: One Network, 1.1 Billion Viewers," *Adweek,* February 5, 2007.
58 See the work of Adams Bodomo, based at the University of Hong Kong, quoted in Evan Osnos, "The Promised Land," *The New Yorker,* February 9, 2009, Vol 85, Issue 1, p50–55.
59 Jacques Vinson, "Review of Shooting People: Adventures in Reality TV by Sam Brenton and Reuben Cohen," *The Velvet Light Trap,* 54 (Fall), 2004: 80–82; see also Annette Hill and Gareth Palmer, "Editorial: *Big Brother," Television & New Media,* 3 (2002): 251–54; Paddy Scannell, *"Big Brother* as a Television Event," *Television & New Media,* 3 (3), 2002: 271–82; Minna Aslamma, "Flagging Finnishness: Reproducing National Identity in Reality Television," *Television & New Media,* 8 (1) (2007): 49–67.
60 Some exceptions are Laura Hubbard and Kathryn Mathers, "Surviving American Empire in Africa: The anthropology of reality television," *International Journal of Cultural Studies,* 7 (4) (2004): 437–55; Nick Shepherd and Kathryn Matters, "Who's Watching Big Brother? Reality Television and Cultural Power in South Africa," *Africa e Mediterranei* 38 (2002): 67–69.

Chapter 13

Making populations appear

Nick Couldry

Introduction

Reality TV is more than just a series of texts or generic variations. At the very least, reality TV needs to be understood as a form whereby objects, mechanisms of representation, and people (producers, participants, audiences) are arranged so as to sustain claims – plausible at *some* level – that social "reality" is presented through these means. This social form (in many varieties) has persisted for nearly two decades across an ever-expanding range of countries. Five years ago, the death of reality TV was widely predicted, yet we are now debating its political implications on a global scale. This persistence is not guaranteed into the future, but so far it has surprised many, and so too needs explanation. If "reality production" proves an enduring social form in late twentieth-century and early twenty-first-century media – even as media interfaces undergo huge transformation – then we need to understand why.

Dominant so far have been explanations that prioritize economic factors and one type of political factor (neoliberalism and/or biopolitics). While I will acknowledge those explanations' importance, I will link them to wider dynamics. We need here to separate long-term factors from shorter-term, more "local" (and more obviously contingent) factors. My wider aim will be to formulate ways of thinking about the phenomenon of reality TV that facilitate international comparative research. In so doing, I will extend aspects of my earlier analysis of how media rituals contribute to media's role in the development of modernity.[1]

Long-term contexts for interpreting reality TV

Many analysts dismiss the "reality" claims of reality TV, as if the word "reality" was here just a dead metaphor. Of course audiences discount such claims, if made explicitly. But that doesn't mean audiences (any more than marketers) treat these claims to "reality" as trivial. As research by Bev Skeggs, Helen Wood and Nancy Thumim and even more recently by Katherine Sender brings out,[2] whether or not people say they discount such "reality" claims does not affect whether they act on them, for example, by treating reality shows as sources of knowledge or as presenting real moral choices. Authenticity is something people look for in reality TV, as Annette Hill's audience research has brought out.[3] Ignoring this cuts us off from recognizing a wider process of which reality TV is part: the constant, contested but generally naturalized construction of media institutions as privileged sites for accessing "our" social "realities," and the myths associated with that construction. So it is exactly from this reality claim that our framework for analyzing reality media should start.

Reality TV and the myth of the mediated center

Media invest a lot of effort in reinforcing the legitimacy of their symbolic power,[4] or even better its naturalness – when they tell us that we must watch because everyone is watching (*Big Brother, American Idol*), when they tell us they know what a nation thinks (*Daily Mail, New York Post*). In English such claims are even condensed in language. As Todd Gitlin notes,[5] we often slip the definite article in front of the word "media" – *the* media. But what object is referred to by this term? What is at stake in this language?

There are of course many media, and important contrasts between them; recognizing that has never been more important, as media interfaces have proliferated in the past decade. But I highlight the term "the media" in order to emphasize that this term's apparent naturalness is part of a much larger, ongoing social *construction* whose relevance extends far beyond the vagaries of the English language. In my book *Media Rituals* I called this construction "the myth of the mediated centre,"[6] by which I mean the *claim* that "the media" are our privileged access-point to society's center or core. This myth enfolds another myth, "the myth of the center," the idea that "societies," nations, have not just a physical or organizational center – a place that allocates resources – but a center in a different sense, a generative center that explains the social world's functioning and is the source of its values. In isolating this myth, I was attempting to extend an earlier analysis of media power,[7] and the highly dispersed processes whereby that power is legitimated, that in turn had drawn on late twentieth-century readings of power as pervasive and decentered (Foucault, Bourdieu, Actor Network Theory). The broad, seemingly ever-expanding phenomenon of "reality media" can be productively analyzed both as a site of media rituals[8] and as an instantiation of the myth of the mediated center. Indeed that myth is a good starting-point for developing a framework for analyzing comparatively how reality TV is embedded in institutional settings across the world.

The mythical object – "the media" – is not a trivial construction. *Socially*, it sounds like an answer to Durkheim's question about what bonds sustain a society as a society.[9] Durkheim's account of how social bonds are built through ritual has remarkable overlaps with how we have talked about "the media" – as what everyone is watching, as the place where we all gather together.[10] We must be wary of course of functionalism in our readings of society and media, yet some version of that functionalism is a real force in everyday life, and that discourse helps sustain media institutions (in all their particularity) as a site of general importance in our lives. *Politically*, the idea that media provide a representative space for a social "totality" is crucial to how languages of politics in modernity have developed, since by this fiction, media can be treated as providing the means through which governments can plausibly assume they appear to "their" populations, and their populations appear to them. This is not to claim media's representational spaces are co-terminous with "our world," or provide our only space of politics: it is the functionalism of such claims that I seek to avoid by emphasizing the *constructive* work necessary to sustain the fiction of "the media." In the *economic* domain, media's role in focusing attention in particular directions, and the cultural work necessary to sustain this role, is relied upon not just by media industries (ratings) but by marketing industries generally. This is part of the cultural *supplement* to political economy explanations of media power; in times of economic instability, particularly in media markets, it is even more important that we think about how this cultural supplement works in tandem with economic pressures.

In these interlocking domains (social, political, economic), then, a great deal is at stake in "the media's" claimed ability to make populations appear, and to make a "world-in-common" appear to populations. The emergence and continuity of reality TV as a social form needs, I suggest, to be interpreted as part of this process. But this process is itself subject currently to various complex transformations to which I now turn.

Challenges to the myth of the mediated center

If reality TV should be first understood as part of a wider construction of "the media" as socially central, it is necessarily caught up on the tensions to which the myth of the mediated center is now subject. Those tensions require ever more work if that myth is to be sustained.

Socially, if the claim of "liveness" was an essential component in the construction of "the media" as socially central[11] because "liveness" captures our sense that we *must* switch on centrally transmitted media to check "what's going on," then we must note how new forms of "liveness" are emerging through online interfaces and mobile media that are primarily *interpersonal* and so potentially more continuous than mass media have ever been.[12] Is there emerging a sense of social "liveness" – mediated, yes, but not by central media institutions? Manuel Castells and his co-authors suggest that a new "mobile youth culture" is emerging that helps young people "set up their own connections, bypassing the mass media."[13] So will interpersonal media become people's primary mode of connection, with "the media" increasingly incidental to our checks on what our friends are up to? Will this challenge our notion of media as socially central? This is unlikely but, to see why, we need to consider some other dimensions.

Politically, the remarkable events of Barack Obama's 2008 election should not allow us to forget the more pessimistic narratives in recent decades about the declining trend of engagement in mainstream politics, in many countries including the USA (Pharr and Putnam 2000).[14] Outside of the USA, where voter turnout rose in 2008, the broader context – longer-term fears in some countries that turnout, particularly among the under-25s, will stabilise below or close to 50 per cent[15] – provides a troubling context for considering whether governments will be able in future to assume that media provide an effective means for making "their" populations appear and for them to reach those populations. Although the Obama campaign *did* tap into social networking sites for political mobilization, and benefited from huge attention from mainstream media also, the question for the future is whether, in less exceptional circumstances, governments will be able to use these extra-media focuses of social attention as sites for reaching populations: Barack Obama's one million "friends" on Facebook may prove an exception, not the norm.

In the *economic* domain, the uncertainty is of a different nature. As the search for advertising audiences intensifies, marketers are already using the counter-space of social networking sites as an important alternative to television for reaching consumers: media institutions from the BBC and NBC to music majors to commercial brands are all building profiles in social networking sites to create a "buzz" about bands, products and programs. Consistently with the above analysis, falling advertising revenues have *generated* a cultural response, that is an attempt to renegotiate where and how "we" must focus our attention. Long-term, I suspect, new interpersonal media, far from being divorced from centrally produced media flows, will become increasingly intertwined with them in a sort of *double helix*. There is a complication, for sure, since this dynamic – the attempt to recreate the general pull of fashion in new ways – will interact with a competing dynamic (whose source is also intensified economic competition): the pressure to narrowcast audiences and to obtain their loyalty by differentiating consumers' needs and performance (what Joseph Turow has recently called "niche envy").[16] We cannot be sure how these contradictory economic pressures (aggregating and disaggregating) will play out. But the aggregating pressures condensed in the construction of "the media" are likely to remain an important part of the mix for the foreseeable future.

A potential comparative frame

So far I have argued that reality TV is best seen as part of a much wider process that I have called "the myth of the mediated center." By examining the tensions to which that myth is now subject, at least in particular territories, I have brought out how this broad analytic framework allows us to get a broader perspective – that *links* social, economic and political dynamics – on how reality TV's claims have come to matter. Clearly my account of the myth of the mediated center and its tensions, formulated above in terms shaped by media's role in Europe and North America, remains a hypothesis to be tested and possibly reformulated afresh for other parts of the world. No assumption is made here that such tensions are universal: Indian and Chinese media/advertising markets, for example, are (subject to the current economic downturn) in a phase of long-term growth, leading to the possibility that in those countries "the myth of the mediated center" may, in relation to a large proportion of the population, be digitally enhanced from the outset. Nor, of course, can we assume there is one form of modernity or ignore the highly particular ways in which, for example, histories of state formation or the institutionalization of religion have shaped modernity in different places, and media's varying role within such processes.

I will return more explicitly at the end to the comparative implications of this long-term framing of the phenomenon of reality TV. I want first to turn to some other dynamics of reality TV that are more directly contingent. Under this category, I will deliberately, if provocatively, include neoliberalism, sometimes discussed as if it was universal.

Contingencies

If the continuing pressure to sustain media institutions' status as a privileged access-point to "what's going on" is, I would suggest, a feature of all states where media institutions have been an important feature of modernity – with reality TV one clear form for working through that long-term pressure – there is still a great deal to say about the particular pressures that have encouraged this form, this particular "solution," to that broader problem. Here is where I rejoin other accounts of reality TV, since there is something like consensus on some of the key factors.

The economics of form

Few would disagree that economic factors were crucial to the initial emergence of reality TV. While similar factors affected many countries,[17] in the UK growing competition in the television market with satellite and cable expansion, alongside the Thatcher government's pressure on public broadcasting to cut costs and operate more "commercially" (the Peacock Report), quite obviously favoured program forms that were cheap, yet in economic (audience) terms sustainable. Even if the *idea* of presenting so-called "ordinary people" (that is, those outside media institutions)[18] as actors had its source in a longer documentary tradition and, quite plausibly, in rising tensions about the representative authority of "the media" themselves, the economic advantages of early reality TV formats were of overriding importance.[19]

The ways in which such basic economic pressures translated into formal patterns has, however, particular interest.[20] Because the point of reality TV is to attract regular audience attention for non-professional performers, but without the expense of a formal plot, it needs a temporal structure targeted at "*events*" which "cannot" be missed. It is not accidental that reality programs which a few years ago tried to narrativize observation (observing staff at an airport, a hotel, and so on) have in part been replaced by programs that, as John Corner puts it,[21] "build their own social" – within event-structures constructed for the purpose (*Big Brother*, *Survivor*, *American Idol*). Those event-structures require critical moments – how better to generate these than through *judging* behavior between characters, who thus become "contestants"? (Clearly there are older lineages of popular culture – the singing contest, the talent show[22] – to draw on here.) This in turn requires recognizable *forms of authority* through which decisions are rati-fied. In reality TV, media draw on various external forms of authority in order to fill out their wider authority to present "the social": the psychologist as judge of the "facts" of general human nature, the industry expert (music producers, professional chefs and so on) as judges of skill. The economic advantages of *game-like* structures (as ways of generating events based on judgements) have further consequences: game-based forms shield media's underlying claim to social knowledge from direct criticism (it's only a game!), and guarantee a structure whose detailed rules are difficult to challenge (if you're playing the game!). It is rare for contestants explicitly and publicly to challenge the rules of reality TV and those who do get treated harshly. In the UK *Big Brother*'s third series one contestant reacted to the tedium of the house, quite rationally you might have thought, by reading a book in the bedroom – he got voted off and heavily criticized in public for this by the show's presenter (29 and 31 May 2002).

Teaching and judging "reality" in the UK

Various pressures then (above all economic) encouraged particular resolutions of the problem of how to embody media institutions' authority and make populations "appear" in new popular entertainment formats. But equally important are the factors favoring particular inflections of the basic forms of reality TV as meaningful. I want to resist the temptation to reduce all such content-related factors to just one, neoliberalism, for reasons that will become clear later on. My discussion will focus on the UK.

In the UK (and perhaps other countries) an important factor behind the growth of reality TV may be not so much neoliberalism, as the growing opacity of the social world. Individuals, if we follow Axel Honneth's recent analysis, operate in a social world with fewer clear signals about values, more incitements to mark themselves off from others through consumption, and increasingly abstract measures of their "performance" – a conflict that Honneth claims is "making [individual] lives into fiction."[23] The "fiction" that results from this gap between people's lives and the narratives available for making sense of them is, arguably, filled through reality TV's various forms of instruction and guidance. This incitement towards "instruction" is inflected, without doubt, by wider fea-tures of UK society, particularly its growing inequality and indeed inhospitability as a place for receiving instruction! If we exclude housing, the top 10 per cent share of UK national wealth increased (by more than 20 per cent) to 71 per cent between 1986 and 2003, while in terms of income the UK top 10 per cent purchasing power is nearly 14 times more than that of the bottom 10 per cent (this is according to the UNDP's comparative figures); the latter figures suggest the UK is twice as unequal as Germany and Sweden and three times more unequal than Japan (in the US however the multiple was nearly 16). That opaque and increasingly unequal world is one that has provided poor conditions for young people as they grow up. A much cited 2007 UNICEF report on child well-being placed the UK bottom out of 21 rich countries and identified the UK as one of only 2 countries where less than 50 per cent of children found their peers "kind and helpful."[24]

Underlying pressures towards formats where "ordinary people" compete at everyday tasks have in the UK intersected with an older tradition of media's pedagogic authority (one of the staples of the Reithian BBC): from television in the UK we can learn not only how to cook or undergo "extreme adventures" but also how to decorate our rooms, move house, go on a date, even see potential criminals learn what prison is "really like" (*Banged Up*, Channel 5 2008). This last example illustrates how such pedagogy is often purely *vicarious*: one is encouraged to watch others very distant from oneself undergo a pedagogic experience before the hybrid authority of television. Note also the equally bizarre *Fast Food Junkies Go Native*, Channel 4 2008, which took overweight people to remote rural Pakistan to experience the local diet and work routine. In the UK, such reality-based pedagogy has become an arena where barely disguised judgements of *class* have become acceptable again,[25] notwithstanding Tony Blair's vision of a "classless society."

Political irony aside, what is most striking about this new popular version of "the media's" social and pedagogic authority is how it works, not through impersonal instruction delivered to an unseen and anonymous audience (as in cooking and gardening programmes till the 1980s), but through *judgements* meted out *in public* on *the bodies of "ordinary people"* in all their particularity and vulnerability. While aspects of this process are specific to the UK's tortured class politics, the USA for example shares the increase in inequality in recent decades and, as Ouellette and Hay demonstrate,[26] offers many examples of pedagogy through "reality-based" media judgement.

Neoliberalism

It is only at this point in exploring the dynamics of reality TV that we need to consider what impact neoliberalism has had. By neoliberalism here I mean the complex of forces – discursive/economic/organisational/political – which have converged to sustain a view of the social world that gives absolute priority (in terms of explanation, organization and values) to the market,[27] and have therefore helped marketize social space and the relations between government and governed. This does not, whatever the rhetoric, involve a simple withdrawal of the state from social space, but on the contrary the installation as common sense of new principles of organization that Rose calls "degovernmentalization" (1996), because it involves forms of power that seek, so far as possible, *not* to rely on the explicit orders of the state.[28] An analogous process has been under way in the corporate domain whereby power in corporate settings is displaced in new forms of "self-management" that, because of the norms they entrench, are wholly consistent with the increasing arbitrariness and violence of authority's actual operations.[29]

Take the UK version of *The Apprentice* where the US show's Donald Trump is replaced by the abrasive working-class entrepreneur Sir Alan Sugar. Here the most important rule is that Sir Alan Sugar's personal authority overrides everything else;[30] indeed contestants show *character* by submitting to that authority in all its arbitrariness. A clear illustration came towards the end of Series 2 when Sir Alan confronted Paul (who had been on the winning team in every previous task and so hadn't yet appeared to defend himself before Sir Alan in the programme's "Boardroom"). Here's Sir Alan: "the fact that you've won all the tasks doesn't mean jack shit to me because *I* haven't talked with you yet. So you speak to me now, you speak to me now, because, I'm telling you, it's getting close to that door." So the message was clear – playing by the rules, doing all the approved tasks, counts for nothing, unless you have proven yourself *in front of* Sir Alan. This rule fits rather well with working conditions in those neoliberal democracies where, as Richard Sennett says,[31] corporate authority is increasingly personalized and charismatic. The argument can be extended to shows such as *Big Brother*, where the arbitrary authority and compulsory emotional labor of today's workplaces is translated, in disguised form, into the rules of harmless play, within what I have called a "secret theatre."[32]

There is no doubt a strong case for the convergence in the UK and USA between wider social and economic regulation under neoliberalism and reality show formats,[33] with US shows offering a clear case of television "filling out" domains of social instruction and guidance from which federal governments have withdrawn, telling citizens to rely on self-discipline. Neoliberalism is not, however, a master-narrative for understanding reality TV. Reality TV is better seen as a site where the authority of "the media" – their distinctive claim, however playful, to give us a privileged access to the social world – is doing work, in alliance with other types of authority, to present the social world in a consistent way: as a place where the complexity of people's experiences and motives is easily reducible to *rules*; where one key rule is that submission to continuous *surveillance*[34] and the judgement of *external* authority is necessary for "self-improvement" or self-development. The result is a new form of mediated authority, enacted in public, in which not just neoliberalism but multiple overlapping factors – of varying sorts and temporalities, economic, social and political – converge. This causal complexity suggests that reality TV is not just a format, but something more like what the great German sociologist Norbert Elias called a "*figuration*" which in highly condensed form enacts, through the bodies and judgements of individuals, the outcome of many types of mutual dependency and pressure.[35] So far all I have done is recharacterize an emerging consensus about the deeper social and political implications of reality TV's particular way of making populations appear, particularly among North American and European writers. But it is clear we can't stop the story here.

Complications

There are two types of factor which require us to complicate the story told so far: first, international comparison; second, the site of the audience.

Marwan Kraidy's work[36] has brought out how in the Middle East, with its distinctive constellation of media, political and social authority, reality TV becomes an important site for rearticulating issues of national identity and religious authority, while neoliberalism, for example, is rarely directly relevant as a frame of analysis. Indeed we would expect the stakes in an overdetermined figuration such as reality TV to vary from place to place (Elias was one of the classical sociologists most committed to comparative analysis). Comparative research into reality TV requires the largest possible set of reference-points and framing reality TV as part of a wider social conflict over the construction of "the media" provides this. Within this broader frame, we can expect a number of possibilities:

1   cases where the very construction of "the media" is interpreted not consensually, but as acting *against alternative* constructions of society's "center" (for example, religion or secular authoritarian power);
2   variations in the range of forces competing over "the media" (in some places religious organizations, in others competing political forces, in still others competing models of economic organization);
3   cases where the territory over which a given reality TV form circulates does not match with the boundaries of political or state power (the Middle East with its regional television flows being a key example), creating obvious conflicts of authority;
4   variations in the degree to which the act of *becoming visible in media* as an "ordinary person" (essential to reality TV) is itself socially regulated or constrained for particular groups, for example women or ethnic minorities.

To the extent that in any location one of these axes coincides with wider social or political faultlines, then we would expect that a discourse dominant elsewhere (such as neoliberalism) will *not* be the primary reference-frame for reality TV in that location, even before we consider the uneven global circulation of neoliberal discourse itself. In addition, there may be uncertainties whether "the myth of the mediated center" has been successfully constructed at all in a particular location, or, even if it has, whether it is now subject to collapse (a more radical version of the tensions discussed earlier). These are the sorts of possibilities that a comparative analysis of reality TV could hope to explore.

The second complicating factor is what, for shorthand, we can still call the "audience." My point is not the banal one that analyzing the effectivity of texts requires an account of audiences' possibilities of resistant interpretation. The default assumption that audience "decoding" is a site of freedom has long been exploded.[37] Texts become embedded in action, thought and belief – with significant implications for power – far beyond any initial act of "reading," and a key aim of analyzing reality TV and other "media rituals" was to highlight this point. My point instead is that, in so far as media forms such as reality TV carry traces of wider contests over authority and power, we need to find out rather more than we currently know about *how* those forms get embedded in everyday life. Do traces of neoliberal models of self-government in a reality show get circulated in forms of everyday talk ("the Apprentice" as office joke?) or in individual forms of playful acting-out? What forms of informal collective play (for example the exchange of comments and opinions at the climax of a show such as *American Idol*) are now common? But reality TV formats may also be embedded in quite different ways, for example in the form of crisis, as where reality TV formats have attracted political or religious attention in Brazil, the Middle East or Southern Africa.[38] At this point, we come face-to-face with a larger difficulty for comparative media analysis, which is the lack of work to date on how to compare "media cultures" rigorously (Hepp and Couldry forthcoming), a topic with which I have no space to deal here.

It is important therefore that our accounts of reality TV do not close down the possible complexities of how cultural formations around reality TV work. Here the overwhelming emphasis of governmentality approaches such as Ouelette and Hay's on discourse runs into some difficulties. Their excellent deconstruction (following Foucault and Rose) of US reality TV only talks about the action of reality TV's discourses on US society, as if social space itself was simply a plane of discourse. Their language for describing television – as "everyday technologies of the self,"[39] as "an integral relay within the entrepreneurial network of welfare provision and private social support"[40] – offers precious little scope for asking the crucial question: *how, by whom, under what circumstances and to what practical ends* does such pedagogy get accepted and internalized? To write, as they do, that "television's lasting value may have to do with its rootedness in daily life, as a serialised framework for personal regimes"[41] only indicates the site of the problem, not the answer. In this, they risk repeating the explanatory foreshortening in Nikolas Rose's work, when he depicts "mass media" as merely one among "a plethora of indirect mechanisms that can *translate* the goals of political, social, economic authorities into the choices and commitments of individuals, *locating them* [citizens] into actual or virtual networks of identification through which they may be governed."[42] This notion of "translation" ignores the question: through what mechanism exactly is it that individuals are "formed," indeed reformed, as subjects?[43] It is here that the reference-point of the myth of the mediated center – related on the macro-level to media's widest claims to social authority and on the micro-level to the minutiae of media's ritualization – can complement governmentality accounts to broaden our understanding of how reality TV works in "society."

Conclusion

The subject of reality TV is complex and multidimensional, and our understanding of it no doubt still incomplete. This chapter has reflected on how best to frame reality TV, as we enter the age of more seriously comparative international research.[44] Unhelpful is any account which reduces reality TV to the operations of one causal dimension, whether of discourse (for example "neoliberal discourse") or the economy, expression of national community, or television history. Reality TV is everywhere a multidimensional (social, political, economic and cultural) process, whose variations need to be understood within a comparative frame that recognizes this complexity.

Our analysis also needs to be in touch with media's broader claims to present social "reality" within the various forms that modernity has taken; "reality media" as an example of those claims has significant political implications. The claim of particular media institutions anywhere to present central social "realities" will always be clothed in language that is variable, often ironic, perhaps discounted by those who encounter it, and multiply determined. But just as the claim to present "reality" is not trivial, neither are the stakes involved in such claims trivial, since behind them lies a contest of wider long-term significance: the continual struggle within modernity to *make populations appear*, whether to governments, markets or to themselves, and so help sustain the plausibility of key assumptions on which modern politics, economies and societies depend.

That is why I suggest we analyze reality TV as first, but not only, an example of media institutions' attempts to claim social authority for themselves, and other institutions' practices of underwriting or buying into such claims. Such processes will play out very differently in different locations, and this variation is something a fully international media studies must explore, along the axes of comparison mentioned above and no doubt more. The modest aim of this chapter has been to provide a framework within which such comparative work might develop.

Notes

1 Nick Couldry, *Media Rituals: A Critical Approach* (London: Routledge, 2003).
2 Beverley Skeggs, Nancy Thumim and Helen Wood, "'Oh Goodness, I *am* Watching Reality TV'; How methods make class in audience research," *European Journal of Cultural Studies* 11 no. 1 (2008): 5–24; K. Sender, "Audiences as Citizens: Management and Meaning in the Reception of Makeover TV Shows," paper presented to ICA preconference on the Global Public Sphere, Montreal, May 2008.
3 Annette Hill, *Reality TV* (London: Routledge, 2004) and *Restyling Factual TV* (London: Routledge, 2007).
4 John Thompson, *The Media and Modernity* (Cambridge: Polity, 1995) and Pierre Bourdieu, *Language and Symbolic Power* (Cambridge: Polity, 1991).

5 Todd Gitlin, *Media Unlimited* (New York: Henry Holt, 2001), 5.

6 Couldry, *Media Rituals*.

7 Nick Couldry, *The Place of Media Power* (London: Routledge, 2000).

8 Couldry, *Media Rituals*, chapter 3.

9 Emile Durkheim, *Elementary Forms of Religious Life* (Chicago: Chicago University Press, 1995 [o.p. 1915]).

10 I have discussed this in much more detail elsewhere: Couldry, *The Place of Media Power*, 14–16, *Media Rituals*, 6–9.

11 Couldry, *The Place of Media Power*, 42–43; Jane Feuer, "The Concept of Live Television" in E. A. Kaplan (ed.), *Regarding Television* (Los Angeles: American Film Institute, 1985), 12–22, at p. 12.

12 See Nick Couldry, "Liveness, 'Reality' and the Mediated Habitus from Television to the Mobile Phone," *The Communication Review* 7, no. 4 (2004): 353–62 for early speculation about the role of mobile phones here, before social networking sites became so dominant.

13 M. Castells, M. Fernandez-Ardevol, J. Qiu and A. Sey, *Mobile Communication and Society: a global perspective* (Cambridge, Mass.: MIT Press, 2007), 1.

14 Susan Pharr and Robert Putnam (eds), *Disaffected Democracies* (Cambridge, Mass.: Harvard University Press, 2000).

15 For the UK, see The Hansard Society, *Fifth Audit of Political Engagement*. www.hansardsociety.org.uk (2008).

16 Joseph Turow, *Niche Envy* (Cambridge: MIT Press, 2007).

17 Richard Kilborn,. "'How Real Can you Get?' Recent Developments in 'Reality' Television," *European Journal of Communication* 9, no. 4 (1994): 421–40.

18 Couldry, *The Place of Media Power*, 46–48.

19 See Ted Magder, "The End of TV 101: Reality Programs, Formats and the New Business of Television" in S. Murray and L. Ouellette (eds), *Reality TV* (New York: New York University Press, 2004), 137–56, and Chad Raphael, "The Political Economic Origins of Reali-TV" in S. Murray and L. Ouellette (eds), *Reality TV* (New York: New York University Press, 2004), 119–36 for helpful accounts of these economic pressures.

20 For an interesting and different reading, see Colin Sparks, "Reality TV: The Big Brother phenomenon," *International Socialism* 114 (2007), www.isj.org.uk.

21 John Corner, "Performing the Real: Documentary Diversions," *Television and New Media* 3, no. 3 (2002): 255–69.

22 Stijn Rijnders, Gerd Rooijakkers and Liesbet van Zoonen, "Community Spirit and Competition in *Idols*: Ritual Meanings of a Television Talent Quest," *European Journal of Communication* 22, no. 3 (2007): 275–93.

23 Axel Honneth, "Organized Self-realization: Some Paradoxes of Individualization," *European Journal of Social Theory* 7, no. 4 (2004): 463–78, at 478.

24 Sources: [UK] Office of National Statistics, 2008, www.ons.gov.uk/; UNDP Human Development Report 2007/8, www.undp.org

25 Angela McRobbie, *The Aftermath of Feminism* (London: Sage, 2008); Deborah Philips, "Transformation Scenes: The Television Series Makeover," *International Journal of Cultural Studies* 8, no. 2 (2007): 213–29.

26 Laurie Ouellette and James Hay, *Better Living Through Reality TV* (Malden, MA: Blackwell, 2008).

27 Pierre Bourdieu, *Acts of Resistance* (Cambridge: Polity, 1998); David Harvey, *A Short History of Neoliberalism* (Oxford: Oxford University Press, 2004), 2; Toby Miller, *Cultural Citizenship* (Philadelphia: Temple University Press, 2007).

28 Wendy Brown, "Neoliberalism and the End of Liberal Democracy," *Theory & Event* 7, no. 1 (2003): 1–23.

29 Richard Sennett, *The Culture of the New Capitalism* (New Haven: Yale University Press, 2006).
30 Nick Couldry and Jo Littler, "Work, Power and Performance: Analysing the 'Reality' Game of *The Apprentice*," *Cultural Sociology* (forthcoming).
31 Sennett, *Culture*.
32 Nick Couldry, "Reality TV, or the Secret Theatre of Neoliberalism," *Review of Education Pedagogy and Cultural Studies* 30, no. 1 (2008): 3–13.
33 Ouellette and Hay, *Better Living*.
34 Mark Andrejevic, *Reality TV: The Work of Being Watched* (Lanham, MD: Rowman and Littlefield, 2004).
35 Norbert Elias, *The Civilizing Process* (Malden, MA: Blackwell, 1994 [o.p. 1939]).
36 Marwan Kraidy, "Saudi Arabia, Lebanon and the Changing Arab Information Order," *International Journal of Communication* 1 (2007): 139–56.
37 Nick Abercrombie and Brian Longhurst, *Audiences* (London: Sage, 1998).
38 Esther Hamburger, "Politics and Intimacy: The Agrarian Reform in a Brazilian Telenovela," *Television and New Media* 1, no. 2 (2000): 159–79; Kraidy, "Saudi Arabia, Lebanon and the Changing Arab Information Order"; Sean Jacobs, "*Big Brother*, Africa is watching," *Media Culture & Society* 29, no. 6 (2007): 851–868.
39 Ouellette and Hay, *Better Living*, 15.
40 Ibid., 31.
41 Ibid., 31.
42 Nikolas Rose, "Governing 'advanced' liberal democracies" in A. Barry, T. Osborne and N. Rose (eds), *Foucault and Political Reason* (London: UCL Press, 1996), 37–64, at p. 58, added emphasis.
43 Judith Butler, *The Psychic Life of Power* (Stanford: Stanford University Press, 1997), 1–2.
44 See the special themed issue of *Global Media and Communications* 3, no. 3, November/December (2007).

Chapter 14

Reality television in new worlds

Marwan M. Kraidy

The Politics of Reality Television stages two conversations. In the first, an established literature grounded in the critique of neoliberalism and located in the US–UK nexus converses with an emerging literature on the social and political lives of reality television in the Global South. In the second, empirically based studies enter in dialogue with a first wave of largely theoretical discussions of reality television. Through these two exchanges, this volume captures not only the expansion of a television genre beyond industrialized Western countries, but attends to a gamut of thematic, conceptual and epistemological challenges that arise when the subject and methods of study cross into new terrains.

Reality television reflects, more conspicuously than other genres, the multiple entanglements of temporalities, scales and narratives that characterize the contemporary media industries: the convergence between "old" and "new" media, new relationships between viewer, text, and context, a fluid articulation of "global" and "local" in the context of the global march of market fundamentalism and local reactions to neoliberal ideology and practices. In a context of privatization, free trade, and media and worldwide liberalization of media and telecommunications, a comparative examination of reality television enables a renewed appreciation of the complicated economic, political and cultural implications of convergent media industries.

By examining changing social relations empirically and across several sites, this volume addresses the ways in which the social and political lives of reality television in France, India, South Africa, the ex-Yugoslavia, Norway, Singapore, Australia and Arab countries, at once re-affirm and challenge approaches and themes forged by scholars studying reality shows in the United States and United Kingdom. As it suggests ways for re-tooling our approaches to reality television, *The Politics of Reality Television* does not aim to stipulate a definitive agenda for the globalization of reality television studies; rather, our objective is to initiate a process of inquiry that takes the globalization of reality television studies as an opportunity to re-think broader connections between media and politics, historically and globally – reality television as a prism refracting the complexities of the contemporary global formation.

A changing political economy

The worldwide popularity of reality television reflects an emerging media environment combining the national and transnational expansion of commercial television, format-adaptation, convergent media platforms, and new labor relations. Reality television is emblematic of the rise of an economic model for television[1] based on the convergence of mobile telephony and the internet with television, on uncompensated amateur labor, and on viewer involvement through nomination and voting. This qualitatively new confluence of technology, labor and affect unfolds in a space formed by the intersection of the global with the national and the local, a junction enabled and regulated by the global trade in television formats. Worldwide, most reality shows are adapted from formats owned as intellectual property by a handful of European companies like Endemol and Fremantle. Format-adaptation is attractive because it eliminates program development costs, standardizes production, and minimizes the risk of commercial failure. A combination on the one hand of convergence between telephony, the internet and television – which requires bottom-up viewer participation – and on the other hand, the political economy of formats – which grafts local sensibilities onto global production norms – undergirds an unstable cultural economy prone to conflict and controversy. The various polemics that have arisen around *Big Brother*'s national (UK, France, Germany) and transnational (pan-African and pan-Arab) versions reflect the propensity of reality television to trigger contentious politics. Grasping how (local) contexts shape the production and reception of (global) reality format adaptations enables a fresh perspective on how we think about the global–local dialectic in media and cultural studies at large.

The success of the reality genre, premised in large part on the rise of convergence and formats, reflects a new stage in media commercialization. Just as reality television in the UK reflects a shift from public service broadcasting values enshrined in the British documentary tradition (Palmer), in Norway (Kjus) reality television emerged as a crucial way for new commercial channels like TV 2 to lure viewers away from public television. In the United States, shows like *American Idol* and *Dancing with the Stars* have rejuvenated the venerable networks which have for two decades been embattled in an era of cable television, niche markets and audience fragmentation. Elsewhere, reality shows have underwritten the expansion of national channels like M-Net in South Africa (Jacobs, this volume) and LBC in Lebanon to major transnational players with new names (respectively MultiChoice Africa and The Lebanese Satellite Channel) reflecting their new geographic reach. In addition to attracting large audiences, the new "interactivity" (nomination, voting, etc.) between viewers and text that is at the heart of the business model of reality television has given marketers more precise information about consumers and fuelled the rise of corporate research on audience "engagement." This worldwide phenomenon is especially important in parts of the world where the audience ratings industry remains woefully underdeveloped.[2] By enabling the capture of increasingly precise information about viewers, interactive features in reality shows close the loop of the new relation between viewer-consumer and text. This, in addition to the increased mobility of the field of media consumption, calls for a re-thinking of terms such as "audience" and "reception," forged in the good old days of broadcasting and family-room television viewing.

The Politics of Reality Television also reflects a crucial contribution of reality television studies to global communication scholarship: labor. With rare exceptions,[3] scholarship on global media has systematically ignored labor issues. As Grindstaff, Andrejevic, Jost, and Wood and Skeggs show, participants in reality television programs produce identity within the constraints imposed on them by the genre and the producers – institutional, legal, dramatic, etc. Andrejevic demonstrates the importance of social class and status by exploring how different groups are treated differently, with children, women and ordinary people's labor remaining unpaid, while celebrity labor is lavishly compensated. Grindstaff's focus on the emotional labor involved in crafting personalities that are both ordinary people and celebrities shows the gendered and ethnicized nature of such labor. Jost shows how reality television contestants can deploy interpretations of the law that enables them to recuperate labor rights. Wood and Skeggs explore how viewers derive positions of moral authority refracted through gender and class, which enables, for example, working-class women to gain agency through the trope of motherhood. The tension between being and acting/laboring spawns a gamut of possibilities ranging from submission to exploitation via uncompensated labor under surveillance, to a partial and contingent recuperation of human agency.

The scales of mediated politics

Contributions to *The Politics of Reality Television* reflect the multiple geographical and political scales of the reality television phenomenon. Reality television's reliance on local adaptations of global formats enables a heuristic perspective to scalar issues, including how the national scale relates to political and economic forces upwards (supra-national) and downwards (subnational). While higher incomes in industrialized countries underwrite *national* reality television shows, lower socio-economic capacities elsewhere have pushed producers to pursue *transnational* audiences in search of economies of scale across geo-linguistic markets: thus in Western Europe each nation-state has had a tailored version of *Big Brother*, but African (Jacobs) and Arab versions of the show addressed multinational audiences.[4] Market size, however, can mitigate low purchasing power, as suggested by the case of *Indian Idol* (Punathambekar), which introduces another scale to the discussion, the sub-national/regional/local. Reality television thus becomes a prism through which to re-evaluate communication processes globally, enabling a felicitous exit from the global–local dialectic that has dominated the field to a more flexible framework that takes into account myriad articulations of the global, the supra-national/regional (i.e. the Arab countries), the national, the sub-national/regional (i.e. Meghalaya in India), and the local.[5]

The articulation of multiple scales exacerbates reality television's potential to generate controversy. The debates that the continental *Big Brother Africa* (Jacobs),[6] the pan-Slavic *To Sam Ja* (Volčič and Andrejevic), and the pan-Arab *Star Academy*[7] activated within and between nations suggest complex and contingent interactions between local, national, regional and global scales. Designed ostensibly to reconcile Bosnians, Croats, Macedonians, Montenegrans, Serbs and Slovenes, *To Sam Ja* incited sectarian tensions between members of those post-Yugoslav nations. In contrast, *Indian Idol* (Punathambekar) re-reshaped how the Northeast states of Meghalaya and Assam, politically and economically marginalized from national life, related to the Indian nation. French reality television (Darling-Wolf) enacts a double gesture, reasserting at once the (local) importance of French traditions and the (global) centrality of France in today's world. This phenomenon includes the United States, where, as several contributors to a volume on the topics have shown, anxieties, discourses, and myths of national identity permeate makeover reality shows.[8]

The worldwide salience of national identity in both textual constructions of reality shows, and public discourse generated by these shows, suggests that *nationalism mediates neoliberalism*.[9] This could mean a seamless takeover of the former by the latter, like in the US and the UK during the 1980s, when Ronald Reagan and Margaret Thatcher combined neoliberal economic policies with a pugnacious nationalism; it could also mean various degrees of appropriation and contestation: multiple contributions to this volume underscore that neoliberalism and nationalism have a complex – and not necessarily antagonistic – relationship. Through the notion of "commercial nationalism," Volčič and Andrejevic explore a specific articulation of the two; Palmer describes reality television's subversion of British documentary's claims to reality; Jacobs shows how *Big Brother Africa* bolsters South African business expansion by promoting the country as a "cool" brand to its neighbors. Regardless of the direction and nature of the relationship between nationalism and neoliberalism, *The Politics of Reality Television* contributes to the restoration of the media/nationalism nexus which has for at least a decade been lost in the multi-disciplinary debate on globalization. The nation, *The Politics of Reality Television* demonstrates, persists as a locus of identity construction and political contestation.

As it is recruited into national projects in need of makeover, sustenance and repair (Darling-Wolf, Jacobs, Lewis, Volčič and Andrejevic) reality television highlights the fluid, in-the-making, and contested dimension of national identity. This, in turn, reflects how neoliberalism is appropriated, resisted and changed by different national and regional contexts, and the ensuing need to fine-tune neoliberal critique in reality television studies. The case of *al-Ra'is*, the pan-Arab version of *Big Brother*, is instructive in that regard. On March 1, 2004, the Saudi-owned, Dubai-based MBC Group shut down *al-Ra'is*, produced in the island nation of Bahrain, after a few hundred people demonstrated against *al-Ra'is* in Manama, Bahrain's capital, on February 27, ostensibly because a Saudi male kissed a Tunisian female on the cheek. This occurred in a minuscule country (population 750,000[10]) that nonetheless has sixteen major political formations, including several Islamist parties and the Economists' Bloc, a (neo) liberal party representing the interests of the business community. To reduce dependence on dwindling oil reserves, developing an infrastructure of financial services has been a central element of national policy.[11] With more than 400 licensed financial institutions, 30 specializing in Islamic finance, Bahrain has successfully branded itself as a transnational financial hub, integrating its financial services in the global economy and focusing on attracting foreign investments.[12] Becoming a member of the General Agreement on Tariffs and Trade (GATT) in 1993 and a founding member of the World Trade Organization,[13] and signing a free trade agreement with the US in 2004, Bahrain is considered a strong proponent of free trade in the Arab world.[14]

Bahrain's economic policies put the country at the neoliberal vanguard among Arab countries, but these policies are intensely contested. As I explored at length elsewhere,[15] the *al-Ra'is* polemic reveals a struggle to define national identity (of Bahrain). This contest is shaped by regional geo-political actors (Saudi Arabia) and global economic forces broadly defined as neoliberal: Bahrain's trade and investment liberalization policy and the global television formats industry embodied in the *al-Ra'is* contract between MBC and Endemol. During field research in Dubai I learned that during pre-production preparation, MBC sought "permission" from Saudi authorities to satcast the show. This was necessary because MBC was Saudi-owned and because of the importance of the wealthy Saudi market for the pan-Arab television industry. According to MBC staff I interviewed, a Saudi committee representing the ministries of the Interior, Culture and Information, and Religious Affairs considered the request and advised against *al-Ra'is* unless the show (1) were not shot in Saudi Arabia (Bahrain was suggested) and (2) enforced strict gender segregation.[16] MBC decided to shoot the program in Bahrain in a studio featuring gender-segregated sleeping quarters and bathrooms, in addition to prayer rooms, an innovation on the original format.[17] The living room was the only space shared by men and women.

As production started, MBC's contractual obligations to Endemol, the drive for ratings, and worries about Saudi objections to the show created a tense atmosphere. High-level MBC officials micro-managed production, with producers *in situ* in Bahrain receiving "contradictory and constantly changing instructions: one day, it was 'show more skin'; the next day: 'you're showing too much skin'; the third day: 'you are not showing enough skin'."[18] In contrast to experienced producers and directors, the crew, mostly consisting of poorly trained Bahrainis, was unprepared. "One major mistake," a producer told me, "was committed when the video channel was showing the girls' room while all 8 audio channels were left open (the 4 audio feeds from the boys' room were supposed to be shut off), giving the impression that there were boys in the girls' room" by producing an audio-track with both male and female voices.[19] Concerns over *ikhtilat*, the illicit social mixing between unmarried men and women, exploded in street demonstrations on the fourth day of the show, after the infamous Saudi–Tunisian kiss.

The shutdown of *al-Ra'is* and its aftermath reflected a battle between proponents and opponents of neoliberalism. Several members of parliament (MPs) defended the show with claims that it would foment economic growth by boosting tourism, promoting foreign investment, and creating new jobs.[20] A prominent businessman stated that the show would bring in more than US $15 million in direct investment and provide work for 200 nationals. "What the MPs are doing will only discourage potential investors," the businessman said.[21] A prominent columnist criticized MPs for "trying to score political and election points at the expense of national policies that encourage investments and an open economy."[22]

A parliamentary committee discussing the impact of *al-Ra'is* considered "ways to protect investments and preserve Bahrain's Islamic ethics"[23] – a balancing act increasingly typical of worldwide local reactions to the advances of neoliberal trade and fiscal policies. As the head of the committee stated, "there are people who want to cancel the contract with the producing companies, but this is opposed by the businessmen who fear that such a decision would hurt Bahrain's reputation and undermine potential investment agreements."[24] Raising the trope of national reputation – frequently used to suppress activists or journalists critical of Arab government policies – in reference to Bahrain's fitness for foreign investment reflects the rise in Arab public discourse of free-market ideals, unfettered trade, and the search for competitive advantage to lure global capital – modernity as neoliberal governance. Whereas the victorious opponents of the show attacked it on moral bases, defenders of *al-Ra'is* articulated strictly economic arguments; both, however, couched their arguments in the rhetoric of national identity.

Nationalism, however important, is not the only social force that comes in focus when we focus on reality television globally and contextually. The Indian, pan-African, and pan-Arab contexts demonstrate that ideological contests triggered by reality television focus on social and political issues like political pluralism, citizenship rights, political economy, and gender equality that interact contingently with both neoliberal and nationalistic forces. The downside of nationalism, of course, is its treatment of internal difference, a fraught issue that is nonetheless made visible by the representational energies spawned by reality shows, and their impact on various registers of identity and difference in terms of citizenship, lifestyle, sexuality, or race.[25] As it takes into account this wide gamut of social relations, reality television scholarship has an auspicious opportunity to shed light on important issues that transcend reality television itself – most importantly the rise of localized neoliberalisms.

Localizing neoliberalism

The preceding indicates that local and national forces contest and resist the worldwide spread of neoliberal ideology, and that multiple ideological sources inform public arguments over national policy, even when governments adopt neoliberal economic policies. Here it is useful to recall that the term neoliberalism refers to several things at once, including macroeconomic policies emphasizing low inflation and low public debt, trade liberalization, financial deregulation, privatization of state assets, and finally the withdrawal of the welfare state. So far, reality television studies in the UK–US have been chiefly concerned with the latter meaning of neoliberalism, focusing on how the reality genre makes over individuals into self-responsible, entrepreneurial citizen-consumers. The field has largely ignored more structural and macro-implications of extreme free market ideology. Thus, an important distinction that ought to be made within the critique of neoliberalism, one between seeing reality television as a space for the training of citizen-consumers in synch with the demands of neoliberal ideology, and another focused on how neoliberalism as government fiscal and trade policy is resisted by social and political actors. One way of looking at this issue is to tease out different kinds of neoliberalisms, focused on remaking not only individuals but also institutions (Couldry, Palmer), societies (Couldry) and nations (Darling-Wolf, Jacobs, Punathambekar, Volčič and Andrejevic).

Re-thinking the juncture of media and governance via the prism of neoliberalism does not entail dismissing the salience of neoliberal ideology; rather it calls for a focus on investigating and understanding the manifold ways in which neoliberalism is resisted, changed, and appropriated around the world. By describing how reality shows in Singapore reflect a locally inflected strand of neoliberalism that co-exists with a strong regulatory state, Lewis shows that the case of Bahrain is not unique. This volume explores the global trajectories and local forms of market fundamentalism three decades after Reagan and Thatcher launched the neoliberal revolution. It accomplished this task in at least two ways, one focused on the changing structure and content of the global reality television industry, the other through an examination of variations on the reality genre's typical rituals and affects.

A structural-textual shift

Our collective examination of reality television in its global context reveals a structural-textual shift from systematic format adaptation to locally created (not adapted formats) reality programs. This localization of the global can be glimpsed in many parts of the world. In Slovenia alone, seven local reality shows appeared between 2003 and 2007 (Volčič and Andrejevic). In China, India, and Singapore, government and privately owned television channels have launched local versions of Western shows (Lewis). Whereas in 2004 most Arab reality TV shows were formats licensed from European or American companies and adapted to the Arab market, by 2008 a majority (15 out of 26) of Arab reality TV shows were original local creations.[26]

This shift involved experimentation with global ideas and practices that culminated in local creations with historically resonant topics.[27] The substitution of adapted European formats with locally created shows reflects broader processes of cultural translation that lay at the heart of the local–global dialectic. This shift towards the indigenization of global neoliberal norms and practices is not restricted to the "Global South" but can be glimpsed between US and UK or US and Australian versions of reality shows. According to Lewis, Australian shows display a less aggressive competitive streak than their US counterparts, and elsewhere Kavka notes that whereas UK reality shows tend to focus on domestic scenes, US shows emphasize the individual and body as a locus of transformation.[28] Structural and textual elements in global reality television mitigate neoliberal ideology.

Ritual/social differences

In societies permeated by neoliberal ideology, such as the US and UK, reality TV programs compel participants to unveil the most intimate personal details, thus aiding in the creation of self-reliant, self-governing citizen-consumers. In these contexts, reality TV's underlying premises center on individuals – the exacerbation of desire and emotional conflict, the exaltation of individualism, and the promotion of self-revealing behavior.[29] Likewise, reality TV in the non-West contributes to the creation of modern composite citizen-consumers. This refashioning is manifest in several reality shows worldwide, where European and North American influence is discernible in the makeover theme based on personal metamorphosis. Reality TV's promise of individual transformation has some resonance beyond the US–UK junction.

But in contrast with many American and British shows, reality TV in Africa, India, China, the Arab countries, and even the ex-Yugoslavia, provides a platform to reclaim things social and political. Contentious debates arise over *liberal* values and practices – the rights of the individual, gender and regional equality, political participation – triggered by reality TV, in a manifest difference from the focus on *neoliberal* values and practices – survival-of-the-fittest social behavior, willing submission to surveillance, individual assumption of the state's role, that characterizes much of the dominant scholarship on reality TV. Though neoliberal practices are present, they are trumped by the contest over liberal values, themselves often transcended by social traditions. Thus the neoliberal trope is not universally applicable because social fabrics in the Global South are not as thoroughly penetrated by capitalism as some Western societies.[30] For example, several Arab reality shows draw on social norms and traditions: *Millionaire Poet* reenacts traditional oral poetry contests in Arabian Gulf countries; *Green Light* requires participants to accomplish good deeds according to religious customs;[31] *Al-Qur'an Caravan* appropriated the reality genre to stage competitive

Qur'anic recitals. These shows have imbued reality shows with local resonance while maintaining the competitiveness and plebiscitary nature of the genre.

The ways that neoliberal ideology becomes practice is visible in cross-national differences in the shaming rituals characteristic of the reality genre. As Sender convincingly argued, "if neoliberalism involves both self-monitoring and increasing adaptability in new economic and geographical circumstances, *shame should be seen as the quintessential neoliberal affect*, offering a highly efficient means to govern at a distance."[32] One of the most striking things I noticed in my research during the last five years is that Arab reality TV is remarkably less debasing and more didactic than its Western counterparts. The absence of humiliation rituals familiar to viewers of US and UK reality shows, and MBC's naming the Arabic version of *The Biggest Loser*, *al-Rabeh al-Akbar* [*The Biggest Winner*], reflect negotiated textuality and affect, a compromise that at once affirms and mitigates neoliberal ideology.

Chapters in this volume suggest various paths to understanding the global–local articulations that create context-specific versions of neoliberalism. Some contributions reaffirm the dominant trope in reality television studies, what the political theorist Nikolas Rose called "responsibilization," in which neoliberal discourse is at work to forge the ideal citizen-consumer whose sense of self-responsibility is matched by individual initiative and personal entrepreneurship. Several chapters exemplify the kinds of empirical work that are required if we are to make sense of how reality television mediates the morphing of neoliberal ideology into everyday life practices.[33] Other contributions to *The Politics of Reality Television*, rather than focusing on reality television exclusively as an instrument that trains individuals to become better neoliberal citizen-consumers, show that reality television provides a social space where neoliberalism is mediated, contested and transformed by issues of social authority, sexuality, class, labor, and a variety of group identities – ethnic, national, regional – operating on the local-to-global spectrum. One major lesson to draw from this volume is that neoliberalism is experienced in various locales in various forms and with different levels of potency.

Tensions between neoliberalism and these various loci of human meaning and action are important theoretical issues that enable us to use the globalization of reality television studies in order to re-visit how we think about the connections between media, politics and governance globally and historically. In some cases explicated in this book, rather than promoting the privatization of social life and its separation from government concomitantly with throwing societies and individuals at the mercy of market forces, which is the essence of neoliberalism, reality television shows brought governments back into the realm of cultural and social life. In Africa and the Arab countries, some politicians intervened to ban, censor or simply attack reality shows, while others ostensibly sought to be associated with the popularity of *Star Academy* and *Big Brother Africa*. In some countries, most notably Kuwait and Malawi, national legislatures debated the impact of reality shows and sought to prohibit and restrict their broadcasts. In both regions, reality programs spawned broad debates about globalization and its impact on society, creating a space where facets of neoliberalism came under systematic attack. In Singapore, a strong state oversees a free market, creating a neoliberalism that in David Harvey's description blends Confucianism, cosmopolitanism, and nationalism (Lewis). An important lesson we can carry away from *The Politics of Reality Television* is that government and governance matter as much as governmentality.

Consideration of various neoliberalisms through a comparative and contextual analysis of reality television and its social and political consequences worldwide helps establish a potentially important link with another important contemporary debate across the humanities and the social sciences, which focuses on how to understand modernity itself as a locally and nationally-inflected experience. Understanding multiple modernities, which the eminent Canadian philosopher Charles Taylor believes to be the single most important task of the social sciences, requires a global and comparative approach that is at the same time locally contextualized and attuned to fine-grained differences in culture, economics and politics. Though in this volume, only Lewis makes explicit reference to this problematic, considering "the lifestyle genre as exemplary of the multiplicity of culturally hybrid modernities currently being worked out" (Lewis, Chapter 6), it is a productive avenue that enables us to think freshly and inquisitively about the world through the prism of reality television. From that perspective, *The Politics of Reality Television* provides a global and comparative vista of neoliberalism's attempts to flatten all of us into consumers and commodities, and underscores that neoliberal practices have not fully succeeded in subduing the dizzying complexity and difference of our world.

Notes

1 See, for example, Kjus, this volume; Mark Andrejevic, *Reality TV: The Work of Being Watched* (Lanham, MD: Rowman & Littlefield, 2004); Nick Couldry, *Media Rituals: A Critical Approach* (London: Routledge, 2003); Marwan M. Kraidy, *Reality Television and Arab Politics: Contention in Public Life* (Cambridge, UK and New York: Cambridge University Press, 2009).

2 Kraidy, *Reality Television and Arab Politics*.

3 Miller et al, *Global Hollywood* (London: Global Film Institute, 2001); Paula Chakravartty, "Labor in or as Civil Society? Workers and Subaltern Publics in India's Information Society," in *Global Communications: Towards a Transcultural Political Economy*, ed. Paula Chakravartty and Yuezhi Zhao (Lanham, MD: Rowman and Littlefield, 2008): 285–308. See also the recent book by Vincent Mosco and Catherine McKercher, *The Laboring of Communication* (Lanham, MD: Lexington Books, 2009), on labor issues in the US and Canada.

4 Kraidy, *Reality Television and Arab Politics*.

5 See Marwan M. Kraidy, "Glocalization as an International Communication Framework?" *Journal of International Communication* 9 no. 2 (2003): 29–49; and Joe Straubhaar, *World Television: from global to local* (Sage, 2007).

6 See also Sean Jacobs, "*Big Brother*, Africa is watching," *Media, Culture and Society* 29 no. 6 (2007): 851–68.

7 Kraidy, *Reality Television and Arab Politics*.

8 Dana Heller, ed., *The Great American Makeover: Television, History, Nation* (New York: Palgrave Macmillan, 2006).

9 In addition to contributions in this book, see Minna Aslama & Mervi Pantti, "Flagging Finnishness: Reproducing National Identity in Reality Television," *Television and New Media* 8 no. 1 (2007): 49–67; and Kraidy, *Reality Television and Arab Politics*.

10 Bahrain Economic Development Board 2008, http://www.bahrainfs.com.

11 Rasheed Muhammad Al Maraj, "Vigorous Economic Growth in Bahrain." Speech by His Excellency Rasheed Muhammad Al Maraj, Governor of the Central Bank of Bahrain, at the Strategic Forum on the Bilateral Trade and Investment Opportunities in Banking and Finance, London (January 10, 2008).

12 Moin A. Siddiqi, "Bahrain: Financial Hub of the Middle East," *Middle East* 313 (June 2001): 37.

13 "The Endeavours of Gulf Countries to Meet WTO Requirements," *Arab Law Quarterly* 16 no. 1 (2001): 49–51.

14 See Kenneth Katzman, *Bahrain: Key issues for U.S. policy* (Washington, DC: Congressional Research Service, March 14, 2005); Michele Wallin, "U.S.–Bahrain Accord Stirs Persian Gulf Trade Partners," *New York Times* (December 24, 2004): W.1.

15 Kraidy, *Reality Television and Arab Politics*: Chapter 2.

16 Author interview with Paul Hitti, Special Projects Manager, MBC, June 22, 2005, Dubai, United Arab Emirates.

17 Author interview with Safa Al-Ahmad, *Al-Ra'is* Story Producer, Middle East Broadcasting Center, June 19, 2005, Dubai, United Arab Emirates.

18 Author interview with Safa Al-Ahmad.

19 Author interview with Safa Al-Ahmad.

20 Neil MacFarqhar, "A kiss is Not Just a Kiss to an Angry Arab TV audience," *The New York Times*, March 5, 2004.

21 "Bahrain MPs Seek to Grill Minister on Reality TV Show," *Gulf News*, February 26, 2004. Available http at: www.gulf-news.com. See also F. Davies, "Al-Rais has Fallen Silent." EBU, 2004.

22 "Bahrain MPs Seek to Grill Minister on Reality TV Show."

23 "The Reality of Reality TV in the Middle East," www.albawaba.com/ news/print-Article.php3?sid = 271966& lang = e, 7 March 2004.

24 "The Reality of Reality TV in the Middle East."

25 On sexuality in reality TV, see Sender, "Queens for a Day: *Queer Eye for the Straight Guy* and the Neoliberal Project," 131–51. On race, see Minna Aslama, & Mervi Pantti, "Flagging Finnishness", *Television and New Media* 8 no. 1 (2007): 49–67; K. E. Bell-Jordan, "Black. White. And a Survivor of the Real World: Constructions of Race on Reality TV," *Critical Studies in Media Communication* 25 no. 4 (2008): 353–72; R. M. Boylorn, "As Seen on TV: An Autoethnographic Reflection on Race and Reality Television," *Critical Studies in Media Communication* 25 no. 4 (2008): 413–32; R. E. Dubrofsky and A. Hardy, "Performing Race in *Flavor of Love* and *The Bachelor*," *Critical Studies in Media Communication* 25 no. 4 (2008): 373–92; M. C. Hopson, "'Now Watch me Dance': Responding to Critical Observations, Constructions, and Performances of Race on Reality Television," *Critical Studies in Media Communication* 25 no. 4 (2008): 441–46; M. P. Orbe, "Representations of Race in Reality TV: Watch and Discuss," *Critical Studies in Media Communication* 25 no. 4 (2008): 345–52; J. H. Park, "The Uncomfortable Encounter Between an Urban Black and a Rural White: The Ideological Implications of Racial Conflict on MTV's *The Real World*", *Journal of Communication* 59 no. 1 (2009):152–71; D. C. Smith, "Critiquing Reality-based Television Black Fatherhood: A Critical Analysis of *Run's House* and *Snoop Dogg's Father Hood*," *Critical Studies in Media Communication* 25 no. 4 (2008): 393–412.

26 Andrawes Snobar, *Arab Reality TV Shows* (Amman, Jordan: Arab Advisors Group, May 2008).

27 Kraidy, *Reality Television and Arab Politics*.

28 Misha Kavka, "Changing Properties: The Makeover Show Crosses the Atlantic," in *The Great American Makeover: Television, History, Nation,* ed. Dana Heller (New York: Palgrave Macmillan, 2006): 211–29.

29 Damien Le Guay, *L'empire de la télé-réalité: ou comment accroître le "temps de cerveau humain disponible"* (Paris: Presses Universitaires de France, 2005).

30 Even though Australia is linguistically and culturally "proximate" to the US and Britain, Australian reality television shows tend to display less aggressive behavior than their US and UK counterparts, for example in *The Biggest Loser*. I am grateful to Tania Lewis for this information.

31 "Green Light: A Reality Show of Another Kind," *Al-Riyadh* (June 1, 2005) [Arabic].

32 Katherine Sender, "Queens for a Day: 'Queer Eye for the Straight Guy' and the Neoliberal Project," *Critical Studies in Media Communication* 23 no. 2 (2006): 131–51, emphasis added.

33 In addition to contributors in this volume, see B. Skeggs, N. Thumim, and H. Wood, "'Oh Goodness, I *am* Watching Reality TV': How Methods Make Class in Audience Research," *European Journal of Cultural Studies* 11 no. 1 (2008): 5–24; A. Hill, *Reality TV* (London: Routledge, 2004); Katherine Sender, *The Big Reveal: Makeover Television, Audiences, and the Promise of Transformation* (New York: NYU Press, forthcoming).

Index